The World Is Yours

Also by Glenn Kenny

Made Men: The Story of Goodfellas

Anatomy of an Actor: Robert De Niro

A Galaxy Not So Far Away: Writers and Artists on Twenty-Five Years of Star Wars (editor)

The World Is Yours

THE STORY OF *SCARFACE*

GLENN KENNY

HANOVER
SQUARE
PRESS

Recycling programs for this product may not exist in your area.

ISBN-13: 978-1-335-44962-7

The World Is Yours

Hanover Square Press
22 Adelaide St. West, 41st Floor
Toronto, Ontario M5H 4E3, Canada
HanoverSqPress.com
BookClubbish.com

Printed in U.S.A.

In memoriam Allan T. Kenny (1937–2021), Joseph Failla (1959–2022) and Mary Alice Evans (1942–2023)

The World Is Yours

"But we must go on doing what we like doing best as if it were the illusions of humanism which are real and the realities of nihilism that prove a nightmare."

—Cyril Connolly, *Enemies of Promise*

CONTENTS

PROLOGUE

WHISKEY AND COKE

Every amendment to the US Constitution tells a story. The Eighteenth Amendment's is a killer.

The first section of that amendment, which was passed in 1919, a mere three months after the Armistice of World War I, reads: "After one year from the ratification of this article the manufacture, sale, or transportation of intoxicating liquors within, the importation thereof into, or the exportation thereof from the United States and all territory subject to the jurisdiction thereof for beverage purposes is hereby prohibited." If you're wondering why so many US soldiers suffering from PTSD chose to stay in France in the immediate aftermath of the Great War, it's not entirely frivolous to point out that in France they could drink legally. (For good fictional references, see not only Ernest Hemingway's 1926 novel *The Sun Also Rises* but the 1931 film melodrama *The Last Flight*, in which Richard Barthelmess,

David Manners, and future real-life alcoholic Elliot Nugent portray dead-drunk demobbed pilots doing their Lost Generation thing all over Paris.)

The so-called temperance movement that triumphed with Prohibition dates back all the way to the 1830s; among its engines were the Church of Latter Day Saints and the Young Men's Christian Association. Its philosophy, distilled to an essence, was that alcohol abuse was a moral failing, and that morality could indeed be legislated. In the post-Prohibition twentieth century, that view was supplanted by the notion that alcohol addiction is a disease. (Even, of course, as consumer culture arguably continued to normalize alcohol abuse.) In any event, if alcohol abuse at the turn of the nineteenth century was killing our menfolk (women, domestic workers, or one-time domestic workers for the most part were among the most vociferous temperance leaders) by turning them into sotted layabouts, Prohibition killed in different ways. Murders and suicides went up. One is shocked that according to statistics of the time, only one thousand persons a year died from drinking poisoned alcohol—casualties from bathtub-distilled gin, it would seem, had to be greater in reality.

What the thirty-first US president, Herbert Hoover, dubbed a "great social and economic experiment" was a failure almost from the get-go. Protean journalist H.L. Mencken observed in 1925, "Five years of Prohibition have had, at least, this one benign effect: they have completely disposed of all the favorite arguments of the Prohibitionists. None of the great boons and usufructs that were to follow the passage of the Eighteenth Amendment has come to pass. There is not less drunkenness in the Republic, but more. There is not less crime, but more. There is not less insanity, but more. The cost of government is not smaller, but vastly greater. Respect for law has not increased but diminished."

The oil millionaire John D. Rockefeller expressed a not dissimilar disillusionment: "When Prohibition was introduced, I hoped that it would be widely supported by public opinion and the day would soon come when the evil effects of alcohol would be recognized. I have slowly and reluctantly come to believe that this has not been the result. Instead, drinking has generally increased; the speakeasy has replaced the saloon; a vast army of lawbreakers has appeared; many of our best citizens have openly ignored Prohibition; respect for the law has been greatly lessened; and crime has increased to a level never seen before."

It can be argued that Prohibition invented the American gangster movie. The criminal groups of 1912's *The Musketeers of Pig Alley* and 1915's *Regeneration* (landmark films for canonical directors D.W. Griffith and Raoul Walsh, respectively) were more gangs than mobs. Bootlegging gave such go-getters some focus, so to speak.

The most iconic gangster films, the ones that set the template for all American gangster pictures to come, were made before the election of Franklin Delano Roosevelt, who won the presidency in 1932 in part due to his promise to end Prohibition, which happened with the adoption of the Twenty-First Amendment in 1933. (The in-between amendments were the Nineteenth Amendment, which gave women the right to vote, and which took more than forty years to ratify, and the Twentieth, which put the country's vice president in direct line of succession to the president in the event of that president's death. The Twenty-First was ratified through the process of state rallies, which greatly streamlined the process to meet populist expectations.) *Public Enemy* and *Little Caesar*, both made in 1931 and released by First National, which later became Warner Brothers, were furious, tough-as-nails crime stores anchored by still-startling lead performances by outsize performers James Cagney and Edward G. Robinson. *Scarface*, a ruthless case study that saw Yiddish theater stalwart Paul Muni portray feral Italian-American mob king Tony Camonte, followed in 1932.

These films rarely if ever detailed the mechanics of getting booze into the States. The bootleg action more often than not consisted of tough guys with beer kegs storming into speakeasies and replacing the extant goods with their bosses' goods. As Robert Warshow noted in his seminal 1948 essay "The Gangster As Tragic Hero,"

> The gangster's activity is actually a form of rational enterprise, involving fairly definite goals and various techniques for achieving them. But the rationality is usually no more than a vague background; we know, perhaps, that the gangster sells liquor or that he operates a numbers racket; often we are not given even that much information. So his activity becomes a kind of pure criminality: he hurts people.

The repeal of Prohibition vaguely coincided with the enactment, in Hollywood, of the Production Code, which had the effect of softening the content of movies across the board. Historical dramas got more tame—no more nipple-revealing milk baths for Claudette Colbert, or impaled Christians in the Roman arena, both among the visual treats of Cecil B. DeMille's 1932 *The Sign of the Cross*. The skimpy lingerie regularly sported by the likes of Joan Blondell in Vitaphone musicals got a lot more substantial. And the crime-does-not-pay messages of gangster movies got a lot more priggish emphasis, to the point of achieving banality.

And without bootlegging, the gangster movie lost a primary theme. Filmmakers soon had to look backwards to get their kicks: see 1939's *The Roaring Twenties*, evoking an exciting bygone era and its pure criminality right there in the title.

In real life, Alphonse "Al" Capone, nicknamed "Scarface," was the most prolific, arguably the most vicious, and most feared of Prohibition's gangsters. So feared that the movies shied away from portraying him indirectly or directly until after his death. The 1932 *Scarface* was a notable exception to this rule, and as we'll see later, the movie did attract Capone's attention.

In his book on Prohibition, *Last Call*, Daniel Okrent muses on Capone's enduring pop culture notoriety: "Over the years Capone has been played by Rod Steiger, F. Murray Abraham, William Devane, Eric Roberts (*Eric Roberts!*), Robert De Niro, Ben Gazzara, and Jason Robards, Jr. (not to mention Paul Muni as Tony Camonte, a fictionalized version of Capone, in the original *Scarface*, and Al Pacino in its remake). If Capone hasn't exactly been portrayed as a hero, all that celluloid has enabled him to maintain a reputation that would delight any narcissistic mobster. More than fifty years after Capone's death, a browser on eBay could make bids in a single day for Al Capone wristwatches, trading cards, bobblehead dolls, belt buckles, and T-shirts. Other items included a two-sided Al Capone Dog Tag Necklace; a 'tiny piece of hat owned and worn by Al Capone, with Certificate of Authenticity'; a photocopy of Capone's death certificate; from the Franklin Mint, an Al Capone Collector's Knife; and a Hugo Boss 'Al Capone-style' suit, available in 40, 42, or 42 long. Literary offerings included several biographies, as well as *Black Hat: A Novel of Wyatt Earp and Al Capone*; *The Travel Guide to Al Capone's Chicago*; *Al Capone was a Golfer: Hundreds of Fascinating Facts from the World of Golf*; and a much-honored children's book entitled *Al Capone Does My Shirts*—also available in Spanish as *Al Capone Lava La Ropa*."

Cocaine, which can be snorted, injected, applied topically, or, after modification, smoked, made its pop culture debut in Arthur Conan Doyle's novel *The Sign of Four*, first presented in serial form in February 1890 and published in a single volume later that year. *Four* is the second novel Doyle, a physician turned fiction writer, authored about the eccentric consulting detective

Sherlock Holmes. The story opens with Holmes's amanuensis, Dr. Watson, recounting with undisguised distaste the detective shooting up (whether subcutaneously or intramuscularly, Holmes scholars and annotators still cannot be sure, although it's agreed he's definitely not doing it intravenously) "a seven percent solution."

"Would you care to try it?" Holmes asks after letting out a "long sigh of satisfaction." Watson "brusquely" refuses, protesting, "My constitution has not got over the Afghan campaign yet. I cannot afford to throw any extra strain on it." (Watson is a veteran of Britain's Second Afghan War.)

Holmes, master of deduction that he is, notes Watson's objection and tries to mollify his friend by describing the drug's effects. Cocaine is, he says, "so transcendentally stimulating and clarifying to the mind that its secondary action is a matter of small moment." Recalling Holmes's cocaine hangovers, Watson counters that "the game is hardly worth the candle." Holmes allows him the point but insists: "My mind rebels at stagnation… I abhor the dull routine of existence."

The lure of cocaine, which at the time was mostly used as a dental anesthetic, was a kind of crystal revelation. Proper cocaine, which is not what is sold on the streets nowadays (to put it mildly), was said to focus the mind in a particularly exhilarating way. That was Sigmund Freud's idea of the drug, after he witnessed its use on Bavarian troops by an army brass seeking to lengthen the endurance of the individual soldier. Scholars have speculated that Conan Doyle must have been familiar with Freud's paper "Uber Coca," and drew from it the inspiration to give the master detective the habit.

Holmes's trait coincided loosely with the introduction of the soft drink Coca-Cola. There's an urban myth that the original formula for Coca-Cola contained cocaine. What *is* true is that the inventor of the first Coca-Cola formula, John Pemberton, had a medical degree, was a morphine addict as a result of wounds sustained in the Civil War, and concocted his "medical tonic" using the African kola nut to provide the "stimulating" caffeine that the soda still contains. While there's some conflict as to whether Pemberton also used the South American coca leaf, from which cocaine is derived, in his recipe, it wouldn't be exactly the same thing as actually spiking the beverage with cocaine. Amusingly, Coca-Cola was originally marketed as a "temperance drink." In any event, when Beatle John Lennon, whose main experience with drugs by this time was with Benzedrine and other forms of speed (he and his bandmates needed to be on their toes for the punishing gig schedules of their Hamburg years), put a Coke bottle to his nose and took a little sniff in the 1964 film *A Hard Day's Night*, his cheeky joke perpetuated a probable fallacy.

The thing is, Pemberton could have put cocaine in his drink if he'd had a mind to; the drug was entirely legal and could be had, in limited doses, over the counter. It was not classified as a narcotic until 1914, and its prohibition did certainly cut down on its recreational use, not to mention its use as an ingredient in common medicinal tonics and such. Damian Chazelle's 2022 depiction of silent-era Hollywood, *Babylon*, which begins in the mid-'20s even as its depiction of filmmaking seems rooted in the early teens, shows the inchoate Tinseltown as a burg where cocaine was as plentiful as tap water. Filmmaker Kenneth Anger, in his scurrilous 1959 alternative history *Hollywood Babylon*, delightedly informed readers that no less a star than derring-do maestro Douglas Fairbanks appeared in a comic short in 1916 playing an unusually alert detective named "Coke Ennyday." But as the drug became more difficult to procure, its mainstream cultural cachet diminished. In part because it stayed underground for so long, it was difficult to enumerate the ways in which cocaine could physically harm one's health, whereas the liabilities of alcohol had been plain since the days when they called gin "blue ruin," if not before.

★★★

When I read Sherlock Holmes in boyhood, the references to cocaine didn't really spook me; they went over my head. My first education in cocaine came from a *New York Times Magazine* article from September 1974, when I was fifteen (my parents regularly brought home the paper, believing it to be "improving," and I was a fiend for the magazine, the book review, and the Arts & Leisure section). Bylined to Amy Crittenden and Michael Ruby, it bore the headline "Cocaine: The Champagne of Drugs." Well now. (Above the main hed, though, in thinner type, were the words, "Highs, horns and bugs crawling," which painted a far less enticing picture. Balance!)

The piece opened with an ostensibly charming anecdote about how Freud became fascinated with the drug. It then spoke of how the substance was gaining a new cachet: "Once the nearly exclusive province of pimps and prostitutes—street people of the night—the drug has spread—into widening circles, if not into the light of day. Its users encompass all social and economic categories but are particularly concentrated among what one drug-abuse specialist calls 'the glitter people.'" I recollect, from my readings in *Rolling Stone* and other rock magazines, such as the freewheeling *Creem*, rock musicians being not at all shy in describing their pharma enthusiasms. One gritty-voiced singer from Scotland raved about the synthetic heroin he was able to score on tour in the States, while another gritty-voiced singer, London-born but of Scottish extraction, bemoaned his inability to score pharmaceutical-grade cocaine. I am happy to report that both of these individuals are still with us as I write this.

The Crittenden/Ruby piece, in some sections, made cocaine seem like a wonder drug of sorts; after an account of an unpleasant OD, it went on: "Such overdoses are extremely rare, but there are indications that while many people can take cocaine or leave it, others develop a powerful, compulsive craving for its euphoric delights. As Dr. Jerome Jaffe, a psychopharmacologist at Columbia Presbyterian Hospital in New York, has written: 'Repeated use of the drug...does not produce addiction, but...addiction arises when persons with emotional difficulties encounter drugs which have ameliorative effects....' The drug's tendency to produce psychological addiction was recently described by one heavy user: 'I can go without coke, but when I have it around, I feel like I've got to take it.' While there have been few controlled tests on humans, recent experiments on rats would seem to confirm cocaine's tremendous appeal. Animals taught to push a lever for a reward did so up to 250 successive times for caffeine, 4,000 times for heroin—and 10,000 times for cocaine."

The idea of cocaine as non-addictive had tremendous appeal for some who struggle with recreational drug use. Some accounts of his life tell that, after a long and painful ordeal kicking heroin, the great jazz pianist Bill Evans took up cocaine in the highly mistaken belief that this white powder was not addictive. It is, of course, and it helped ruin Evans's health: he died in 1980 of a combination of bronchial pneumonia, a peptic ulcer, cirrhosis, and untreated hepatitis. He was fifty-one.

Nevertheless, cocaine's fortunes as a recreational drug rose inexorably. The drug became, unfairly or not, synonymous with the disco culture that seemed to dominate the 1970s. For early '80s President Ronald Reagan, escalating the war on drugs was a major policy plank that was played as a moral imperative. As it happens, the drug war is as much an engine, if not more of an engine, of human tragedy than Prohibition. In concocting a gangster epic for the 1980s, making your Capone figure a cocaine lord was an inspired choice. And not just because it played with a formula out of Hegel and Marx, reiterating initially tragic history as a deluxe variant on a rough-and-ready genre movie.

1

DE PALMA'S COMPLAINT

By 1981 or 1982, many parties agreed: "New Hollywood" had been fun while it lasted. If, in fact, "New Hollywood" had ever really existed.

For every film history narrative constructed by a journalist, a theoretician, or anyone moved strongly enough by a nostalgia for more vital times—or anyone just with an axe to grind—there's a counternarrative. But the dominant narrative in the here and now, still, was constructed by my former colleague Peter Biskind in his 1996 book *Easy Riders, Raging Bulls*. It's been iterated endless times, so this reiteration will be brief. Beginning, aptly, with the film *Easy Rider*, a shoestring-budget counterculture chronicle no one in straight Hollywood knew American audiences wanted, the imploding studio system enabled and empowered and funded a loosely organized (if organized at all) group of filmmakers who festooned American screens with maverick works. And a couple of these filmmakers wound up codifying the franchise blockbuster ethos along the way.

In his recent book *Cinema Speculation*, Quentin Tarantino cites a number of other volumes that celebrated this possible movement, some of them published as the phenomenon was happening: James Monaco's *American Film Now*, Diane Jacobs's *Hollywood Renaissance*, Michael Pye and Lynda Myles's *The Movie Brats*. But none of these volumes spoke to the popular imagination—nor, for that matter, to a subsequent generation of American filmmakers, which included Tarantino—the way Biskind's book did. And this book was arguably more pronounced in depicting the raucous behavior of directors and screenwriters than chronicling their galvanic work.

In any event, the phrase "movie brats," which Biskind was not immune to, pinpointed a particular phenomenon. The self-conscious filmmaker, the product of film school, the director ostensibly with a pronounced sense of *himself* (it was almost always a "himself") as his film's primary author—or, as an oft-misunderstood film critical practice imported piecemeal from France to the United States would have it, *auteur.* This figure was the fabricator of New Hollywood "personal" films that nevertheless hailed back to grand artistic forefathers like John Ford, Raoul Walsh, Samuel Fuller, Howard Hawks and others.

In the earliest part of the twentieth century, you could become a filmmaker by accident, fall into it—Ford and Hawks did, kind of. (Ford came to Hollywood and worked as an assistant to his ex-vaudevillian actor brother; Hawks was an engineer-in-training and tennis champ who got into the business through a summer job.) Now it was something you could go to school for.

In an interview with *Premiere* magazine's Anne Thompson in 1998, Brian De Palma insisted, given the ups and downs of his career, that he never let scoring a big hit make him feel as if he were invincible. "I never once had one of those successful hits and thought I was God." He reminded Thompson that the names of his friends by themselves could keep him relatively humble: "Just remember my group. Steven Spielberg, George Lucas, Francis Coppola, and Marty Scorsese." Of these five, it was only Steven Spielberg who never studied film or theater at a collegiate level. Coppola was a student at UCLA's inchoate film division in 1960; Lucas was in the legendary USC program, one of the oldest in the country; De Palma's theater studies at Sarah Lawrence morphed into film activity almost immediately; Scorsese was part of NYU's 1960s film program, which subsequently expanded into one of the country's most respected. Scorsese himself now has a school there named for him.

Lucas and Spielberg were for all intents and purposes native Californians. Scorsese and De Palma were New Yorkers whose paths had taken some time to cross while on the East Coast. Coppola, partially raised in New York, lit out for California in 1960, well before De Palma and Scorsese were getting started. When they met, they were united by youth, cinephile enthusiasm, and the fact that they were all learning the ropes by butting heads with execs who wanted to mess with their visions. Coppola was the veteran, with several feature pictures under his belt by the end of the 1960s. Spielberg was the precocious one, and the one who played relatively well with executives. Lucas had been an incorrigible avant-gardist. De Palma and Scorsese were, well, the New Yorkers—street-smart, hardheaded, fixated on telling their visions.

And so we got, from this group, the likes of *The Godfather, The Conversation, Jaws, Close Encounters of the Third Kind, Taxi Driver, Raging Bull, A New Hope* yclept *Star Wars, Carrie,* and *The Fury.* Those last two were De Palma pictures, and while they're now considered genre classics, they were explicitly genre films in a way that even *Star Wars* and *Close Encounters* weren't, quite.

In 1982, De Palma was in a reasonably good position relative to a few of his friends. Martin Scorsese was in a form of movie jail following the box office disaster of *The King of Comedy*, which had, in addition to failing financially, alienated critics and cost a lot of Scorsese's personal energy—in the service of a project that had been pressed on him by actor Robert De Niro. Francis Ford Coppola was in the process of losing his Zoetrope film studio, killing a dream of independence. In the wake of *Star Wars*' phenomenal success, George Lucas stopped directing. Steven Spielberg, with the success of *E.T.* and more, could arguably write his own ticket—it's never quite that simple—and was moving towards a sort of moguldom. De Palma's understanding of the business contributed to a kind of equanimity in occasionally accepting the role of the gigging filmmaker.

Decades before Steven Spielberg concocted his own cinematic origin story with 2022's *The Fabelmans*, De Palma gave an account of his own youth, sort of, in the 1980 thriller *Dressed to Kill*. If, in *The Fabelmans*, Spielberg depicts his younger self becoming a kind of voyeur into his own life, *Dressed to Kill* shows, in an indirect way, how De Palma discovered the uses of voyeurism before connecting the dots between peeping and making cinema. The plot engine of *Dressed to Kill* involves a tech wizard teen using primitive homemade computers and hidden recording devices to solve his own mother's murder. In later interviews, De Palma revealed that the character, played by future director Keith Gordon, was directly based on himself. On discovering that his father was having an adulterous affair, he followed his parent, photographed him, tracked him down at a tryst, and threatened him with exposure. "He was a bit surprised, to say the least," De Palma recalls in the documentary *De Palma*, by Noah Baumbach and Jake Paltrow. (For all that, De Palma also allows that he owes his father a temperamental debt of sorts: dad was an orthopedic surgeon who allowed his son to witness some of his work, which gave the younger De Palma a strong stomach when dealing with blood and gore.)

In his early features, De Palma had transposed the sense of betrayal onto the young male protagonists who served as a stand-in for the filmmaker. Never shy about acknowledging Alfred Hitchcock as a primary cinematic model (and it's worth remembering that Hitchcock, like Buñuel, pursued filmmaking while very directly inspired by the work of Fritz Lang), one of his first features was a microbudget suspense film with the very New York grindhouse-friendly title *Murder a la Mod*. His late 1960s features *Greetings* and *Hi, Mom!* were energetic, inventive, trenchant satires that mixed De Palma's personal obsessions and his political concerns with an anarchic abandon. Both films starred Robert De Niro in the role of Jon Rubin, a draft-dodging bookstore haunter in *Greetings* and a wannabe pornographer (sort of) in *Hi, Mom!*

In *Hi, Mom!*, Rubin takes an experimental approach to pornography. He moves into a ratty storefront apartment that's directly across from a modern complex with a grid of forward-facing windows. At his own window he positions a movie camera, and soon starts moving in on a female tenant, played by Jennifer Salt. Rubin bares his soul to her about his bad luck with girlfriends, recounting a time when he came home with flowers to surprise one amour on her birthday: "I opened the door very quietly and crept in and I heard the shower running. Well I opened the door to the bathroom, and I hear some voices. And all of a sudden I open the shower curtain and uh…there she is with another person. They were naked." De Palma would actually film an incident not unlike this for the beginning of his 1984 *Body Double*, the film he made directly after *Scarface*. (And in the film, the nude cheating girlfriend is played by an actress named Barbara Crampton, who in 1985 would take her first step to scream-queen immortality in *Re-Animator*.) In any event, Rubin's confessions are aimed at gaining the trust of Salt's character. His scheme is to get her to sleep with him, and film the result with his camera across the street. A convoluted way to create pornography, but De Niro's De Palma surrogate is nothing if not ambitious.

The movie delivers some genuinely scathing satire in its second half, when Rubin gets a job playing a policeman in a theatrical project titled *Be Black, Baby.* Here, white bourgeois theatergoers are invited to ask any questions of a Black performing troupe (they even accommodate the request "can I touch your hair," later to become a kind of trope in contemporary antiracism grifter Robin DiAngelo's pitch) before the tables are turned on them, and they are brutalized in the way Black Americans were, and still are. After being beaten bloody, the audience members praise the experience. De Palma's metatextual critique goes way beyond Brechtian. The movie then pulls back to all but endorse a Wile-E.-Coyote-style terrorist bombing of the exclusive apartment building's laundry room. The TV coverage of that event provides the movie with its punchline and its title.

Hi, Mom! in particular garnered fierce interest from New York critics and New York filmgoers. Like Robert Downey Sr.'s 1969 *Putney Swope*, *Hi, Mom!* was an underground movie that wasn't quite an underground movie. Gritty-looking, to be sure, but sophisticated in its film language and telling a coherent narrative with a "sick" sense of humor related to that of counterculture icon Lenny Bruce. De Palma would soon decamp to Los Angeles, at the invitation of Warner Brothers, to make *Get to Know Your Rabbit*, a film about a magician in training.

It would hardly be an overstatement to note that De Palma entered the world of corporate filmmaking with some ambivalence. Of the directors in his group, he was the most overtly politically minded. Scorsese came in a close second. (Coppola would, with *Apocalypse Now*, ostensibly critique the madness and "the horror" of American intervention in Vietnam, and Lucas would draw inspiration from the Vietcong to create Ewoks, but this was relatively mild and entirely acceptable to the conventional wisdom of the day relative to the political consciousness

De Palma and to a lesser extent Scorsese partook of.) In 1968, inspired by the general strike and the student rebellion in France, Jean-Luc Godard, the critic turned New Wave filmmaker who was a model for many New Hollywood types, changed his way of making pictures. Rejecting the bourgeois individualism of auteur-centric filmmaking, he formed the Dziga Vertov group and went about creating films (some would call them anti-films) that were calls to political action at their core. Thus inspired, Martin Scorsese, whose 1967 short *The Big Shave* has been interpreted by many as an allegory of US involvement in Vietnam (log line: man shaving can't stop cutting himself, turns his face into a bloody mess), helped form a collective called Cinetracts. Its sole production was a rarely seen documentary called *Street Scenes*. Before *Greetings* and *Hi, Mom!*, De Palma shot *Dionysus in '69*, which captures the theatrical collective The Performance Group enacting a decidedly counterculture-inflected (that is, it had a lot of nudity) version of *The Bacchae*. In interviews after *Greetings* and *Hi, Mom!* started getting attention, De Palma toed a radical line. I remember as a kid reading one interview in which I could swear he said, "The only way to deal with the bourgeois state is to blow it up." Just like the laundry room in *Hi, Mom!* Unfortunately I have yet to locate an actual source for this. But De Palma later recollected "talking about revolution" in a subsequent interview when he was older and savvier.

The making of 1972's *Get to Know Your Rabbit*, in any event, was dogged with unpleasantness. It was during this period that Jay Cocks, the critic and screenwriter who was later to collaborate with De Palma, and who would prove a crucial figure in the fight to get *Scarface* an R rating, met the director. He had known Martin Scorsese since the late '60s, and it was while all three were in California that this introduction was made. "Brian and I met in Malibu. We [Cocks and his wife, the actor Verna Bloom] were staying at a friend's house on the beach. Marty had been out there working for a while, and he would've been at Warner Brothers with Brian, where they were both having a terrible time. Brian had, of course, been fired from *Get to Know Your Rabbit* after losing an aesthetic battle of wills with Tommy Smothers. Marty was unhappily directing these hack music documentaries, the spawn of *Woodstock*. And Marty remembers both of them sitting on the curb outside of Warner Brothers studio, two guys literally sitting on the curb with their heads in their hands. And Thelma [Schoonmaker, Scorsese's friend and future editor] comes by in a car, she's waving at them like the Queen of the May. She's there working with Wadleigh [Michael Wadleigh, director of *Woodstock*, on which Scorsese and Schoonmaker worked] or something, but they knew each other from there and from before from NYU. Brian has actually known Marty a little longer than I have. Anyhow, Marty came out to visit us, Verna and me, at this place in Malibu that a friend had lent us." We will pick up Cocks's story in a later chapter.

De Palma's "aesthetic battle of wills" with star Tommy Smothers, and then studio execs, resulted in a picture that pleased no one, and sent De Palma back to New York, where he found independent financing via producer Ed Pressman and made a nasty, grisly, innovative thriller called *Sisters*. It was a movie that got talked about; its follow-up, *Phantom of the Paradise*, also financed by Pressman, was something very much but not wholly other, an eccentric and mordantly funny Faustian rock opera about a musical genius who's written a Faustian rock opera. Its genesis was in De Palma's bemusement at how notions of authenticity in rock and roll had mutated in the postmodern pop space. De Palma's return to Hollywood was not entirely on his own terms, but on better terms, and in 1976, after collaborating with critic-turned-screenwriter Paul Schrader on *Vertigo*-inspired thriller *Obsession*, with mixed results, he made it pay with *Carrie*, his committed, blood-drenched adaptation of Stephen King's first novel. It was material De Palma knew he could make a meal of, and he did. Less than an hour and forty minutes long, the movie is practically ruthless in its narrative momentum and rife with bravura virtuoso use of split-screen and near sadistically ingenious jump scares. The movie's success had a not entirely welcome effect. Studio forces wanted more of the same, and De Palma's next movie also took on teens with paranormal powers. *The Fury* had gifted adolescents Andrew Stevens and Amy Irving—both of whom can make people bleed just by looking at them funny—kidnapped by an unnamed and very shady government agency; it's a paranoid thriller by way of EC Comics. De Palma applied more than customary brio to the work: the movie actually ends with the villain exploding, his flying body parts covered by multiple camera angles in slow motion.

The successes of the two films gave De Palma breathing room. He used it in a variety of ways. For one thing, he returned to Sarah Lawrence College in Yonkers, where he had studied in the early '60s, to teach this time. There he concocted a group project for his students, an actual motion picture comedy that, like *Dressed to Kill* would, drew on the family dynamics of De Palma's youth, only this time in the context of a self-help satire about how to avoid being "an extra" in your own life. *Home Movies* did what De Palma hoped: it gave his students a chance to work on a real set, with real stars (Kirk Douglas of *The Fury*, and De Palma's then-wife Nancy Allen, who'd been one of the villains in *Carrie*) on a movie that got actual distribution (while confusing both critics and audiences).

The next two pictures were both written and directed by De Palma. 1980's *Dressed to Kill* was audacious both formally (you didn't see many mainstream pictures go for twenty minutes without a snatch of meaningful dialogue, as this film does early on) and in its content, kicking off with a shower sex scene that flirted with vaginal penetration and moving on to a slasher killing that practically grabbed viewers by the hair to make them register every laceration. It riled up critics (the *Village Voice* ran dual reviews by Andrew Sarris and J. Hoberman, the older auteurist calling the film "derivative" while Hoberman, hip to De Palma's avant-garde formal bona fides, hailing it as "dazzling") and captured a substantial audience curious as to what all the fuss was about. Or perhaps just hungry for sex and violence, as one was in the early '80s. Absolutely the nastiest date movie of its summer.

De Palma spent a lot of time in this period on another project, an adaptation of a nonfiction crime book, *Prince of the City*, in which he'd hoped to cast Robert De Niro as corrupt cop Robert Leuci. When the project went over to director Sidney Lumet, De Palma was sufficiently resentful that he lifted a scene from Leuci's life and planted it in the middle of *Blow Out*, itself a personal project in a different way from *Dressed to Kill*. As Vincent Canby astutely noted in his *New York Times* review of July 24, 1981 (yes, it was only a year between *Dressed to Kill* and *Blow Out*; even as film studios were dying, they kept directors working at what now looks like a spanking pace): "[M]ore important than anything else about *Blow Out* is its total, complete and utter preoccupation with film itself as a medium in which, as Mr. De Palma has said along with a number of other people, style really is content." Its whole subject and reason for being, Canby argues, is "the manner in which sound and images can be spliced together to reveal possible truths not available when the sound and the image are separated." An audio gloss on Antonioni's *Blow-Up*, De Palma's film finds a mordant poignancy in those mechanics. Reuniting now-big-movie-star John Travolta with Nancy Allen—they played evil boyfriend and girlfriend in *Carrie*—*Blow Out* nevertheless proved a box office disappointment. A younger generation has since embraced the picture as a masterpiece.

Having developed over the years a philosophy that a working filmmaker should devote time to projects not his own, as both a labor exercise and a way to remain viable within the industry, De Palma was now ready to take on such a project. Here's how director Quentin Tarantino imagines De Palma's attitude, in his book *Cinema Speculation*: "De Palma had seen directors come and go. He knew in this industry nothing was more important than to keep being allowed to make movies. Also, despite his troubled relationship with Warner Bros., he didn't want to go back to the shoestring, run-and-gun world of independent filmmaking. He *liked* having permits. He *liked* shutting down the street with police control. He *liked* being able to afford a crane. And the only way to keep in business—unlike Jim McBride, unlike Shirley Clarke—was to make commercial movies people wanted to see." (McBride and Clarke were New York City underground filmmakers and De Palma influences who, in different ways, ran afoul of Hollywood in the courses of their careers.) At this point Tarantino is actually talking about the *Get to Know Your Rabbit* phase of De Palma's career. Tarantino also recollects a piece of advice De Palma gave him after seeing Tarantino's first feature, *Reservoir Dogs*: "Quentin, don't be too esoteric with your subject matter. If you want to be allowed to keep making movies, you've got to give them a *Carrie* every once in a while."

It's hardly beside the point to ask: Where had De Palma's politics gone as he was making commercial movies? And the answers are complicated. A couple of his movies of the late '70s–early '80s have notes of almost giggly racialist reactionism. In *The Fury*, Andrew Stevens's paranormal tyro Robin, who believes that his dad has been killed by Arab terrorists, is brought to an amusement park by his keepers. He sees a couple of Arab men, wearing kaftans and kaffiyehs, boarding a "Paratrooper" ride. Once they're airborne, he uses his powers to unscrew the nuts that hold the ride's seats to its spinning mechanism, sending a couple of them flying to their deaths—projecting them directly into a restaurant where others in their group are dining, probably killing those guys too. Good aim! In *Dressed to Kill*, Nancy Allen's call girl character is fleeing from the movie's overcoat-wearing, sunglasses-and-wig-disguised killer. On a subway platform, she's noticed by three young Black men, one of whom is carrying a boom box, who threaten to "break her fucking ass." She gets on a car where she confronts a Black police officer (playwright Stan Shaw), who doesn't believe her account. Once the cop gets off the train, the Black guys, now a gang of five, take up their cause again, but when they see the razor-wielding killer hiding between cars, they bug out and flee, wide-eyed and jaws agape in what one could call the "classic" Stepin Fetchit "feets don't fail me now" mode. It's only if one recalls that this is the director behind *Be Black, Baby* that one can see a formal, pointed lampooning of standard Hollywood racist practice in these sequences.

The threads of political paranoia in the work are consistent: the shadowy CIA-like organization of *The Fury*, the Chappaquiddick-redolent political cover-up of *Blow Out*, and so on. Over the years the personal voyeurism that informed De Palma's work grew into a vision of an entire society of sanctioned voyeurism, indulged by both the powerful and their prey. Reviewing De Palma's 2019 film *Domino*, I observed, "The death-dealing, all-voyeurism-all-the-time world that De Palma has been imagining in some form or another since the late '60s, has, he recognizes, finally come into actual being, and it's worse than he, or anyone, ever imagined. At times during *Domino*, the director seems practically giddy about it." When the protean downtown New York musical force Bill Laswell teamed up with the former Sex Pistol Johnny Rotten, now going by his real name, John Lydon, to make an album in 1986, the critic Robert Christgau noted that the duo shared "a disappointed revolutionary's professional interest in power." One senses this current in De Palma's work over the years, to be sure.

By 1980, after his friends Steven Spielberg and George Lucas had transformed the industry, De Palma knew what was what.

He told Jean Vallely of *Rolling Stone*: "When I made *Greetings*, I found myself on talk shows, talking about the revolution, and I realized I had become just another piece of software that they could sell, like aspirin or deodorant. It didn't make any difference what I said. I was talking about the downfall of America. Who cares?" De Palma came to a hard earned realization: In America, "Everything is meshed into a product."

De Palma may have maintained a vivid, unruly, violent imagination throughout his creative existence, but, in keeping with the meticulousness of his visual style, he kept an orderly life. He worked with his wife but did not make a show out of it. He was not tabloid-chased. He did not get involved with drugs. (According to Oliver Stone, the writer of *Scarface*, he'd never touched cocaine.) He is conspicuously absent from all the accounts of bad behavior in restaurants featured in Biskind's book.

And even as he behaved himself (a matter-of-fact person generally, he could be brusque on film sets but never acted out ragefully) and made his ostensibly commercial films, De Palma felt squelched, condescended to. He had fought with the MPAA ratings board over the sexual content and harrowing violence of *Dressed to Kill*; the back-and-forth was "you can't do that" versus "aren't we all adults here?" There was never any question of a milder rating than an R, but the MPAA kept holding the box-office-poison threat of an X over the movie. De Palma found it exhausting and exasperating, and in addition, he felt he was not getting the support he deserved from the studios. When he accepted the offer to make *Scarface*, he again knew that he was going to have to deliver an R picture, but believed, for various reasons, that the movie would have more cachet than *Dressed to Kill* or *Blow Out*; this was going to be a studio epic that could not be dismissed as a mere genre picture. De Palma saw in its potential value the opportunity to get some revenge on the forces that were slighting him.

On the set of *Scarface*, he told the journalist Lynn Hirschberg: "As soon as I get this dignity from *Scarface*, I'm going to go out and make an X-rated suspense picture. I'm sick of being censored. *Dressed to Kill* was going to get an X rating and I had to cut a lot. So, if they want an X, they'll get a *real* X."

But first, of course, he had to get the "dignity" from *Scarface*. Which was not exactly what he got.

It was not for nothing that upon seeing De Palma's film, Scorsese remarked to both De Palma and the movie's costar Steven Bauer, "They'll hate it, because it's all about them." "Them" being the moguls, the studio bigshots. Louis B. Mayer, after watching Billy Wilder's *Sunset Boulevard*, a direct shot at the studios, told Wilder he should be ashamed of himself, and Wilder told Mayer to go shit in his hat—at least that's how Wilder told it. And now Scorsese looks at a movie about guys who chainsaw people's limbs off and takes it as a statement about corporate criminals in the entertainment industry.

But it's only *because* De Palma made it that *Scarface* can be seen as being about "them." Because the people who hired De Palma had no interest, of course, in that kind of statement.

2

THE FIRST *SCARFACE*

In 1968 the British Film Institute published a book-length study of American director Howard Hawks by the critic Robin Wood. Not too long after that, Andrew Sarris's *The American Cinema, Directors and Directions 1929–1968* would see print, introducing many readers to what would become known, for better or worse, as "the auteur theory." Sarris's method of categorization enshrined Hawks as a "Pantheon director." Hawks had come a long way. Back in the 1950s, Eugene Archer, a film critic and a friend of Sarris's, checking out the cinephile scene in 1950s Paris, where a cadre of critics (many of them future filmmakers) were singing the praises of a select group of American directors, wrote to Andrew: "Who the hell is Howard Hawks?"

Hawks was, as his biographer Todd McCarthy put it, a "boy of privilege." His father was a prosperous paper manufacturer who began spending extended time in California believing the climate would improve the health of his wife, Howard's mother Helen. Born in 1896, Howard was ten when he first walked in the warm California sun. Schooled in New England, he trained to be an architect, and got his first taste of the movie business in 1916, when he worked on an unspecified Cecil B. DeMille picture. The next summer, he made his first substantial connection in the business, with James Wong Howe, the brilliant cinematographer, who at the time was working as a slate boy. An avid reader and lifelong anecdotalist, Hawks made an alliance with Douglas Fairbanks Jr. and his then-wife Mary Pickford and volunteered to direct a sequence in a Pickford picture on a day when the actual director didn't show up. He was only twenty-one. His first solo feature, the 1926 *The Road To Glory*, is a lost film.

Looking at the entirety of Hawks's prodigious career, what amazes is how adept he was in any genre. His *Bringing Up Baby* and *His Girl Friday* are quintessential screwball comedies. *Red River* and *Rio Bravo* are timeless Westerns. *Only Angels Have Wings* and *To Have and Have Not* are stirring adventure pictures. *The Big Sleep* is the snappiest Bogart/Bacall picture. And *Gentlemen Prefer Blondes* is, um, a musical starring Marilyn Monroe and Jane Russell. You get the idea.

Scarface was only Hawks's fourth sound film. In Robin Wood's volume on Hawks, he divides his favorite films by genre, and he leads off his section on Hawks's comedies with, yes, *Scarface*. His opening is one that film criticism connoisseurs can quote by heart: "It may be perverse to approach the comedies via a gangster film of exceptional ferocity, almost the only Hawks film in which the protagonist dies. But *Scarface* belongs with the comedies."

Wood's point was that the movie was animated by a kind of energy that was essentially comedic, and that energy's primary source was the lead character, Tony Camonte, patterned after the real-life gangster Al Capone and played with a frequently apelike demeanor by Paul Muni. Raised in Chicago, the stomping ground of Al Capone and then Tony Camonte, he gained fame in New York's Yiddish Art Theater and graduated to Broadway in the 1920s.

Muni was one of those actors who made a point of being chameleonic. His first Broadway role, which he undertook when he was barely in his thirties, was of a much older man. One of his stage triumphs, *Seven Faces*, saw him playing seven distinct roles. As he demonstrated during his storied film career, he thrived when changing his appearance. As such, he was the kind of actor you might expect to inspire someone like Robert De Niro, whose preference is to build a character from the outside in. It's interesting to note that while De Niro and Al Pacino are longtime friends, and the public tends to link them together categorically, their approaches to acting are somewhat opposed. Al Pacino studied with Lee Strasberg, whose instruction emphasized psychology and encouraged the performer to try to simulate a character's experience. De Niro was a devotee of Stella Adler, who spent time in New York's Group Theater collective with Strasberg but came to reject Strasberg's theories and practices and pressed students to study characters in detail and simulate their mode of being, which sounds kind of similar but is an entirely different kettle of fish. (One of the only interesting features of the 1969 ostensible Mafia movie *The Brotherhood*—an effort so thoroughly misguided that it almost dissuaded Paramount from undertaking *The Godfather* a couple of years later—is a wedding scene in which Susan Strasberg, Lee's daughter, plays a bride, and is hovered over by Luther Adler, Stella's brother and also a Group Theater alum. What might they have talked about between camera setups?)

Prior to *Scarface*, Muni had tried to ditch Hollywood after a couple of unsatisfactory outings, including a film adaptation of *Seven Faces*. The one-two punch of *Scarface* and the searing realist torn-from-the-headlines drama *I Am a Fugitive from a Chain*

Gang brought the actor into the movie-going public's consciousness with a vengeance. Nevertheless, it would be several years before Muni hit his stride playing a variety of History's Great Men, starting with Louis Pasteur in 1936. He went on to play Emile Zola and Benito Juarez in portrayals that were stolid, reverent. But in *Scarface* and *Chain Gang*, Muni was electric. His acting crackled with the kind of energy that would make his contemporaries James Cagney and Edward G. Robinson into screen icons. One wonders just why he opted not to capitalize on it further. In any event, you can draw a through line from these films to the tough-guy portrayals of John Garfield, to the idiosyncratic exertions of Marlon Brando, and to Pacino and De Niro, the more self-conscious and ambivalent carriers of a very particular masculine legacy.

As both Hawks and screenwriter Ben Hecht were enthusiastic, sometimes hyperbolic, storytellers, their accounts of how the scenario of *Scarface* came to be are frequently contradictory. Hawks recounted to interviewer Joseph McBride that the incestuous attraction of Tony Camonte to his sister Francesca was his idea, and that he was inspired by the ancient example of the Borgias (the politically powerful Italian renaissance family of the fifteenth century). "Well, Ben, I've got an idea that the Borgia family is living in Chicago today. See, our Borgia is Al Capone, and his sister does the same incest thing as Lucrezia Borgia," Hawks has himself saying to Hecht. Naturally the movie-hating Hecht, sometimes a self-styled classicist, claimed the Borgia angle was his. In any event, the movie never goes Full Borgia, so to speak. Tony's attraction to Cesca is not reciprocated, to say the least. (The real-life Capone had two sisters; one died in infancy. The other, Mafalda, married a relative of a Capone henchman and became a successful bakery proprietor later in life. Al himself seemed to have a generally normal relationship with her.)

Todd McCarthy cites the treasure trove of fact that Hecht mined in concocting a scenario for Hawks: "As reworked by Hecht, with Hawks's enthusiastic participation, the resemblance of *Scarface* to the career of Al Capone became a great deal closer than the pronounced facial feature that, in the real gangster's case, extended along his jaw and across his neck, the result of an unsuccessful attempt to slit his throat. The film's magnificent opening scene, in which fat-cat mobster 'Big Louie' Castillo is robbed out in a phone booth after an all-night party, was based on the killing of Chicago racketeer 'Big Jim' Colosimo by Capone and Johnny Torrio in an attempt to take over the Chicago underworld. The next to go is the unseen O'Hara, an obvious stand-in for Deanie O'Banion, 'the last of the first-class lady killers,' whom Hecht and especially [Charles] MacArthur had known well. His death prompted a retaliatory raid on Capone's headquarters—reproduced in the film almost exactly in the attack on a restaurant that Scarface survives by lying flat on the floor, just as Capone had done. The St. Valentine's Day Massacre, while not reenacted, is depicted in its bloody aftermath, and Hecht slipped in innumerable details based on his knowledge of how things actually happened in Chicago."

As for just what Hecht was reworking, the property originated with a novel by pulp writer Armitage Trail. Hecht, in interviews and his autobiography *A Child of the Century*, never mentions it. It may well be the case that he never read it. Hawks mentions it in passing to McBride, thusly: "The original story had two brothers in it. The script didn't have the brother." Lest anyone believe that here is yet another case of a noble prose author being given the shaft by snakelike film folk, I am compelled to state not only does Trail's *Scarface* have very little of what became the movie's story in it, but also that it is an altogether atrocious novel. Among other things, its prose is so consistently stilted and leaden that one need only open the book to a random page to find passages worthy of wholehearted condemnation. For instance:

> It was after midnight. He saw no one on his way out. He had seen no one on his way in. He felt sure he was safe from identifying witnesses.
>
> Two blocks away he hailed a taxi and gave the driver the name of one of the best hotels in town. The police, even if they were looking for Tony Guarino, would never think of looking for him in a hotel like that.
>
> There were many uniforms on the streets and even in the lobby of the rather expensive hotel to which he went.

"Rather" expensive hotel. Oh dear. "[T]o which he went." Oh, dear again. And so on.

Ben Hecht had a livelier style, in both prose and screenwriting. His aforementioned autobiography, *A Child of the Century*, is doorstop-thick but reads like a breeze. Hecht was also notable for his speed, something he advertised with no false modesty. He claimed he could crank out a full screenplay in two weeks or less. His alacrity reflected, among other things, his contempt for motion pictures and the people who made them. In *A Child of the Century*, he writes: "The movies are one of the bad habits that corrupted our century. Of their many sins, I offer as the worst their effect on the intellectual side of the nation. It is chiefly from this viewpoint I write of them—as an eruption of trash that has lamed the American mind and retarded Americans from becoming a cultured people." While Hecht declines to talk smack about his Hollywood collaborators—who, besides Hawks, also included titans such as Hitchcock and megaproducer David O. Selznick, and a raft-load of others—he only designates one of them a true artist: the cinematographer Lee Garmes. Who, in fact, shot Hawks's *Scarface*. (He also shot several

Dietrich/Von Sternberg pictures, the underappreciated Rouben Mamoulian melodrama *City Streets*, portions of *Gone with the Wind*, and many more, including the eccentric films Hecht himself codirected with his writing partner Charles MacArthur.)

One thing Hecht really loved about Hollywood was the money. In 1925, Herman J. Mankiewicz, a writer and wit whose path crossed with Hecht's at the *Chicago Tribune*, and who was now comfortably ensconced at a studio, sent Hecht the legendary telegram inviting him to join the fold: "Will you accept three hundred per week to work for Paramount Pictures. All expenses paid. The three hundred is peanuts. Millions are to be grabbed out here and your only competition is idiots. Don't let this get around." (Mankiewicz would go on to coauthor the screenplay of Orson Welles's *Citizen Kane*.)

Hecht entered into business with Howard Hughes warily, according to his own account: "I would work for [Hughes] only if he paid me a thousand dollars every day at six o'clock. In that way I stood to waste only a day's labor if Mr. Hughes turned out to be insolvent." Not much later in *Child*, he amplifies his insouciant fearlessness—he is cowed by neither tycoon nor gangster!—in recounting a visit from some real-life tough guys. Two scowling associates of Capone showed up at Hecht's hotel, brandishing a copy of the *Scarface* script. "Their dialogue belonged in it," Hecht notes. Their question as to whether the script is about their boss is met by a faux-shocked, "God, no. I don't even know Al" from Hecht. The Chicago expatriate exchanges some small talk about mutual associates with the thugs—the names of Jim Colosimo, Mosey Enright, and Peter Gentleman are dropped—before explaining to them that the movie's not about Capone, but is titled after his disliked nickname as a matter of marketing. And that sort of thing has been cooked up by Howard Hughes, described by Hecht to the flunkies as "the sucker with the money." That kind of talk they understand; mollified, they say "[to] hell with him," and leave Hecht be.

So Hecht tells it. Entertaining? Sure. True? No man living today could say.

For Hawks, making *Scarface* was an act of professional rebellion—which he made a crucial part of his own myth. When Joseph McBride asked him about the movie in the 1970s for his 1982 volume *Hawks on Hawks*, the director said, "*Scarface* is my favorite picture, even today, because we were completely alone, Hughes and I." At the time, he was a reasonably well-regarded director, but even as he sought out work, he balked at the studio system's habit of shackling directors with exclusive contracts. Unhappy with an assignment from First National, he more or less goaded the studio into suing him as he moved into an independent deal with Hughes. The tycoon was excited by Hawks's pitch: "I said, 'I haven't got any plot, but there have been several gangster pictures made, and I will double the casualty list of any picture to date, and we'll have twice as good a picture. *The Secret Six* killed off about eight people. I will kill off twenty, and we'll have the audience right in our hands.'" (*The Secret Six*, all but forgotten today, was a 1931 gangster picture whose Al Capone was renamed Louis "Slaughterhouse" Scorpio, played by roughneck character actor Wallace Beery—a major star at the time. It was directed by George Hill and featured future marquee attractions Clark Gable and Jean Harlow in supporting roles.)

Hawks can take full credit for the casting of Muni; the director was, according to biographer Todd McCarthy, an aficionado of Yiddish theater. He had Muni in mind from the get-go, and had to persuade the actor, who became diffident on being presented the opportunity, to take the role. George Raft, a one-time gangster associate in real life, became fast friends with the more staid Muni upon introduction, and it was he whose career would lean more to tough-guy roles hereafter than Muni. (It was in this picture that Raft first demonstrated the signature tic that defined his persona, his character's habit of idly flipping a coin. Decades later, playing the gangster Spats in Billy Wilder's farce *Some Like It Hot*, the now-venerable Raft would upbraid a young coin-flipping hood—played by Edward G. Robinson Jr., as it happened; Wilder didn't miss a trick with his meta jokes—by grabbing the coin and asking, "Where did you pick up that cheap trick?") Raft was responsible for bringing Ann Dvorak on board. Hawks had worked with the stately British actor Boris Karloff, who would make an international sensation incarnating Frankenstein's monster, in the 1930 prison picture *The Criminal Code.*

The picture was shot at lightning speed. Photography began at the end of June 1931. By July 8, Hawks and Hughes were submitting test scenes to the Hays Office. Although the official Production Code that served as a form of self-censorship in Hollywood from the mid-'30s until the early '60s had yet to go into effect, the so-called Hays Office, which had been formed in the late '20s and had the Code formulated by 1930, was already putting the screws on filmmakers. Hughes himself was someone who consistently balked at it—his exploits defending another Hughes/Hawks collaboration, the shot-in-1941 but released-in-1943 *The Outlaw,* are entertainingly fictionalized in Martin Scorsese's 2004 picture *The Aviator*—and prior to the shoot, he instructed Hawks, by telegram: "Screw the Hays Office. Start the picture and make it as realistic, as exciting, as grisly as possible." The shoot concluded in September, and negotiations with the Hays Office dragged on into the winter of 1932. As McCarthy observes, the movie's mid-May release date meant that the movie missed "the height of the gangster craze." The movie "did very well at the box office, but it did not clean up as it might have" had it caught that wave.

Nowadays, when media professionals deign to consider older movies, they tend to tread lightly in certain areas, afraid of alienating readers who, they imagine, demand and crave only the most up-to-date "content" for consumption. Hence, warnings that film X or Y may not be "relatable," may contain material that is "alienating" to "contemporary sensibilities," all that sort of thing. Additionally, popular commentators on film openly disdain pictures of a certain vintage. The pop culture polymath Shea Serrano freely espouses that in the 1930s, filmmakers were "still figuring thing out" and, when compiling for video a compendium of top scenes from gangster movies, completely and purposefully ignored the pictures from the 1930s that created the template for contemporary gangster movies on the grounds that they're "not fun." These pronouncements elicit the usual disapprobation from certain critics, while the rest of the world either shrugs or agrees wholeheartedly.

I confess that while watching the Hawks *Scarface* during the researching of this book, my mind wandered away from what was actually in front of me and into a realm of speculation and second-guessing. What still counted as "a gangster film of unusual ferocity" for Robin Wood in 1966 will not register as such for certain viewers; this is undeniable.

Some of its dramatic devices feel quaint; for instance, in an interrogation scene early in the picture, a cop, Guarino (C. Henry Gordon), butts in on Camonte as he's relaxing in a barber shop with a hot towel and hauls him to headquarters after Camonte uses his badge to strike a match. At the police station, the chief detective (Edwin Maxwell) essentially predicts Camonte's fate, delivering his speech in the rat-a-tat-tat syncopated style that became a commonplace of Hawks's later screwball comedies: "Listen to me. You come into this town and you think you're headed somewhere, don't you? You think you're gonna get there with a gun, but you're not. Get me? You know why? Because you've got thousand-dollar bills pasted right in front of your eyes. And someday you're gonna stumble and fall down in the gutter. Right where the horses have been standing. Right where you belong." And this is literally how things resolve, at least in the version Hawks first delivered to audiences: in a rerelease version, Camonte is lifted from the gutter and delivered to the gallows via the bureaucratic arm of law enforcement.

If elements of the movie can't help but play as "corny" for viewers disinclined to shift their expectations into a different realm than what they're comfortable with (a realm in which storylines and character dynamics are in point of fact even cornier than what 1930s films offer; pick any random picture in the *Fast and the Furious* franchise, with its windy fake pieties about "family" and so on), Muni's performance, and the peculiar expressionism of Hawks's visual style, are still bound to impress.

For most of Hawks's career, he preferred to work with a more or less invisible eye. His shots were rarely designed for overt visual beauty, and his cutting had a steady, reliable rhythm that never contrived to jar the viewer in ways either classical or postmodern. For *Scarface*, however, he and Lee Garmes luxuriated in the shadows of criminality's Night World, and brought in a fantastic recurring visual emblem: most times a murder is committed in the film, a giant "X," either in the local architecture or in shadow, appears on the screen. The X of course signifies death and is also more or less the same shape as the scar that decorates Tony Camonte's face and gives him his nickname.

"I got it in the war," Tony laconically explains to his boss's girlfriend, Poppy, whom he is soon to claim for his own. "War! With a blonde in a Brooklyn speakeasy," laughs Johnny Lovo, the boss in question. He's played by Osgood Perkins, father of Anthony Perkins. Lovo speaks of his accomplice with amused affection, having no reason yet to fear Tony.

Adventurous viewers looking at this movie for points of comparison will perhaps be surprised at how closely the more sprawling later picture follows the story arc and adheres to the major themes of the De-Palma-Pacino-Stone-Bregman opus. As written by Hecht and others, Muni's Tony Camonte is a more immediately clownish character than the one that Pacino would create. Upon being released from arrest by a slick lawyer working for Lovo, Camonte spouts a goofy malapropism, citing a "writ of hocus-pocus." Tony Montana doesn't do much wordplay, instead eliciting mordant laughter perhaps with observations like "I kill Communists for fun" and "this town is like a giant pussy, waiting to be fucked."

But Karen Morley, as Poppy, who Camonte wins to his side after usurping Lovo, initially regards Camonte with the same icy disdain that Michelle Pfeiffer's Elvira has for Montana. Muni's Camonte shows his ambition early on, vowing, "Someday I'm gonna run the whole works."

"First you get the power, then you get the money, then you get the women," Montana tells Manny. In Hawks's film, Camonte's philosophy is a bit different: "Do it first, do it yourself, and keep on doing it." Also worth noting: Montana's mantra is prefaced by, "In this country." The Hawks *Scarface* doesn't really aspire to say anything meaningful about the so-called American Dream. Its prime imperative, in a sense, is the thing that Hawks promised to Hughes: slaughter. And loud slaughter. "How many barrels did you say you wanted? Six. Well you're gettin' ten."

Several scenes in the Hawks are explicitly elaborated in De Palma. A scene in a nightclub in which Tony Camonte beats on a guy trying to make time with Ann Dvorak's hotsy-totsy Cesca is expanded into a set piece of around twenty minutes in De Palma's movie. A phone call to Lovo in Hawks is reprised as a phone call to Robert Loggia's Frank Lopez in the 1983 film. Ann Dvorak's death scene isn't as big as Mary Elizabeth Mastrantonio's, but it's pretty big. And so on.

In 1947, after the film's rights changed hands, the movie was withdrawn from circulation and viewable, according to McCarthy, "only overseas or at clandestine screenings, where the prints shown were almost invariably awful 16 mm bootleg dupes of who knew what version of the film." For there were at least two, the cut Hawks initially approved, and a Hays Office–approved version with a drippy variation of a "crime does not pay" message that the original, in its way, also carried. Certain of the overseas screenings were held in Paris, at a place called the Cinémathèque Française, and it was here that the reputation of Hawks in general began its metamorphosis.

Because by the mid-1950s Hawks, despite putting "A Howard Hawks Production" at the head of many of his films, was something of a lesser-known quantity. After a lengthy string of hits (and flops, commercially at least) in numerous genres spanning the late '30s to the early '50s—the aforementioned *Bringing Up Baby* and *His Girl Friday* in comedy, *Only Angels Have Wings* and *To Have and Have Not* in adventure, vivid pictures of adventure and romance, ineffable noir detective picture *The Big Sleep*, sweeping Western epic *Red River*, all of these featuring the most iconic stars of their time, including Cary Grant, Katharine Hepburn, Humphrey Bogart and Lauren Bacall—he was now producing rather less immediately noteworthy fare including the post-screwball *Monkey Business* and the cumbersome ancient epic *Land of the Pharaohs*.

Peter Wollen's essay "Who the Hell Is Howard Hawks," included in his excellent 2002 collection *Paris Hollywood: Writing on Film*, chronicles the making of Hawks's reputation. It begins with Henri Langlois, the founder and curator of the Cinémathèque, who, at the age of fifteen, saw Hawks's 1928 silent *A Girl in Every Port* and was struck, as so many filmgoers have tended to be, by the sight of beautiful screen siren Louise Brooks. "He remembered the film vividly all his life," Wollen writes, "and his life-long respect for Howard Hawks could almost seem a kind of by-product, praise for the man who launched Brooks' career." And so, at his Cinémathèque, among the most innovative and free-wheeling of repertory cinemas anywhere (inveterate collector and pretty much anti-neat-freak Langlois would store prints in his bathtub when he had to), he regularly showed Hawks films. And "it was at Langlois' makeshift little cinema [...]

that the group of young cultists who wrote for *Cahiers du Cinema* first saw Hawks' work." These cultists included critics who would turn filmmakers, major ones at that: François Truffaut, Jean-Luc Godard, Jacques Rivette, Éric Rohmer, all of them mentored at one point or another by protean critic André Bazin. And they, as Wollen puts it, "launched Hitchcocko-Hawkism on a bemused public."

Hence the origin of the letter that Eugene Archer, living in France on a Fulbright scholarship, wrote to his friend, the then freelance critic Andrew Sarris: "Who the hell is Howard Hawks?" Archer had no clue as to why the filmmaker was being "taken seriously," Sarris recalled.

They found out. And a decade later, Sarris would put Hawks in his pantheon.

Scarface was acquired by Universal in the late 1970s and was featured in a good print at the 1980 New York Film Festival. Despite the fact of those atrocious bootleg prints that were the only means of seeing it up until then, the movie had become, as *Cahiers du Cinéma*–driven auteurism took a firm hold of a certain sector of film criticism, an object of a particular kind of critical worship. Wollen sees the diversity of Hawks's work as the key to why his reputation has ridden on a (wholly positive!) "roller coaster." He is different things to different observers: "the constructivist of film (Henri Langlois), the master of pulp, operetta, and action (Manny Farber), the French classicist, the Corneille (Jacques Rivette), the Greek tragedian, the Sophocles (Andrew Sarris), the serious moralist (Robin Wood), the bard of the male group (Peter Wollen), or of the Hawksian woman (Molly Haskell)."

The accounts Farber and Wood give of *Scarface* are worth airing here. Farber, the American critic of whom Susan Sontag said, "[his] mind and eye change the way you see," enthused on it, in a 1969 issue of *Artforum*, thusly: "*Scarface* is a passionate, strong, archaic photographic miracle: the rise and fall of an ignorant, blustery, pathetically childish punk (Paul Muni) in an avalanche of rich, dark-dark images. These people, Italian gangsters and their tough, wise-cracking girls, are quite beautiful as varied and shapely as those who parade through Piero's religious paintings… [I]t is a movie of quick-moving actions, inner tension, and more angularity per square inch of screen than any street film in history." I like Farber's coinage, "street film," and am sorry it never really caught on; it's potentially useful. I also like Farber's vivid imagery, which kind of matches that of Hawks's film: "The whole population in *Scarface*, cavemen in quilted smoking jackets, are like the first animals struggling out of the slime and murk toward fresh air."

The British-born critic Wood catches a piece of Farber's wave when he compares the Hawks film to Godard's feral 1964 war satire *Les Carabiniers.* Citing the infantile behavior of Tony and several supporting characters in the Hawks film, Wood writes: "Both here and in *Les Carabiniers* we are made to feel the frightening discrepancy between the achievements of civilization and the actual level of culture attained by the individuals who are its by-products." For all that, though, Wood notes: "The film shows remarkably little society either to outrage or defend. Hawks' 'naturalism' is highly selective: he works by simply eliminating society."

This will also prove to be true, in a sense, of De Palma's movie. Except for a detour into potential guilt and shame when Montana visits the house of his mother, there isn't anything like "normal" life in the movie. And there wasn't meant to be.

3

THE LEGEND OF MARTY BREGMAN

The story of the 1983 remake of *Scarface* has many beginnings. The Hawks film, of course. Al Pacino, whose first viewing of the Hawks film made him want to star in a new *Scarface*. Original director candidate Sidney Lumet, who had the inspiration to replace booze bootlegging with cocaine smuggling and distribution. Screenwriter Oliver Stone, who took that theme and ran with it. Brian De Palma, whose visual virtuosity and willingness—no, *determination*—to push all boundaries of depiction gave the 1983 film its irreproducible distinctiveness.

But mostly, the story of the 1983 *Scarface* begins with Martin Bregman. Born in 1926, educated in business at Indiana University and NYU, he began his professional career selling insurance. He found his entry into arts and entertainment via nightclubs, as an agent. Clients included Barbra Streisand and Woody Allen, then a cabaret singer and standup comedian, respectively.

Like many other New York theatergoers, Bregman was electrified when he first saw Al Pacino on stage. It was in a 1968 off-Broadway production of Israel Horovitz's play *The Indian Wants the Bronx.*

Horovitz's one-act is a disturbing urban parable of racism and all-too-typical New York City mook behavior. The premise is simplicity itself: a South Asian man who speaks little English is trying to find a bus to take him to the Bronx to visit his son; he is accosted by two adolescent punks who make nasty sport of him before committing a completely pointless assault. The two punks are Joey and Murph; Pacino originated the role of Murph, while in early productions, Joey was played by Horovitz himself. (Horovitz's son, Adam, born in 1966, the year *Indian* got its first tentative staging in Connecticut, would go on develop a blustery juvenile delinquent persona as Ad-Rock in the rap trio Beastie Boys decades later.)

According to Pacino biographer Andrew Yule, Bregman had been tipped off to Pacino by Faye Dunaway, a management client of Bregman's whose 1967 work in *Bonnie and Clyde* had catapulted her to movie stardom. Bregman was so impressed by Pacino's energetic, frightening portrayal that he went backstage and promised the world to the young actor. Whether becoming a screen icon was part of the world Pacino was coveting at the time is open to question. In numerous interviews, Pacino has averred that the most crucial times in his existence—not merely his professional existence, but his whole life—are those times when he's on the stage. "I love what [high wire artist Karl] Wallenda said," Pacino told Lawrence Grobel, going on to paraphrase Wallenda's response to a question about how he could get back up on the wire after a fatal accident took one of his own. "[H]e said 'Life is on the wire. The rest is just waiting.' That's where life is for me. That's where it happens." Given his subsequent approach to Tony Montana on the set of *Scarface*, he regarded the soundstage as both theater and laboratory. But this environment had been afforded him by the clout he had built up in the film world up until that point, which might not have even been a glimmer in Pacino's eye when Bregman turned up and offered to do his bidding.

As it happened, doing Pacino's bidding, or what he took to be Pacino's bidding, did some good for Bregman's other clients as well. Pacino's first film appearance was in 1969's *Me, Natalie*, a brief bit in the beginning, as a rough guy who tries to pick up Patty Duke's title character at a dance. He might have made an impression, but the movie did not. Winning a Tony for his work in *Does a Tiger Wear a Necktie?* started the film offers rolling. In consultation with Bregman, Pacino turned down offers from high-profile directors like Otto Preminger and Mike Nichols. He instead took the lead role in a low-budget but high-pedigree picture called *The Panic in Needle Park*. While Bregman was not a credited producer, according to Yule he had some involvement in securing backing for the film. The nominal producer was Dominick Dunne; the screenwriters were Joan Didion and John Gregory Dunne, the "It" literary couple of the time. The movie is a chronicle of the desperate lives of young junkies on Manhattan's Upper West Side; its director, Jerry Schatzberg, was a Bregman client. (Schatzberg had directed Dunaway in *Puzzle of a Downfall Child* in 1970.)

Discovering that the border between artist management and film production could be profitably porous, in 1971 Bregman started a company called Artist Entertainment Complex. "We were a public company; we went into career management and production, ostensibly with the idea of working with our clients in finding and developing properties for them to produce, which was kind of a very ambitious idea," Bregman recounted to journalist Tom Hawley in the mid-'70s. "Having been a manager and having put together packages for clients, producers, directors, writers, was a natural transition." Their first picture was a Raquel Welch roller derby potboiler called *Kansas City Bomber*.

"That was done for a million dollars and did very, very well. It wasn't a great film but it was a good film." I skipped guitar lessons to see it when I was a wayward 12-year-old and not only is it not a good film, I've regretted my lack of discipline in pursuing guitar studies ever since.

The company's conception was prescient. Years later, at the agency CAA (Creative Artists Agency), Michael Ovitz made a specialty of packaging projects from a huge stable of clients working both behind and in front of the camera. Some called it "creative synergy"; others called it less complimentary things. In any event, Martin Scorsese's *Goodfellas* was among the motion pictures that benefited from Ovitz's way of doing business, so it was all worth it.

When it came to *The Godfather*, Pacino's breakthrough movie, Bregman's role was to encourage Pacino to continue pursuing a role that Pacino was convinced nobody wanted him for. For a while, Pacino was right, except the one person who wanted Pacino was Francis Ford Coppola, who did not back down. "Okay, you got your midget," mega-producer Robert Evans recalls telling Coppola after finally deciding to give him his way. (Among Evans's preferred Michael Corleones was his French best friend Alain Delon, who barely spoke English.)

Pacino followed up *The Godfather* with another picture with Schatzberg, *Scarecrow*, a shambling narrative of lost souls on the roads of America very in keeping with a particular mode of alternative Hollywood filmmaking of the time. Pacino was paired with Gene Hackman, so the movie was also something of an actor's duet. But the principals didn't click. "We didn't communicate, didn't think in the same terms," Pacino told an interviewer.

Serpico, on the other hand, was a kind of aria, the story of the ultimate alienated man, based on the true case of Frank Serpico, a New York City cop who exposed the rampant corruption of his profession and got, among other things, a bullet in the face for his trouble. Investigative journalist Peter Maas published his biography of the man in 1973, and the movie was made and released the same year. Maas's book was dynamite, and a hot property for a film adaptation. The Italian biographers of mega-producer Dino De Laurentiis depict him calling Maas and offering him nearly half a million for the rights at a point when Maas was months from anything resembling a completed manuscript. He then pursues Pacino, negotiating with him in Italian. Andrew Yule's biography of Pacino calls the De Laurentiis version of the story "long discounted."

One thing that was true: De Laurentiis had adapted Maas's previous nonfiction crime best-seller *The Valachi Papers*, about a Mafia informant, into a (meh) picture. So he was in a good position with respect to Maas. And De Laurentiis had convinced Paramount's Charles Bluhdorn to put out the cash for the rights to Maas's book. The men would coproduce the picture. De Laurentiis at first looked out for the story, commissioning a screenwriter, trying out a director. Bregman looked over the Italian producer's shoulder intently, especially because Pacino himself needed some prodding in order to commit to the role. After spending time with the real Serpico and finding good pace in a new script by Waldo Salt (Salt's third draft; Bregman considered the first version Salt turned in "very political," which quality was apparently something of a bugbear for the producer), Pacino was in.

The eventual director was Sidney Lumet, at the time among other things something of a quintessential New York filmmaker. If *Serpico* was an urban epic par excellence, the next Bregman-Lumet-Pacino collaboration, 1975's *Dog Day Afternoon*, went one better. It told the only-in-New-York story of Sonny Wortzik, woefully inexperienced in criminal endeavor, who attempts to rob a bank to pay for his partner's sex reassignment surgery. (For film purposes, the name of the real-life figure, John Wojtowicz, was changed.) What had been intended as a cash grab turned into a day-long siege and a harrowing kind of street theater. Working again with cherished friend and colleague John Cazale, his costar in *The Indian Wants the Bronx* who went on to play Corleone brother Fredo in the first two *Godfather* movies, Pacino gave one of those performances that critics like to say "burns a hole in the screen."

With *Serpico* and *Dog Day*, both critical and popular successes (Pacino's outlaw charm in *Dog Day* had audiences either accepting or forgetting that his character was devoted to what you'd now call a gender-fluid personal relationship), Pacino, Bregman, and Lumet seemed to be on a roll. But Bregman and Pacino's pursuit of a particular project gummed up the works for both their professional and personal relationships.

In his exceptional memoir *Chasing the Light*, writer/director Oliver Stone recalls being summoned by Bregman to the latter's office in the mid-'70s. At the time, he was trying to get his Vietnam war picture *Platoon* made. The script was setting off tremors throughout the movie industry, but nothing was enough to get anyone to actually back the project.

> I was impressed with his busy secretaries, accountants (for his tax and money management business) and the massive electric door that opened only from the inside when he buzzed me in to his private office. He stood up, wearing braces; while the effects of his childhood polio were not as severe as Roosevelt's, it no doubt made getting around difficult. He reeked of authority with a commanding, no-bullshit sensibility. He brought in Al Pacino from a secret back office, who, like his Godfather persona, was restless, edgy, sensitive, and tough to read; he didn't really look me in the eye, and I felt nervous. He didn't speak much. He was sizing me up like he would a boxer in training. All

that mattered was the part, "the play." Everything else was "hanging around."

Marty invited me to join him at the well-known Elaine's restaurant uptown, introduced me with conviction as a coming young writer, and the conversation with his celebrity friends dazzled me. Marty was genuinely trying to make *Platoon,* but it was uphill all the way. Sidney Lumet, who'd directed Al in *Serpico* and *Dog Day Afternoon* with Marty producing, had been sent the screenplay and said that as good as the script was, he was too old now to chase around a jungle like he'd done earlier in his life (which in fact he'd never done). He was a man of the New York neighborhoods through and through, a man of interiors and raw dialogue; *12 Angry Men* (1957) was his first film. And Al, well, he was already in his mid-thirties, not close to the *Platoon* protagonist's twenty-one. Marty, in that first phone call to me, had done his job well as the producer; he created excitement, which is crucial to birthing a project. But in this case, excitement was all there would be.

Stone was excited to have Bregman involved in his career: "He was also dark and handsome like Bugsy Siegel—altogether a dramatic persona you don't forget. He'd become a major figure in my life, both good and bad, but right now I was his 'boy.' He felt he'd discovered me with *Platoon*, and he'd test me to my limits with *Born*."

Born is *Born on the Fourth of July*, the 1976 memoir by Vietnam veteran Ron Kovic, about his experiences growing up as a child inculcated by patriotism, fighting in the Vietnam war, sustaining the wound that paralyzed him from the chest down, and founding the organization Vietnam Vets Against the War. Bregman bought the option for the book. At this point in time, the story of an anti-Vietnam-war activist was just political enough. (*Coming Home*, in which Jane Fonda dealt with not one but two traumatized Vietnam vets, became a zeitgeist-defining hit in 1978; Pacino turned down the role in that film that would earn Jon Voight a Best Actor Oscar.) Bregman struggled to get financing for the film, even as locations were scouted. (I remember as a teenager being told by a friend that Dumont High School, in the New Jersey town from which I had moved in 1975, was to be used to stand in for Kovic's high school, and that Pacino had been spotted checking it out.) The first director to sign on was William Friedkin. He dropped out and was replaced by the more staid and conventional Daniel Petrie. Years later Pacino would enigmatically tell interviewer Lawrence Grobel that the project didn't happen because it was "too close." Despite the assurance of German tax shelter money to finance the picture, it fell apart.

Stone writes: "Stories had it that Al had lost confidence in Dan as a director; in those days, Al was extremely suspicious and tough on directors he hadn't previously worked with, trusting mostly his own instinct. Soon we all stopped coming to the rehearsal hall, and the prep week to start locations on Long Island was canceled. Al playing seventeen and going to the prom was going to be a stretch anyway. Our company, which had been so close, simply dissolved. Nothing to do, no place to go in the mornings, no film. Marty's office was a tomb. He'd aged a lot in those weeks. Al was then rumored to have accepted Norman Jewison's … *And Justice for All* (1979) for his next film. Nor would he return Ron's or my calls. Nor, for that matter, did he return Bregman's calls. It was over."

So, too, was Bregman's partnership with Pacino. "It was a series of events that neither of us was responsible for," Bregman told Pacino biographer Andrew Yule. "We had both been heavily into the project, and the rug was pulled from under us." This assertion runs counter to Stone's implication that it had been Pacino himself who got cold feet. In any event: "It was an unhappy, wounding experience for both of us."

He had moved away from personal management as his producing mojo got stronger. He told Yule, "I grew tired of playing nursemaid to gifted but insecure actors." Nevertheless, Bregman continued a fruitful partnership with Alan Alda, an actor with writing and directing ambitions whose clout was bolstered by the incredible popularity of his '70s television series *M*A*S*H.* 1979's *The Seduction of Joe Tynan* brought director Jerry Schatzberg back into the fold, overseeing a script by Alda. The picture, a low-key, earnest examination of political corruption, was a crucial step up for Alda, whose subsequent directorial efforts made him something of a brand in early '80s moviemaking, even if they're not much brought up today. *Tynan* had young Meryl Streep in a showcase supporting role. She took the part while mourning the death of her partner, Pacino's great friend John Cazale.

"I've had screaming fights with Marty, but he fights because he's really trying to make the film better," Alda told Steven Farber in 1987, for a profile of Bregman in the *New York Times.* "[...] He's actually a soft touch. He has given or loaned money to people I wouldn't give lunch to. He has a total inability to fire someone on a movie. On the other hand, if he feels he's been wronged, he does the legal equivalent of killing you.

"He knows people very, very well, in the way that a successful salesperson often knows human nature [...] That helps him to be useful to a writer or director. He'll tell you when something doesn't ring true."

In its 2018 obituary for Bregman, the *New York Times* noted, "By the time Mr. Bregman produced his first film, it seemed like a midlife career change. He was 47."

He would soon make not just a midlife career change but a midlife change, period. It was on the set of *Serpico* that Bregman met young actress Cornelia Sharpe, who had a role in the picture as Serpico's hippie-ish girlfriend Leslie. Serpico meets

Leslie in a Spanish class. When he asks her what she does, she says, "Oh me, I'm an actress, singer, dancer, and a Buddhist."

"I'm a cop," Serpico replies. "Would you believe that?"

"No I wouldn't believe it."

Blonde, lithe, with high cheekbones, Sharpe was undeniably camera-friendly, and Bregman, when speaking of her and their projects together, would praise the aura of glamour she possessed, an aura he believed other contemporary actors of the time were actively, and inexplicably, trying to divest themselves of. (He even once compared his former client, Faye Dunaway, unfavorably with Sharpe.) During the period in which *Born* fell apart, Bregman found a new crusade.

"He was going to make Cornelia Sharpe a star," the producer Barbara De Fina told me in conversation. De Fina, who would be crucial in the making of films including *Goodfellas, Casino, The Age of Innocence, The Grifters* and more, was just starting in the film business in the mid-'70s and was dating a member of the crew of *The Next Man*, Bregman's first vehicle for Sharpe. "His office had a very serious aura, what with its separate private entrance and so on. All the business there was very serious. When his wife [Elizabeth] would visit, there was a bit of a hush. She was invariably referred to as 'Mrs. Bregman.'"

The Next Man was not merely intended as a Sharpe showcase. The story was of a Middle East UN Ambassador who posits a revolutionary scheme for peace with Israel, touching off international controversy and making the diplomat a target for assassination. Speaking to the *Daily News* in the fall of 1976, Bregman waxed philosophical on its ambitious themes: "It was a difficult film to write... [T]he whole Middle East has been considered Neanderthal. We have Connery playing a progressive Arabian—almost like Sadat—who proposes a peace partnership between a united Arabia and Israel." A volatile concept, to be sure. "The film has violence, but it's a picture about violence. We handle it well."

You read correctly, yes, Sean Connery plays the progressive Arab. The year before, he had played a non-progressive Berber in John Milius's *The Wind and the Lion*, so one can say he was possibly expanding his horizons here. Connery's character, Khalil-Abdul Muhsen, is, among other things, almost staggeringly cosmopolitan, well-read, erudite, witty, an enthusiastic chef, a man with the common touch.

Sharpe's role is as Nicole, an elegant, and yes, glamorous beauty who's also an international hit woman. You betcha. Her assignment is to seduce and kill Connery's character. Which, spoiler alert, she does.

Viewed today, *The Next Man* looks less like a political thriller than a form of Bregman wish fulfillment. An inordinate amount of time is spent depicting Sharpe and Connery in courtship mode. They laugh it up at a fish market, get in a little "we love a parade" time, have a ball waterskiing. Sean Connery was still pretty much the best cinematic surrogate a middle-aged white guy could hope for. It all looks like great fun, until Sharpe plugs Connery in the chest with an automatic and splits. Women, am I right?

The movie got moderate-to-poor reviews, with some critics deeming the film's schizoid elements to be somewhat enigmatic—not an entirely unreasonable place upon which to stack their chips, since *Next Man* director Richard Sarafian was also responsible for the counterculture puzzler *Vanishing Point*. It did not do the trick of making Sharpe a star. Some years later, Bregman tried to give Sharpe a boost in television. In January 1980, a faux-breathless item appeared on the *New York Post*'s *Page Six*, announcing a party at Regine's—then a very chic nightspot—celebrating the TV movie *S★H★E*, starring Sharpe. Calling Sharpe a "seductive blonde," and "the new female James Bond," it describes the potential series as one in which Sharpe's character operates using "a variety of disguises and an array of sophisticated gadgetry" and lists a murderer's row of 1960s movie icons—Omar Sharif, Anita Ekberg, and Robert Lansing—as portraying her varied nemeses.

*S*H*E*, incidentally, stood for Security Hazards Expert. The script for the television movie was by Richard Maibaum, whose non-television movies include *Goldfinger*, *Thunderball*, and *The Spy Who Loved Me*. The tagline for *S*H*E* was, "She does it better than he!" In case you were wondering what kind of vibe Bregman and Sharpe were hoping to capture here. Produced as a pilot, *S*H*E* was not picked up, and so the movie did not land Sharpe and producer/party-thrower Bregman a series.

Bregman divorced his first wife, Elizabeth Driscoll, in 1980. He married Sharpe in 1981. That same year he produced *Venom*, a kidnap thriller with a horrible-poisonous-snake-on-the-loose element added for more thrills. Originally to have been directed by *Texas Chainsaw Massacre* and *Poltergeist* frisson-producer Tobe Hooper, it was passed on to British screenwriter and director Piers Haggard after either "creative differences" or, per Haggard, a Hooper nervous breakdown. The cast was stacked with name actors, all of whose reputations for being pleasant and easy to work with no doubt preceded them: Nicol Williamson (rager, alcoholic); Sterling Hayden (possibly recovering alcoholic at the time); Oliver Reed (say no more); Klaus Kinski (say no more). Into this mix Cornelia Sharpe was thrown, in the thankless role of the mother of the mildly irritating child kidnap victim. Under other circumstances the scenario might have produced a normal suspense picture of some quality. These particular circumstances produced something quite a bit more off-the-wall. A shamelessly entertaining mess, call it. Not the kind of picture Martin Bregman wanted to do, one can confidently infer.

After a lengthy period I spent trying to persuade Cornelia Sharpe to speak with me for this book, she ended our exchange with this text: "I read your requests but sadly I have neither the time nor the inclination to get into this kind of thing, but I do wish you all the best with your project."

Here is Andrew Yule's telling of how Al Pacino came to contact Marty Bregman after their estrangement: "Driving down Sunset Boulevard one day while on a visit to Los Angeles, he came across a tiny theater playing Hawks' classic." According to Yule, Pacino had been seeking out this film for some reason. "The movie had a huge impact on him. He was struck by its real, positively grand feeling and especially by Muni's tremendous performance. When it occurred to him a remake might be attempted, the logical man to call was Marty Bregman. 'Look at *Scarface*,' Pacino suggested. 'I think there may be a character there for me to play.'"

There are other versions of Pacino's discovery of *Scarface*. It's clear that Pacino's call to Bregman came at a time when a reunion, particularly on a project of some size, looked especially desirable. He still considered himself a serious producer. And by 1982, the year he would embark on *Scarface*, he'd had enough experience in international production to instruct journalist Howard Kissel, from *Newsday*, on the finer points of just what he did. "Most people don't know what a producer does; they think we have the money," Bregman told the interviewer. "If I had that kind of money, I wouldn't be producing—I'd live in the South of France." He prided himself on working well in the Hollywood system while not being exactly of it. He remained bemused at the paranoid atmosphere he found in Los Angeles. "Sometimes you meet directors out there who talk as if making a picture was like going off to war. I had a director tell me he needed somebody to 'watch my back.'" He kept his base in New York because it was his hometown, but also because it was removed from what he called the "sea of paranoia and competitiveness" of Hollywood. However, he identified one syndrome that was universal in show business. "[P]eople don't like other people's success. When I have made a successful film I don't hear from a lot of old friends. When I have made a disaster, I hear from everybody."

In the wake of *Venom*, it's likely Bregman was tired of hearing from everybody.

4

TONY

It's the evening of April 23, 2023, in New York City. Al Pacino, dressed in black as is his custom nowadays, his hair styled in a kind of salt-and-pepper lion-in-winter mane, sits in an easy chair on the stage of the 92nd Street Y and basks in audience adulation. At their career beginnings, both he and his friend Robert De Niro were "press shy," reluctant to give interviews and somewhat halting and inarticulate when they deigned to do so. For Pacino, a series of exchanges with longtime *Playboy* contributor Lawrence Grobel proved rewarding in terms of allowing Pacino to work out his own motivations and his conversational comfort levels. And these days, he clearly relishes Q and As as a form of performance. Certainly here, he's eager to get laughs from the crowd, surprise them with some unexpected pronouncements, and generally give it what it wants. (While De Niro has over the years grown more comfortable with being interviewed, he's never been able to make the process feel like a show for him; of course, unlike Pacino, who's always kept a close connection to the stage, De Niro all but abjured live theater after he started getting regular work in pictures.)

Pacino's interlocutor this evening is David Rubenstein, a silver-haired, buttoned-down gentleman who is apparently a private equity giant; he sits on the board of the Y and many other organizations, and he probably got this moderating gig by asking for it. The idiosyncrasies of his questions are probably indicative of his larger mindset, which is, after all, that of a billionaire. For instance, speaking of Pacino's Best Supporting Actor nomination for *The Godfather*, Rubenstein notes that in his role as Michael Corleone, he had many, many more lines of dialogue than Marlon Brando, who was nominated for and indeed won the Best Lead Actor Oscar for his work in the film. Didn't that bother Pacino? Pacino puts his palms up and bellows "No," because, you know, among other things, Brando was Brando and Brando was playing the title role in the movie. He's not genuinely offended by the question (and indeed, when Grobel asked him something similar, albeit less inanely phrased, in 1979, Pacino took the question as an opportunity to grouse about awards categories in general) and is able to make a bit out of it. Was he upset that Brando won? "Are you kidding me?" (In any event, Brando did not accept the award; this was the notorious Oscar ceremony where he had sent the actor and apparent Native American impersonator Sacheen Littlefeather to make a speech protesting Hollywood's treatment of indigenous people in lieu of a thank-you to the Academy et al.)

Near the end of the session, Rubenstein reads aloud questions from the audience. One is, "What actor would you really love to work with?" Pacino thinks about it for a minute, and says, quietly, John Cazale. This ought to be a moment for the audience to take in. The sentiment is very moving. For all the fine actors currently now available to work with, the one Pacino has the most yearning for is his friend, someone who was there with him from the beginning, who was his indelible collaborator on three classic films, and who has been dead for almost fifty years. Unimpressed, Rubenstein plows ahead: "What about actress?"

Scarface, when mentioned in Pacino's introduction and elsewhere, elicits especially warm applause from the crowd, same level as the *Godfather* movies.

Michael Bregman, Martin Bregman's son, who knew Pacino from childhood—he recalls that when Pacino would visit the Bregman house on Long Island, Pacino would mostly avoid adult company and play touch football with the kids—speculated in conversation that Pacino really doesn't like talking about *Scarface*. This was during the long period when I was negotiating, with nothing much in terms of results, to interview the actor for this book. "I think Al would like to take *Scarface* off his filmography, because it's still the only movie of his people care about in this particular way. Even Michael Corleone is not the same thing." Bregman might have a point; he went on to speak of how Pacino prefers to talk Shakespeare, but as has been iterated millions of times by now, Shakespearean tragedies and gangster pictures aren't so far apart. Nevertheless—while Pacino may have won his sole Best Actor Oscar for *Scent of a Woman*, that particular film is pretty much, as things stand, precisely nowhere in the public consciousness nowadays. And his signature bit in that movie, about taking a FLAMETHROWER TO THIS PLACE, might as well be out of *Scarface*.

In any event, for the purposes of the exercise at the 92nd Street Y, Pacino understands that, as much as or even more so than the Coppola films, *Scarface* is the source of very entertaining anecdotes. He will not disappoint his crowd.

"I was walking down Sunset Boulevard—a rare occasion, I never went to L.A. NOW I live there. My youngest children are there, so I'm there. There are four or five of us walking down

Sunset, and I see the Tiffany Theater. And I see the marquee: *Scarface*.

"I'd heard of that. I'd been working on plays a lot. And Bertolt Brecht, he loved gangster movies. Of the 30s and 40s. The American gangster movies. And that was one of them. So I went in to see it. And you get that rarely, when you see something, and you are transcendent. And I came out of that and I thought, I loved this performance of this guy, this Paul Muni—great actor. Stage actor. Out of the Yiddish theater.

"So I called Marty Bregman. I made five films with Marty Bregman. *Sea of Love. Scarface. Serpico, Dog Day*, and *Carlito's Way*. Five." After each title, Pacino pauses for applause.

"He looks at it…he got Sidney Lumet. Sidney Lumet sees that, wants to do it, and he said, you gotta make that transition." The transition from Prohibition to cocaine trafficking. "That became the film.

"I think there was a disagreement between Marty and Sidney about the very theme of it. I think Sidney had another way of looking at it. A more serious way. And then, that was it. He left.

"Brian De Palma is a great director, he had this idea about turning it into an opera, which was very important for Marty, too, and I began to feel it with them, that it should be bigger than life. And they got OLIVER STONE to write the screenplay. Oliver Stone?" Another pause for applause.

Rubenstein is concerned about the dangers of making such a film. The death of cinematographer Halyna Hutchins in the fall of 2021, on the set of a picture called *Rust*, has put film set safety back in a national spotlight, one that persisted as increasingly alarming stories circulated about the presence of live ammunition rounds in the vicinity of the prop department. (When I spoke to the prop master and armorer Robert Griffon Jr. about the safety protocols for the making of Martin Scorsese's *Goodfellas*, he told me he didn't want live ammunition within several miles of the set, let alone on the set itself.) Rubenstein asks,

"When you're shooting a lot of people in *Scarface*, did the armorer person make sure you were set up with fake bullets?"

"Of course. That's the first thing. You have to be prepared. I gotta tell you the one time, doing it. I was in that place… I don't know. You can't imagine the hell it was being there, the smoke, and every day, you get into this mantra, you're doing it, and you're in there fifteen hours. And I'm shooting, and it's 'say hello to my little…'" And the crowd applauds.

"And I get hit, and I go down, and my gun goes down, and I crawl to get it, and I grab it…by the barrel. And my hand gets sealed on to it. And I can't get my hand off." The crowd gasps. "I gotta go to the hospital. And I go to the hospital and I've got blood all over me. And this nurse comes in and says 'Oh, you, you're Al Pacino, right? Yeah. Good. I thought you were some scumbag.'" Because he is indeed in costume as scumbag Tony Montana.

"They stopped for two weeks. But they shot the shit out of that scene. I was away but they were shooting everything. Spielberg came down, had a crack at shooting some of it."

Pacino's claim concerning Spielberg is a myth that has become a meme. It is true that De Palma's good friend came to the set while Pacino was absent and De Palma was shooting different components of the finale. Spielberg did not ask for, nor did De Palma offer, a "crack" at actually shooting. "As I remember," De Palma told me in September of 2023, "I think he came by one day, and we had a bunch of cameras set up, and I said, 'Steven, get over to camera four and…watch the shot.' That's basically what happened. I mean, I placed all the cameras, and Steven was just there watching it being acted out."

During the session, Pacino also revealed that he was writing a book, a memoir or autobiography of sorts. He pointed out his ghostwriter in the audience. The audience was delighted, almost started waving money at him right then and there, while my own heart sank at the implications. Sure enough, when Pacino definitively turned down my request for an interview through his publicist, the book project was the reason. As of this writing, no publication date has been announced.

When people talk about an Al Pacino performance nowadays, they speak in all caps. "HOO HA!" That's *Scent of a Woman*, 1992. "SHE'S GOT A GREAT ASS!" That's *Heat*, 1995. "SAY HELLO TO MY LITTLE FRIEND!" That's why we're here. For some, *Scarface* represents the line where Pacino went from low volume all the way up to eleven. That's not so, of course. His breakthrough role in *The Indian Wants the Bronx* was as a very demonstrative teenage mook. In his first film, 1969's *Me, Natalie*, in which he first sported a hairstyle that made him look a little like Four Seasons singer Frankie Valli, he was a relatively low-key mook but pretty aggressive. "Listen. Do you put out?" he asks Patty Duke.

In Jerry Schatzberg's 1971 *The Panic in Needle Park*, his Bobby is a freewheeling, initially bluff junkie, not much of an introvert at all. A very outgoing guy, with an explosive anger. Here, as in the first two *Godfather* movies, Pacino is also acting with the eyes, a lot. And there are a lot of tics, as junkies tend to have. Bobby's always chewing gum, shifting his jaw. In this film, Richard Bright, who would go on to play Michael Corleone's right-hand man Al Neri in the *Godfather* movies, plays Hank, a well-dressed burglar who brags about never having been caught in the act. Hank will later lord it over Pacino's strung-out character, the "panic" in Needle Park (not even a park but a traffic island on the Upper West Side) being a drying up of the heroin supply.

Watching *Needle Park*, one feels one is experiencing a performer already wholly mature. But not a lot of people watched *Needle Park* when it first came out. It's with *The Godfather* that Pacino galvanized film audiences, and his quietude was almost overwhelming.

"As in many of Pacino's performances, the whole role dwells in his eyes," Isaac Butler observes of the actor's Michael Corleone in *The Method*, his superb book on twentieth century acting. "Later in his career, Pacino would become known for his operatic ability to go over the top, find a new top, and then go over that one as well. But *The Godfather* gives us an Al Pacino of extreme, even brave, restraint. Lee [Strasberg] 'taught me something that I don't do enough of,' he said decades later. 'He said "Sometimes don't go as far as you can go."' There is only one moment where we get a glimpse of the volcanic performances that lay in his future, and it is at the end of the film. Pressed by his wife about whether he had his brother-in-law killed, Michael repeats 'Don't ask me about my business, Kay,' over and over, finally ending the conversation by slamming his hand on his desk and shouting a simple 'No!' The scene, in its repetition and escalation of stakes and its rapid, overlapping, improvisational energy, feels exactly like a first-year exercise in a [Sanford] Meisner classroom. It is the one scene in which Diane Keaton—who by her own admission was lost playing Kay in the film—comes alive, and it contains a multivalent thrill. We are witness to the unveiling of a new and terrifying Michael Corleone, and we are witness to two actors working like great tennis players to provoke each other to new levels of their gifts."

Francis Ford Coppola's struggles to get Pacino cast in the role are the stuff of film legend. As was the case with Keaton, Coppola had first seen Pacino on stage, in his Tony-Award-winning role in *Does a Tiger Wear a Necktie?* In a 2014 profile of Pacino, John Lahr writes: "When Pacino was finally offered the part, he almost couldn't take it. A few months earlier, he'd signed on for an adaptation of the Jimmy Breslin book *The Gang That Couldn't Shoot Straight*, and M-G-M and the producer, Irwin Winkler, refused to release him. Winkler and Horovitz were sharing a house on Fire Island, and Pacino begged the playwright to intercede on his behalf." Winkler, a gentlemanly figure and also a constantly inventive dealmaker, heard Horovitz out but also made the playwright understand his own position. He made a proposition to Horovitz: find him an Italian-American actor as good as the one he'd be giving up. So, according to Lahr, "Horovitz took Winkler to see a performance by a young unknown named Robert De Niro. 'He took De Niro, and he got two options on Pacino and two on De Niro,' Horovitz said."

Winkler did get his shot at working with Pacino, in the film that directly preceded *Scarface*, the misbegotten comedy *Author! Author!*, written by Israel Horowitz and directed by Arthur Hiller. "Al responded to the idea of playing a Broadway playwright with an extended family of children," Winkler writes in his memoir, *A Life in Movies*. "He wanted to get away from the grim characters of Michael Corleone and Serpico to play the sweet but troubled [playwright] Ivan.

"The story was straight out of Horovitz's playbook," Winkler continues. "Ivan has problems at home; his wife is having an affair and is leaving him and not taking the children [...] If Ivan is in trouble, it didn't compare to Al Pacino's relationship with his director, Arthur Hiller.

"Rehearsals in New York started off polite but not particularly warm. Hiller and Pacino danced around each other the first couple of days. By the end of the week, with everyone seemingly comfortable, Pacino asked Hiller about how he thought he should play one potential scene. Hiller told Al that Jack Lemmon (whom he'd directed in *The Out-of-Towners*) could do the scene and wouldn't need to discuss how. I was as surprised as Pacino was by Hiller's reaction. From that moment on I felt as if I was holding out my hands trying to prevent two high-speed trains heading towards each other from colliding. The animosity continued, and after the second week of rehearsals Hiller was so upset with Pacino (and Tuesday Weld), he asked me to fire him. When I asked him why he didn't just quit, he told me that if I fired him, he would get paid; if he quit, the studio would probably sue him, and he certainly wouldn't get paid. I didn't fire him and he didn't quit, and once we started shooting, most active hostility stayed in the background."

At least for a while. Hiller and Pacino were a bad match, and that fact wasn't going to just go away. Pacino told Grobel: "Sometimes people who are not really meant to be together get together in this business for a short time. It's very unfortunate for all the parties concerned. It was just one of those situations where all I needed was to have someone tell me what was going on and I would have responded."

Winkler's recollection has a very aggressive, practically imperial Hiller out-and-out punishing the actor. "[W]e flew up to Gloucester, Massachusetts, for a climactic scene. [...] Hiller set the scene in the bright winter sun, and Pacino, being delayed in makeup, was late on set. When Hiller blocked the actors in their places, Pacino was looking into the sun. He asked Hiller to restage the scene, as he was squinting, was uncomfortable, and it was affecting his performance. Hiller refused and told Pacino that if he had been on time, the sun would not have been shining in his eyes. Pacino calmly apologized for the delay, but Hiller was having none of it. Rather, he brought his anger from rehearsals and the coldness between him and Pacino into a full-blown, angry confrontation. Finally, Pacino walked off the set and into his camper. I tried to calm Hiller down, but he was not to be placated. It was embarrassing for not only Pacino and Hiller but the entire crew, who wished they were anywhere else.

"Pacino suggested he would return to work but wouldn't talk to Hiller and didn't want Hiller talking to him. Hiller liked the idea of not talking to Pacino and agreed that Pacino and Hiller would talk to me, and I would be the voice of both Pacino and Hiller, with Hiller saying to me 'Ask Al to do it again,' and Al saying to me 'Tell him OK.' After about an hour I walked off the set, telling them both I was going to New York and they had better find a way to finish the film. They did." Pacino told

Grobel that the movie "did very well on cable; it works better on television because it's about the home—you can go into the kitchen, come back, and watch it. Why don't we make movies just for cable and movies just for theaters? Keep the big screen going, keep those theaters alive." (This conversation was in 1983, imagine!)

In his *New Yorker* profile, John Lahr writes of Pacino, "Acting, according to Pacino, is about 'getting into a state that brings about freedom and expression and the unconscious.' [David] Mamet compares Pacino's excavations of his characters to the way Louis Armstrong played jazz: 'He's incapable of doing it the same way twice.'" There's an anecdote of Martin Bregman interceding with Sidney Lumet on the set of *Dog Day Afternoon* after Pacino pleaded with his mentor/producer: "I don't have the guy. Let me find the guy." Much of the shooting of *Scarface* would be devoted to giving Pacino the time and space to "find the guy."

5

OLIVER STONE IN MIAMI AND PARIS AND HOLLYWOOD

Oliver Stone had to travel a long way before becoming "Oliver Stone" the prolific, outspoken, provocative Hollywood agitator. The man whose cultural gravitational pull is such that a friend of mine called his book on the man *The Oliver Stone Experience* was a scion of Wall Street affluence, a soldier in Vietnam, a student at NYU's film school who worked under Martin Scorsese, and, by the time Marty Bregman brought him on the *Scarface* project, the director of two films.

Horror films, as a matter of fact. The first, *Seizure*, produced in Canada in 1974, starred Jonathan Frid, then known as the sex-symbol vampire Barnabas Collins on the supernatural network soap opera *Dark Shadows*, as a writer tormented by figures out of his nightmares come to life. The second, 1981's *The Hand*, was a gloss on *The Beast with Five Fingers* in which Michael Caine's pathologically jealous writer loses his hand in an auto accident, and believes that hand is still around, with a life of his own, killing anyone who ticks him off. Neither made much impact on release but both are fascinating artifacts, not least due to the pathologies they treat, pathologies that reflected Stone's own conflicts at the time.

When I interviewed him in 2022, one of the first things I asked was if, upon meeting Brian De Palma, he sensed an affinity with this director who'd also worked in horror. Not quite, as it turns out.

"Well, Brian had been a very successful horror director. I had not. And that was screwed into my psyche by Bregman, and you can believe that. *The Hand*, according to him, was 'a disaster,' blah, blah, blah. But you can look at *The Hand*, it's certainly a psychologically interesting film. But it had not done business. And I was dead in the water, as a director. And Bregman used that, of course. I wanted to direct, badly. I had written and directed and I wanted to continue doing that. But I knew that this was not going to be my film, because I didn't have the experience to do something this size.

"To the contrary, I learned a lot on the film. I was down on my luck, and I had just done *The Hand*, and it had been ridiculed. And I was on cocaine. I was doing cocaine, and I was really an addict, without knowing it."

In a sense, Stone reunited with Bregman because he had to. Stone, Pacino, and Bregman had all fallen out with each other over the collapse of *Born on the Fourth of July*. As far as Stone was concerned, between that and Bregman's inability to get *Platoon* made after teasing him with the possibility, he might as well never work under his aegis again. But in the wake of the failure of *The Hand*, he was in a state. "I never wanted to work with Marty again, after that. It was just so difficult. It's what they call 'masochism,' to work for Marty. You have to really suffer. I'm sure you can tell that. Ask any other writer, they know what's in store for them if they go with Marty: endless re-writes. So,

I had to go through that process. It's a process. And out of that process, I said I didn't want to be with him again.

"And then, my bookie called me up after I had hit bottom again—how many times have I hit bottom? Marty called me and wanted me to do it. I didn't want to do a Mafia story. No interest. Thank you. And then, he called me back a few weeks later. He said: 'Lumet has another idea, and here it is—about the cocaine trade.' That was interesting, and that made it different."

Stone today is not as active a filmmaker as he once was, and many of his observers continue to look askance at what he does produce, like, for instance, a 2022 documentary in which he endorses the use of nuclear energy (and in fairness to Stone, while the default position for a lot of people is to dismiss the idea as outright insane, there are potent and persuasive arguments in its favor). As someone who likes to put the force of his personality behind the promotion of both his films and his social agenda, he's one of those people who, as the saying goes, "understands the assignment" when he's being interviewed. So our conversation was loose, illuminating, and entertaining.

And quite a bit about Bregman, who, not quite a decade after his death, still looms fairly large in Stone's consciousness. As he had been with Al Pacino, and even, to a particular extent, as we'll see, with Michelle Pfeiffer, Bregman was a father figure to Stone, one as contradictory and maddening to Stone as his own father, the Wall Street stockbroker Louis Stone, had been.

So when I mentioned that I liked Stone's comparison, in his memoir *Chasing the Light*, of Bregman to Sinclair Lewis's blustery American preacher/con man Elmer Gantry, Stone immediately warmed.

"Did you ever meet him?" Stone asked me.

Yes. I met Marty Bregman once, under arguably unusual circumstances. The occasion was a press junket for the 1989 film *Sea of Love*, a cinematic comeback for Pacino after the 1985 critical and box office flop *Revolution* drove him out of Hollywood and back to the East Coast, and back to his first and most persistent performing love, the theater. What was unusual was the setup for this Q and A. Not in a ballroom with journalists going from table to table, but in the more intimate setting of a hotel suite, with about a half-dozen journalists, Pacino, his *Sea of Love* costar Ellen Barkin, and Bregman himself, whose bearing was frequently like that of a very protective prom chaperone.

Pacino was slumped in an easy chair; his posture was not unlike the one Tony Montana frequently takes in *Scarface*. Bregman stood at the far end of the room, blocking the door, looming over everything and everyone, but especially over Pacino.

Nobody wanted to mention *Revolution*, the film that spurred Pacino's hiatus from cinema, so naturally *Scarface* came up. It had more in common with *Sea of Love* than the ill-fated *Revolution* had, to be sure. Like *Sea of Love*, it was a contemporary crime film with a strong component of violence. Bregman liked talking about *Scarface*; already it was gaining in reputation despite the initial critical disapprobation. *Sea of Love*, the producer insisted, was a different proposition from *Scarface*. Its writer, novelist and sometime Martin Scorsese collaborator Richard Price (who was more of a marquee attraction than its director, the strong but relatively anonymous Harold Becker), specialized in gritty urban realism and intimacy. *Scarface*, Bregman said, was operatic, and deliberately so, on a different scale from what the cast was dealing with here.

Fair enough, and Pacino didn't disagree. This junket was something of a turning point for the actor. Previously almost as press shy as his friend Robert De Niro, now he was more open to the process of doing what he needed to do to promote this project. The unusual setting of this junket was likely contrived to accommodate his comfort level, and it did.

"Marty and Al were like a marriage that went on and on," Stone said. "And I don't know how many times they divorced and how many times they 'remarried' or whatever. But it was quite a journey and, obviously, had many phases. Al changed a lot when—as you pointed out—he went through a change, and he became much more 'giving.' When was *Sea of Love*? '92 or '91, was it?"

But he'd had his ups and downs prior to that. One of them was directly before *Scarface*, the previously discussed *Author! Author!*

"That was the one that put him in the dumps, I think," said Stone. "In one of the dumps that he was in. Eventually he took a different attitude; he changed. He opened up. He was much more difficult on *Scarface* than he was, for example, on *Any Given Sunday*."

On *Scarface*, Pacino and Bregman were definitely running the show, from where Stone sat. "Once Al said, 'I'm excited by it,' then Marty would go to work and he would do his number—which was get the screenplay together for Al. Because Marty, at that time, was an independent producer. He had tremendous success from *Serpico* and *Dog Day Afternoon*. And Marty also had another client, Alan Alda, who was really making a bundle of success—real big money—for Marty. So, that was his financial base. He put together *Scarface*, really literally, with his own blood. And he was *Scarface*, in a sense, in the making of that film; he was ruthless in getting it done."

Not that it represented a particularly tough sell on Bregman's part, at least initially. "Of course, gangster films are easier to make, in the system. So, he had the cooperation—on that film—of [executive] Ned Tanen and the whole Universal group that had financed Alan Alda. So, they went with him, but it soured quickly because *Scarface* was a hell of a hard number to pull off—many difficulties and way over budget. I think twice the distance. Six months, as I remember. It was scheduled for three months. That's outrageous. In those days, too. It's always been outrageous to go that far over budget, and there was a lot of pissed-off people, including Tanen.

"So, one of the things Marty did was just keep Universal at bay. He was constantly promising them anything—'God will come and solve these problems'—keeping them at bay, keeping them away from Al. He always used to say Al was a monster and would blow up if you ever confronted him. And he kept that as a weapon, to defend the enterprise. But he had difficulties inside the enterprise because, frankly, it was in a very difficult shape. The thing was, there was not a lot of communications. And the assistant director had to be fired after a certain point, Jerry Ziesmer. That's the 'usual sacrificial victim,' right away.

"The pressure on me was enormous because I didn't want to cut the film, because I thought it worked as a whole, and I did get pressure, but I don't remember exactly giving in to it. I think we kind of struggled our way through it. We just doubled the budget, and we doubled the time, and Universal kept betting on Bregman, I think because of Alan Alda's success and his past success with Pacino. But they were kind of pissed off. I don't remember it being a very happy film that opened.

"After the film was over, I had a huge fight with Bregman over the cut, and I never talked to him again, for years. I saw him in the '90s before he died, and we made up. But Marty was a tough character. He was a tough, tough—he was a handsome gangster-type who grew up in the Lower East Side, and loyalty was the most important thing. And if you crossed him, if he felt like you'd been disloyal, he treated you like a gangster. He'd want to kill you. So, the situation was very difficult because he wanted to control the film. He was a control freak."

Bregman did not look over Stone's shoulder much while Stone researched and wrote the screenplay, first in collaboration with Lumet. "Sidney was Al's favorite director," Stone recalled. "The moment he told Marty he wanted to do *Scarface*, they went to Sidney. Sidney liked the idea, he liked Al very much, Sidney had been involved with me on *Platoon*. He'd wanted to make it for ten minutes or something like that, and then he passed. Because he was an older man and he didn't want to go to that degree of exertion. He was very interested in politics, Sidney. He certainly wanted to keep *Scarface* in its political atmosphere of that time. With the Mariel boatlift, with the relations between Cuba and the US, and the other side of the equation: the coke war.

"That's what interested Sidney. Sidney wanted to probe the relationship of the CIA and the DEA to what really was going on in the drug trade and if the United States was involved. And of course, it's a dirty story. It's hard to prove. But you know what? It led, ultimately, to the funding of the Contras in Nicaragua, and the Iran/Contra scandal. It led, ultimately, to the Contra hearings and the accusations—which are accurate—of the CIA turning the other eye to the smuggling in Los Angeles. It was a dirty story. In Sidney's conception the film would explore this, but Bregman did not want to go there."

In order to write, Stone had to get off the cocaine he'd been using to lift his spirits after the failure of *The Hand*. This would prove tricky, as his initial research on the cocaine trade would put him in rather close proximity to, well, the cocaine trade. "I did all the research for *Scarface* on cocaine, in and out of the country. It was quite interesting because I understood that world better than if I had not done it. Al, on the contrary, had never done anything like that. He'd never even done cocaine. So, he didn't know. Marty took me down to Miami, and he introduced me to a dozen people who were very helpful. And then, I expanded my contacts from there, outward.

"I talked to several police departments, and I tried to get as close to the gangsters as I could; but that wasn't so easy. I talked to defense lawyers, of course, who were very important to contact. I went to Bimini to actually confront what was the trade, the nightly trade, going into Miami on cigarette boats. And also, prior to that, I'd been to South America, in Peru. I'd been there on another thing that I had been working on, years before, with a very knowledgeable journalist. This was not the El Salvador guy on whom I based my film *Salvador*; this is another thing completely. I had been in that world, and I'd been ingesting the material. So, I knew a lot in the sense of the feeling of it and the fear of being in that world." It was from that fear that Stone conceived the film's notorious chainsaw scene.

"When I was in Bimini, I was found out. I was with my ex-wife and we were pretending to be Hollywood screenwriters, which we were; I was. But they thought, because I knew a lot of people from Miami and I mentioned a name at this late night—we were coked down in the hotel room with three gangsters. Mid-level people, not high-level. They were the 'shippers.' They were the people who were doing the work of shipping it on cigarette boats into Miami. There was a hotel in Bimini, it was very famous. These shippers were all staying there and there was a lot of boats every night, shipping out all night. You'd hear the cigarette boats going. It was a trade. And this was the grunt work, the shipping via cigarette boat. But I could tell the scale of it. The characters that we grew came from that period. They were people who were killed with chainsaws. And some of these crimes were gruesome. They'd scrawl on the wall of the person they killed, they'd scrawl in blood 'Chivato'—or something like that—like 'Traitor.' Or cut people's eyeballs out. All kinds of gruesome shit. So sitting in a hotel room and feeling 'found out' by a group of them was something I tried to get into the film.

"This was a multibillion-dollar business. Talking to the prosecutors in South Florida—there were three or four different divisions trying to handle it. There was this bureaucratic overlap. It was Fort Lauderdale. It was Miami. It was the US Attorney's Office. There was Miami Beach. There was Miami. It was a mess. And the cops were all over the place. Different police departments had different rates of success. We talked to all of them. And we got a varied picture of it.

"So, this was serious; and, as you know, it's the period when

Escobar started to get really big, going into the '90s. It dealt in a gigantic volume. And it was a great business to be in because you could get away with it so much. It started to change about the time we were making the movie there. And Miami was very paranoid about us being there. In fact, we lasted—and I don't know exactly—I'd say close to two weeks we lasted, in Miami, before they threw us out. Because they didn't want to be associated with that stuff."

Having gotten uncomfortably close to "that stuff," Stone decamped to Paris to write. He presumed cocaine would be more difficult to get a hold of in the City of Lights than it had been in these other climes. "It was a hard thing to get off of, yeah. But I knew I had to make a break because it wasn't working for me and my writing was being hurt. So, I moved to Paris deliberately, after the research was over. I cut off everybody I knew. Getting out of the country to a country where there was not much of it, there—in France, in the winter—it was perfect. And of course, I did have family there, so it was a re-entry to an old world that I knew. And I got off it, and I came back to the States, and I was clean. I was able to do it—that is to say I could socialize on it, but I didn't need it anymore.

"The thing is: cocaine doesn't work. That's clear. And I made it very clear to myself. But I have to say: in the movie, it's all relative. Tony is basically saying, through the movie: 'They should legalize this stuff. That's the only way to beat it. They're not going to cut it down by outlawing it.' Like everything else, when the United States goes to war on something—war on drugs—it becomes like a 'Vietnam.' It's a mess. We don't know how to regulate anything.

"Tony Montana is the ultimate, ultimate free-market proponent. Sort of the Milton Friedman of cocaine economics. And he saw the picture correctly. He saw the hypocrisy. That's what he hated, the hypocrisy. And then, of course, after so much cocaine usage, he becomes tinted with paranoia and he ends up turning on his friends. But for a while there, it was some great business. If he'd just kept his marbles, he would have been able to go all the way and probably retire as a millionaire and get into hedge funds or something. And by the way, there is a link because when I did my film *Wall Street*, I was going up to New York, down to Miami, there was a lot of traffic in cocaine coming to New York from there, at that point, about '85. A lot of people were using cocaine—young people—and they're making big money. So, there was a lot of that similarity exploding in Wall Street, the environment."

Back home from Paris, things did not proceed as planned. "Sidney reacted badly to my first draft, which was pretty close to the final draft—it was violent and vulgar, all those things—and it was too much for Sidney. It was too much for him. He would have gone on his own accord. I don't know where. He would have gone somewhere else. But Marty cut him off quickly. It was ruthless. He just said: 'Goodbye. It's not going to work.' So, right away, he went to Brian because I think he was thinking of Brian, in the back of his head, because Brian had already been involved. On some level." De Palma was amenable to Stone's approach.

"There are two styles to screenwriting. One is to be like the Robert Bolt, where you put everything on paper. The other style is more American, where you put it on paper but it's impressionistic and you direct it, and it becomes—you work on it in the direction. And I'm of both styles. Putting it all on paper is extremely difficult because there's so many variations on the theme. So, I've been both ways. I worked with people like that and I worked with people who are a little looser. Brian's a little looser. He's not a stickler in the ways Marty or Al were." He could take what was impressionistic in Stone's script and run with it.

Stone stayed close to the production, starting with the casting process. He clashed with Bregman over the conception of

Elvira, which Stone saw as an ideal role for Glenn Close. "I could never have directed a film with Marty," Stone recalled with some amusement. "De Palma was much 'looser' than I was at the time, in the sense that he had a little more experience, and he could put up with Marty's control freak nature. Marty would be in every casting session. He didn't even have casting sessions with actresses without Brian being there. I saw those. He'd line up fifteen, twenty blondes in the hallway—because he really felt responsible for the Elvira character. He really wanted her to be his 'dream blonde,' I guess. And I think he found it in Michelle Pfeiffer. I had a fight with him—I realize, now, how stupid it was—but I was defending Elvira as Glenn Close's role. And Marty didn't think she was right, visually. And my point was that Close was a very good actress. Michelle was not as experienced and had to struggle to make things work, and sometimes, I had to change the nature of the role, to make it fit Michelle. But ultimately she was the right choice." When I mentioned Cornelia Sharpe to Stone, he immediately said, "That's the prototype for Elvira."

Once shooting started, Bregman let Pacino do his thing. "Brian had no choice because Al was a force. And Al was tough. Al wouldn't get going—and I said in my book: 'I don't think Al will get going for the first seven takes.' It was just generally the formula, and I couldn't believe it because you don't know how much time that wastes. A day has got so many hours and if you can't get the first five, six, seven takes, you're really fucked. You're not getting many setups every day. And I could see this was coming, and it did go that way. But Brian was not a motivator. He was not. Brian was, as you might say, impersonal maybe.

"Al was outside time. And I can't tell you I understood his thinking. I understood his brilliance. I understood the things he was doing. And his screenplay ideas were always very—I always listened to him. I never belittled him like—Marty would belittle him and say: 'Al was out of his mind. Forget it.' You have to think about it, though. He's saying that maybe it doesn't sound right, but there's something there. You have to think about that.

"There was one time, Al went a little bit crazy when he heard Brian's comment about 'The actors are taking over this insane asylum' or something like that. And he did go nuts on that. I think he disappeared for a few hours into his trailer. Jesus. One thing after another. It was a nightmare. I wouldn't want that on one of my films. It would never happen that way, but it can get out of hand. So, Brian's seen a lot. Yeah."

Nevertheless, Stone sometimes found De Palma's way of working confounding. "I don't understand Brian. He's very obtuse. He doesn't give his emotions away. He certainly had a sardonic sense of humor. Very sardonic, very cynical, it's funny. He's very funny. All I can say is he didn't seem to enjoy himself, at any time, in the movie. Except when he was shooting up something and having a tremendous time. But he didn't seem to enjoy the process of *people*. He didn't seem to like people as much as I would.

"On weekends, usually the director's available because the film is an ongoing, seven-day-a-week affair, but he would actually, literally, cut off Bregman and would not answer his phone calls. So, here we are. And Bregman says: I can't reach the motherfucker.' And Brian's rented a big house and he had a staff and they're telling Bregman he can't be disturbed, he's asleep. He'd be asleep all weekend." As we shall see, De Palma also needed to rest on the set, between scenes at times. "So, he's a strange guy. But he had a divorce going on." Indeed he did, from the actress Nancy Allen. Apparently one source of strain was that De Palma would not cast Allen in the Elvira role.

Briefly putting himself in Bregman's shoes, Stone reflected, "How could you fire De Palma when you're in the middle of this mess that's going on? But Marty's certainly pulling his hair out: 'What can I do to speed this guy up? I'll call him on weekends. We'll have a meeting.' And he won't even talk to you on the weekends. You can understand then Marty's frustration. So, you get to the set Monday morning. You finally see your fucking director, and you can't really say 'You've got to speed it up.' You've got to talk to them in certain ways. It's very hard to motivate two people like Brian, who's into his own world, and Al, who's into his own world. So, you have these two obstacles. I wouldn't want to have been the producer on that movie. I would have probably lost all my hair and ended up three hundred pounds or something, eating doughnuts all the whole time. I would have liked to see Scott Rudin fucking make that picture." (Rudin was a famously prolific theater and film producer known for his prodigious temper; the accusations against him were such that while he's still alive, he's taking an indefinite hiatus from work. Apparently in addtion to being a shouter, he was a thrower of objects. Hence Stone's curiosity. What Would Scott Throw?)

De Palma recalls asking Stone to leave the set on more than one occasion. From his perspective today, he's not unsympathetic to Stone's situation. The guy wanted to direct, *had* directed, and was now relegated to the writer's chair but still hadn't divested himself of the desire. And time would prove him a director of some distinction. But on the set of *Scarface*, De Palma had two primary collaborators cum bosses—Pacino and Bregman—and hence was likely to process Stone's unsolicited suggestions as so much static. But Stone insists he was not banished from the set as such. "He asked me to leave the set maybe three or four times in the course of the shoot. Like for the day, I'd leave for the day. I'd go back to where I was staying, and I'd work. Then Bregman may want me back and Pacino wanted me back. There was no way I was going to leave that set. I was stuck. Frankly, at the end, I was getting tired. It was just too much. Six months is a long time, and especially out of my life at the time. There were other things I wanted to do."

Nevertheless, Stone had a passionate attachment to the film and worried over the finished product. In my friend Matt Zoller Seitz's book *The Oliver Stone Experience*, one of the full-page illustrations is a letter that Stone sent to Bregman during the editing process of *Scarface*. Dated August 11, 1983, here are two paragraphs:

> [...] the film is more important than any single one of us and right now I am convinced there are some major problems, especially in the middle. As a result it just doesn't work—not on the level you or I expected. In parts it's downright embarrassing. Unless we fix it now—while we still can—we will be hiding from disaster, not taking it by the horns now. I think still the picture could be good, not great—but good. Right now it's not even that.
>
> I've given my initial impressions to Brian but in the intervening 36 hours I've been unable to sleep and have jotted down various other notes I didn't cover with him so I am sending him a copy of these notes. I am dealing I think only with things that can be fixed, not with things that cannot be changed because they were directed that way. Nor am I going into the many fine things there are in the movie.

Looking back now, Stone allows that he was likely more privy to the shooting and editing processes than a writer arguably ought to have been. In his book he goes into some detail about the differing factions weighing in on how the film ultimately ought to play. He portrays himself as something of a willing pawn of Pacino. He told me, "The reason I saw the cut was only because Al was so alarmed that he brought my attention to it and he wanted me to go. Marty didn't want me to go. He didn't want me to see the film, as a lot of people know—it's the writer! You don't want the writer to see the bones of the film. Right? Now, I think a writer can bring a lot to the rehearsals and to the film as a whole. Brian had me in the rehearsals, that's true; but he didn't have many rehearsals. He was never an actor's director, that way. He didn't believe that much in talking things out about characters, or much rehearsal." But on the set De Palma rolled with Pacino's requests for numerous takes. "That a crazy way to work," Stone insists. "But you don't tell the actor what to do. The actor doesn't tell the director what to do. The producer does what he's supposed to. It's a strange system, and I guess in the old days it might've worked because they all agreed on the idea that they'd have a thirty-day schedule. But this was not agreed to at all. There was no consensus. I saw the 'rough cut' and I went back to Al, and I shared my thinking with him and then, of course, all hell broke loose because that's what Bregman did not want me to talk to Pacino about.

"So, Brian turned on me. Marty and Brian would not talk to me. They were furious because I had let loose the monster, who, of course, was personified in Al. Marty always put the onus on Al. He always made him into the monster, made him worse than he was. Now, Al could be a monster, but he was also very bright. Al had a great sense of drama and a great sense of what was working and what was not working. So, I think it's wrong to ignore him. I think he's very important to the process.

"Anyway, it did improve after I saw it. But I didn't talk to any of them about it again. Even Al didn't call me, which was hurtful because I had been loyal to Al. I feel divided because a director and a writer are supposed to be combined. And I'd been in a situation where the writer ends up working for the actor and I know exactly what happened in that sense, because the writer and the actor—when they combine—it becomes a number for the director. So, the director has to be in charge of the writing and directing. He has to have that under his control, and in certain respects he has to be his own producer. It's an impossible situation. Brian was able to put up with it because of the way he works."

Stone has made his peace with what *Scarface* is. "When Brian's making a gangster film, he wants it to be big. He wants it to be like a Sergio Leone kind of gangster film. He wants it stylistic. He wants big scenes, a lot of suits, a lot of clothes, a lot of costumes, jewelry. I get it. I didn't perhaps get it as much as I did now. And I like the result. I liked the movie. But you realize at the time I was working off a more realistic palette because I'd been there. And Brian didn't really have that realism in him. Or interest in it. He wasn't that interested in it. I would take him to certain places in Miami and show him the atmosphere, and that's what he loved—he loved the clubs, and all of that. But the realism of the business, how deals were made, how money was counted, all of that, he's not that interested in it."

Ultimately, he looks at *Scarface* as Bregman's film; when wrapping up our conversation, he said, "*Scarface* became Bregman's 'big one.' It became his 'big number.' It was his film. And he became famous for it. He did other successful films: Alda's *Four Seasons*. But I don't think he ever did anything else that matched it, not even *Carlito's Way*."

6

DE PALMA'S VERSION

Whatever regard in which Brian De Palma now holds Sidney Lumet, in the early '80s that New York director's proximity to De Palma's own career probably exasperated him just a little bit. At the beginning of the 1980s, De Palma had begun collaborating with the acclaimed playwright David Rabe, and one of their projects was an adaptation of Robert Daley's 1978 nonfiction book *Prince of the City: The True Story of a Cop Who Knew Too Much*.

Daley's book was the story of Bob Leuci, a spectacularly corrupt New York City narcotics detective. Unlike Frank Serpico, who was squeaky clean when he gave his testimony on corruption in the NYPD, Leuci spent a long time reveling in corruption, and once he started cooperating with investigators, it took him years to tell the whole truth. United Artists had the movie rights, and De Palma and Rabe were developing it for the studio.

"Well, Lumet got interested in the book, and his screenwriter [Jay Presson Allen] got interested in the book," De Palma told me in a summer 2022 interview. "But I had been working almost a year developing it for United Artists with David Rabe, working with Bob Leuci himself. And it was really a great script, and we put a tremendous amount of time into it. But ultimately, the powers that be, United Artists, figured that they'd rather go with Lumet, and they basically paid us off for the script and moved on."

De Palma was sufficiently irritated with United Artists that he lifted a real-life incident from Leuci's story—one that is also present in Lumet's 1981 film—for the film *Blow Out*, with John Travolta and Nancy Allen. A film that beat Lumet's *Prince of the City* into US theaters by about a month, which one infers might have given De Palma a chortle of satisfaction. In *Blow Out*, Travolta's character Jack, a sound effects recordist and mixer for a cheap exploitation film producer, is telling Nancy Allen's Sally about his past life, as a technician for "The King Commission," "a group of politicians that got together to stop police corruption." When Sally pries about why he got out of that line of work, he protests that it's a long story, but then he tells it, and soon the movie flashes back. "I wired their best undercover cop. A guy by the name of Freddie Corso." On one particular case, Corso was setting up a captain who was taking a payoff. Over tense strings we see Jack taping the wire to Corso's torso. Jack's in a car tailing Corso's car, recording the exchange, the parties are talking money, and suddenly Jack hears static. He toys with his tape recorder. "The one thing the fucking whiz kid," Jack says, talking about himself, "didn't think of is maybe that Freddie would get nervous, and Freddie would...sweat." In pain, Freddie asks his associates to pull over at a diner. He leaps out of the car, and even before he can get to the diner rest room, he's desperately pawing at the stuff taped to his flesh. Before Jack can help, Freddie is found out and killed. "It wasn't your fault," Sally reassures him. "Tell that to Freddie," Jack responds. (One of this superb thriller's multiple ironies is that Jack ultimately won't be able to save Sally, either.)

In *Prince of the City*, it's Treat Williams, in the title role of Danny Cielo (Bob Leuci's name was changed for the film), who gets the battery burn. He's wearing a wire for the feds, bopping around bars and social clubs, getting audio. The chapter title in the movie, in lowercase letters and quotes, is "it's a game… I love it." After a meeting at the Airline Diner (years later featured in *Goodfellas*, in the scene where viewers meet the adult Henry Hill for the first time) with a mobster named Rocky Gazzo, Danny's driving with the guy and another associate, and Rocky pulls over and says he's gotta check the other guy for a wire. Danny's the one wearing the wire, and he insists that Rocky frisk him as well, and Rocky won't. The meet ends with the passing of a cash envelope. The next shot has Danny lying down, in pain, saying, "I think the batteries leaked." The cloth belt holding pieces of the rig is peeled off, revealing a grotty-looking burn. In Lumet's film it's a colorful anecdote—it makes no difference to the story's outcome one way or another. In De Palma's iteration, it becomes an essential character-establishing narrative dovetail.

Lumet biographer Maura Spiegel's account of the changeover in directors for *Scarface* is curious. Stone recalls Bregman pretty much firing Lumet. Spiegel states that Lumet "handed" *Scarface* over to De Palma, after Sidney declined Oliver Stone's script. One might speculate what a Lumet *Scarface* might have looked and felt like. Given that *Prince of the City* is almost exactly as long as De Palma's *Scarface*, Lumet would not have balked at telling a story of epic length. We know he wanted for the gangster picture something more political than what Stone had conjured.

While De Palma's movies revel in overt stylization, Lumet's kino-eye was stealthier. But that's not to say he was a strict realist. In his invaluable how-to book/memoir *Making Movies*, he goes into some detail about the stylization he applied to *Prince*, using a variety of distorting lenses to convey the ever-closing-in world of the pursued-from-all-sides Danny. "Photographically, this is one of the most interesting pictures I've done," Lumet wrote. "Going back to its theme (nothing is what it seems), I made a decision. We would not use the midrange lenses (28 mm through 40 mm). Nothing was to look normal, or anything close to what the eye would see. I took the theme literally. All space was elongated or foreshortened, depending on whether I used wide-angle or short lenses. A city block was twice as long or half as long, depending on the choice of lens."

When reviewers praised *Prince of the City* for visual realism, Lumet threw up his hands. (As for De Palma, his main complaint about Lumet's film was what he saw as its failure to capture Bob Leuci's world's-greatest-used-car-salesman charm, which itself in turn gives you some idea of how De Palma would have approached the material.)

In Andrew Yule's Pacino biography, Lumet says, first reflecting on his objections to Stone's script, "Apart from the corny elements I objected to, I also wanted to introduce political ramifications, exploring the CIA's involvement in drugs as part of their anti-Communist drive. I didn't want to do it just on a gangster or cop level. As it stood, it was a comic strip. Marty and I argued about it, Marty disagreed with me and I pulled out."

Speaking with Yule, Bregman begged to differ: "I walked away from Sidney. What he wanted to do was just preposterous. He wanted to make a different film, a political film that showed government involvement in the importation of cocaine. I felt that was a bizarre suggestion. He wanted to rewrite the script and told me it would take six months. I gained the impression that he wanted to stall *Scarface* so he could make another movie first. De Palma and I had no intention of making a comic strip. We wanted to give the film a larger-than-life operatic quality."

De Palma's recollections extend to before any of the beginnings that are widely recounted about the film's making. "My agent, who knew Bregman, said that they wanted to develop a *Scarface* script. And I, having seen the movie said, 'Sure.' And having recently worked with David Rabe, I said David and I will do it. However, David had had a kind of very up-and-down relationship with Bregman and Pacino, and he said he'd only do it if they were not involved with the process. Otherwise, we would do the script, which Bregman said was fine. So, David and I, we'd been working, you know, on *Prince of the City* for a year or so, went right into working on *Scarface*. And what they wanted was a *Scarface* set in the '30s. You know, the classic Al Capone. So that's what we're doing.

"And David is a very meticulous writer, and we'd worked for, I don't know, a couple of weeks and he'd written a couple of scenes, and it was sort of coming along, at which point I got a message from Bregman who said that Al wanted to meet with me. I had never met with Al without Bregman. So this was okay. So Al came down to my apartment on 5th Avenue. And we sat and chatted, and he was sort of interested in how the script was going. I tried to bring him up-to-date on what we were working on. And I thought everything went fine. Subsequent to my meeting with Al, I get this phone call from Bregman who said, 'Al is very upset about the script, and he wants to meet with you and David Rabe in my office tomorrow morning.' And I said, 'Marty, if I tell David that, he's going to quit.' He said, 'I don't care. We want you both in my office tomorrow morning.' I said, 'Okay.' So I called up David. I said, 'David, Al and Bregman want to meet about the script.' And he said, 'I quit.' Okay, so now I don't know what to do. And Paul Mazursky lived in my building, and I ran into him in the elevator, and he had some experience with working with Bregman, who I did not know very well. And I explained to him my dilemma. And we sort of talked it out, and I decided, with his help, that I should quit too, and that's what I did.

"I called up Bregman. And I said, 'David Rabe quit, and I

quit with him.' That was in the days when you supported your writer. When they tried to bring on another writer, you said, 'No, you bring on another writer, I go too.' So that's what happened. And I forgot about it."

For the record, David Rabe's recollections of this period differ substantially. He says he had no objection to Bregman and Pacino. "When Brian and I first started talking about it, when he first approached me, we wanted to set it in Chicago, in the '30s. And that kind of lingo, I felt competent with it. Not too far removed from what we were doing with *Prince of the City*, which we did not get to make, the way it turned out."

Rabe says he left when he learned the milieu would be the present-day cocaine trade in Florida. "I don't know anything about that, I don't know how to write that, and I didn't want to risk being inadequate. I did not have a clue about the idea of making this story in Florida. And it wasn't in me to go down and explore there, and I didn't want to be talked into it."

In De Palma's version, the project bounced back to him about a year after he walked from it. "Bregman had worked with Oliver and Lumet, and they'd done this whole Marielito Cuban thing. And apparently, according to Bregman, Lumet didn't think it was political enough. And maybe he was having some trouble working with Sidney. I don't know what the situation was. He came back to me and said, 'Would you be interested in directing *Scarface*? Here's the script.' So I read the script. And I said yes, because it was an excellent script."

I remarked to De Palma that when watching the Hawks film and the De Palma film back-to-back, I was slightly surprised at the ways Stone's script hewed so closely to the plot points of the Hecht scenario. I asked if that struck him too when he read Stone's script for the first time.

"I'd only seen the original *Scarface* movie once so I wasn't completely conversant with it. But I see what you're talking about. At the time, I really didn't see the closeness that it had to the original. I just thought it was a really good script, and Oliver's done a really good job."

Speaking of the casting, De Palma said, "We came across Manny, Steven Bauer, very early. And because he was Cuban, that worked out, because Al could study his accent. And they sort of palled. So, he was on very early. I really pushed for Mary Elizabeth [Mastrantonio, who plays Tony's sister Gina], because she was going to go do a play. And I said, 'Marty, we've got to cast her, or we're going to lose her.' So I sort of forced that to happen. And then there was, you know, the endless leading lady casting that went on and on. And we ultimately had five women to screen test. And Michelle was obviously the best."

De Palma was not unaware of Michelle Pfeiffer's charisma and warmth and acknowledged that she had to tamp that down in order to play Elvira. "Yeah, at one point, she sort of wanted to warm her up a little bit, and I said, 'Absolutely not.' She absolutely had to be a caustic, cynical, bitter cokehead."

As for Pacino, De Palma noted, "Al had a really strong fix on that character, and did approach it a little operatically, you know? And being the great stage actor that he is, he could, you know, rant and rave with great skill. And it worked, as he gets crazier and crazier and drug-filled as the movie goes on."

I fed De Palma one of my cockamamie film critic theories: "It occurred to me that *Dressed to Kill*, *Blow Out*, and *Body Double* can be seen in retrospect as a loose trilogy of movies about cities that are important to you personally. New York, Philadelphia, which is adjacent to South Jersey, where you grew up, and Los Angeles, that is, Hollywood. And *Scarface* is Miami, which is what to you?"

"Well, I had *visited* Miami because both my parents retired there. But I had to go down and find all the locations. And we started with an art director named Leon Erickson in the summer that we went down and spent a couple of weeks finding all the locations in Miami. But the *Scarface* script was so politically unfavorable to the community, and there was a congressman that literally threw us out of town. We were supposed to shoot the whole thing in Miami. We were thrown out of Miami. And we had to go back to LA.

"And we worked out a situation, or Marty Bregman did, where we were able to go back to Miami at the end of the shoot for two weeks and shoot some exteriors. Obviously, Collins Avenue and some of those blatant exteriors, Al at the phone booth, the spot where they go in to meet the big drug dealer the first time. All those locations I had scouted before. So we spent two weeks down there shooting all these exteriors at the end of the *Scarface* shoot. Needless to say, we were surrounded by bodyguards 'cause people still wanted to kill us."

While *Scarface* is certainly a visually extravagant film, often it's not "full" De Palma. There's no use of split screen, and few detectable diopter shots (that is, shots that keep focus in two discrete sectors of the frame). "The camera moves a lot in *Scarface*, and there are a lot of beautiful and stylish and amazingly composed sequences, but the perspective is more anthropological than voyeuristic," I said to the director.

"Yeah, I choose projects like this, and I think it's very important. I have my own obsessions. I write and direct my own movies. But I think it's very important to get out of your own world and just direct somebody else's script, somebody else's world.

"I storyboarded the whole thing. I did it on these little cards. I was basically serving Oliver's script. I wasn't imposing some type of visual style of my own, I was just trying to interpret his material. But, you know, the motel scene, with going outside to Manny in the car with the girls, and going back inside, and those were some strong visual ideas that worked quite well in that sequence.

"And I just basically work as a craftsman trying to articulate Oliver's vision to the best of my abilities. There are not any elaborate set pieces in *Scarface*. You know, a lot of movies, you know, I just think about the set pieces and how to get the characters to them. Here, I just basically followed the script and directed it."

Stone, of course, had moments where he felt De Palma was not doing that. In *Chasing the Light*, he recounts that while he was frustrated at times, he knew he wasn't the director and understood when to step back. "And sometimes he didn't," De Palma responds when I bring that up. "And that's when I had to ask him to leave the set, because he was talking to the actors, and you can't give an actor instruction from two different directors. But he was with us all the way through. I mean, you know, we had our run-ins occasionally.

"There was one situation, the scene where Al kills Loggia. And we were on a set at Universal. And we built this conference room for Loggia's character, that had a desk. It was the the scene where Al and Loggia confront each other after he's come back from South America. And as we moved into the room, later, for the scene where Loggia was going to be killed, suddenly Al felt there was something not right about it. He just said there was something wrong, there was something wrong about this room. And it took me aback. Now, literally, I'm on the Universal lot. I have executives saying, 'Why aren't you shooting? You're over budget.' And Al's in his trailer, and he wants to talk to Oliver. We've only rehearsed this scene a thousand times, and suddenly Al can't make it work. So, I went down to Al's trailer. I remember saying to the executives, 'You go down there and tell him to come out of his trailer and go on to the shooting scene.' And of course, nobody wanted to go down and talk to Al. So I went down, and Oliver and I sort of listened to it, but I wasn't exactly sure what he was getting at. Was it the line, was it the way Loggia and Pacino were interacting? It didn't quite make a lot of sense.

"But as I watched him sort of describing it, a light bulb went off in my head. And I realized, the set was too small. The room was too small for what Al and Loggia had in mind, the way Frank was going to stalk Tony around that long table. So I walked out, and I said to Marty, I said, 'He's not going to shoot in that room we have. We've got to make it four times bigger.' And that's what we did. We shut down, we shot something else, and came back to the scene, I guess it was a week or so later when we had built the room four times larger.

"A funny story is that in the shootout in the boardroom, the bodyguard, the boss's bodyguard—it's a very complicated scene. I have a bunch of really experienced character actors, each one having their own interpretation of their character, each having their own acting style. I've got Harris Yulin, I've got Steven, I've got Al, I've got Loggia. I've got all these characters, and I'm doing a very complicated scene that got delayed because Al didn't like the size of the room.

"So, there's a lot of tension going on. So, I finally get through the scene and the actor who plays the bodyguard is a big strapping fellow, he comes over to me and looks me straight in the eye like he wants to kill me. And he says, 'You didn't speak to me once.' The most hateful look in his eye, like he wanted to kill me. I said, 'I'm sorry. I had a lot of dishes to juggle here. I'm sorry that I didn't speak to you once.' And then, I think we gave him that line at the end about, 'Do you want a job?'" (The actor Arnaldo Santana plays Ernie. He had been in *Cruising* with Pacino a few years before, although you might not recognize him from that film. In *Cruising*, he plays serial killer victim Loren Lucas, who says to his future murderer, "Terrific. I never made it with a Martian before." Santana is lean and muscular here; he apparently gained about one hundred pounds before appearing in *Scarface*, and not, apparently, on purpose. And *Scarface*, as it happens, was his last film role. He died in 1987.)

The story of the reconstructed room brought the conversation around to Ferdinando Scarfiotti, credited in the movie as the "Visual Consultant."

"He was fantastic," De Palma said. "Unbelievable, unbelievably talented. The whole look of the film can be attributed to him, basically."

Scarfiotti was discovered by the film and stage director Luchino Visconti in the early 1960s. His breakthrough picture was Bernardo Bertolucci's 1970 *The Conformist*. Although he received no credit, his incredibly evocative period production design, wed to Vittorio Storaro's remarkable cinematography and Bertolucci's stealthily innovative direction, knocked American filmmakers of a certain age on their collective ears. Peter Bogdanovich scooped up Scarfiotti for Bogdanovich's unfairly maligned 1974 Henry James adaptation *Daisy Miller*, and Paul Schrader, still finding his way in the visual department, used him for 1980's hyperstylized *American Gigolo* and 1982's also hyperstylized *Cat People*. On Schrader's commentary on the Bluray edition of *Cat People*, he generously and unselfconsciously catalogs all the shots he lifted from *The Conformist* for his film. De Palma had been impressed not just by *The Conformist*, but by Scarfiotti's work on Schrader's films, which, like *Scarface*, were backed by Universal Pictures. But Scarfiotti was not on *Scarface* from the get-go.

"After we got thrown out of Florida, and I was having trouble with Leon Erickson, the film's original art director. I wasn't having a great communication with him. And then the idea for Nando came up, and we could get him, and he could be available. And I immediately said, 'Let's get this guy.' I think I had seen Schrader's movie, and I took to the way it was designed. And I said, 'This is what I need.' Because I was trying to make the antithesis of a gangster movie. I wanted everything to be, you know, bright, everything pastel colors, white suits instead of, you know, what you got in *The Godfather*, dark, dark, dark."

While Scarfiotti and the composer Giorgio Moroder's worked on both *American Gigolo* and *Cat People*, they were not a package deal. Nevertheless, they both wound up working on *Scarface*. De Palma had worked for years with the Italian composer Pino Donaggio, whose dreamy strings often posed a constructive counterpoint to De Palma's violence. For *Scarface* he wanted music more directly tied to 1980s coke-driven glamour. In other words, something to do with disco. "It was fairly seamless," De Palma said. "He got it right away. I liked the way he orchestrated things. It seemed to be the right sound for the material. So, it was a very fruitful collaboration. He was the right guy for this movie."

Scarfiotti's approach combined the Miami pastel ideal with a near mania for red that evokes certain Visconti and Bertolucci frames. And, in keeping with certain De Palma motifs, mirrors are never far from Tony, particularly in the Babylon Club, where the booths he slumps in are encircled by them. While *Scarface* is not, as De Palma notes, a movie in which set pieces abound, the movie's center is a long scene set almost entirely in that club and ends with Tony surviving an assassination attempt. An early portion of the scene, with Tony becoming agitated upon seeing his sister dancing with another man, clarifies the nature of Tony's upset: his incestuous desire for Gina.

Putting that scene entirely together "wasn't that difficult because I've been working in that club set for quite a while," De Palma said. "We had done scenes in there before, the first time Frank takes him to the club. And I had a real idea of how Tony sees his sister with that guy that he has no respect for. And he goes into his rage. When he finally explodes, we played that very simply. He throws the guy out, he slaps her. Manny comes in and consoles her. It's all shot according to the logic of the action.

"I always believe that you spend a lot of time thinking about where the camera is in relationship to the material. The worst word in cinema to me is *coverage.* Any idiot can do coverage, which is what we see a lot of the streaming movies, that basically, the whole story is told through dialogue. And it's, you know, the medium shot, it's a two-shot. And you take a wide shot occasionally when they walk from one location to another. Which is not directing. And that's why in the streaming world, we've gone back to the writer as king. I mean, the directors can be brought in and out. It doesn't make any difference." Still, on *Scarface* De Palma did do what's called coverage, shooting certain scenes from different angles, but using multiple cameras simultaneously rather than breaking the coverage down into discrete single-camera setups.

Because of the sheer amount of footage De Palma was amassing, proper editing didn't begin while shooting was still on. "There were so many rushes. We were in rushes for hours. We had a lot of coverage. We had a lot of long takes. I remember that scene where Al is lamenting over his dead sister. I mean, there were like three hours of rushes on that scene, just him talking to her. I mean, I remember going to rushes. You'd have the whole company there. And then as we worked into the second hour, into the third hour, I'd be basically left with me and the editor. Everybody else would have had to go to bed, 'cause they have to get up, you know, the next morning. So I don't think we did a lot of editing while we were shooting. Just to get through the rushes was a tremendous chore at the end of every day.

"I would shoot as much as Al wanted to do. That scene with him consoling his dead sister, I just kept shooting, you know, to see what would happen. And we had multiple, whenever you have cameras, multiple cameras shooting from, you know, two different angles, three different angles, and you have to see the same take over and over from camera one, and then you see it again from camera two, and then you see it again from camera three. There was a ton of coverage."

Was he indulging Pacino's ego or allowing him his craft? I asked De Palma about working in the past with movie stars like Kirk Douglas. "Had you ever encountered a shoot where you gave the actor that much in terms of what he wanted to do over and over again?"

"I don't think so. I think I followed Al's instincts and, you know, because he's always surprising, you know, comes up with stuff you don't anticipate. And I would just keep shooting."

As far as De Palma saw, this wasn't a source of friction for the other actors. "Al got along with all the other actors. Got along with Manny. Their scenes together went pretty well. Loggia, of course, a very experienced stage actor. Harris Yulin? Great character actor. It's so funny. You see these people in, you know, early Lumet films. I mean, you know, all these people have sort of worked in the New York repertory of character actors."

The shoot was long not just on account of Pacino's working methods. Getting ejected from Miami meant a scramble for equivalent locations in Hollywood. Then there was rebuilding Frank's office. Then there was the mishap with Pacino picking up his gun by the barrel and burning his hand. Although that did not stop shooting: "Al went into the hospital for a week or so. That's why there's so many shots of people shooting at him. I had, like, a week of just having people running and shoot at the camera. So, that went on, and on, and on until I could shoot Al's direction when he came back."

And THEN there was the case of the actual set for the final shootout burning down. "I don't know what happened. Just suddenly the AD said to me, 'The set's burned down.' I remember walking on the stage to shoot the first scene. And he said, 'The set burned down. Go home. We're going to work on something else.'

"For that final scene, we developed a device that synchronized with the camera so that we would see the muzzle flash.

Initially, we were shooting these guns and we would see no flash, because the shutter was not in sync with them. So they developed a device that synced with the gun so that we would see the flash. And that took time, too."

With a sigh, De Palma recalled, "And then, of course, we had our ratings problems. That was quite a drama. I kept on, taking, cutting, a few frames here, then resubmitting it, and I would get an X again. I did it three times and got three X's. And I said, I'm not doing this anymore. We're hurting the movie. You know, we're going to have to go with an X. Of course, the studio was horrified. And then we'd have to go to the board, and, you know, plead our case in front of the whole ratings board, which is what we ultimately did. And the thing I did that really got everybody annoyed was I put everything back in I had taken out. I said to them, 'If it's an X on version one, and it's an X on version two, it's an X on the original version, I'm going with the original version.' They said, 'You can't do that.' I said, 'Yes, you can.' And that's what I did. So it all went back to what it originally was."

The chainsaw scene is the most frequently cited in terms of ostensibly "over the top" violence, but in the scene you never once see the weapon touch flesh, as was the case in the shower scene in Hitchcock's *Psycho*. That feature and the use of the shower aside, the two scenes haven't much in common stylistically. And De Palma notes that this is not a gratuitous scene.

"That came from Oliver's research. I mean, they were literally, you know, cutting people up into pieces and dropping them into trash cans. So, chainsaw was a new element in gangster vengeance, for real."

De Palma told me to go to another party for the full story of how the movie ultimately got an R rating. "We prevailed, and that was a great victory." More will be revealed in a future chapter.

7

ELVIRA

"I did not have a lot of work under my belt, for sure," Pfeiffer recalled of the period before *Scarface*, when I spoke with her in the late spring of 2023. And some of it was not so well-recollected—she seemed a little surprised when I dropped the title *Charlie Chan and the Curse of the Dragon Queen*. The role of Elvira was a breakthrough for her, although what she was asked to do in the film only gave audiences a very narrow look at the extraordinary range for which she became known and acclaimed.

In hindsight, we can understand that over the course of a long and distinguished career, Michelle Pfeiffer overcame a curse: that of her extraordinary good looks. She is today acknowledged for what she's always been, an actor of meticulous sensitivity and abundant natural warmth. Warmth that, of course, she was compelled to tamp down for her work in *Scarface*. It wasn't that Brian De Palma and Marty Bregman didn't appreciate that quality. It was more that it would work against the calculating ultimate survivor character that Elvira is. As it happens, she is the only one of the movie's four central characters who does not meet a violent death.

Acting had not always been an ambition for her. A high school theater class turned her around.

After kicking around in commercials and such, Pfeiffer was cast in the series *Delta House*, a grievously ill-conceived network comedy spun off from *National Lampoon's Animal House*. (Network requirements at the time of course meant watering down the coarse humor that distinguished the definitively R-rated feature film; the result yielded dialogue gems like John Vernon's Dean Wormer calling a particularly obsequious student a "sneaky little son of a snake." The redubbing of *Scarface* for network television, as celebrated in countless YouTube clips, was similarly eyebrow-raising.) It proved a miserable experience for Pfeiffer.

But the series did coincide with several small movie roles, and in pursuing these, Pfeiffer said, she tried to make sure that each one was better than the last. One of them, *The Hollywood Knights*, a raucous comedy of pre-counterculture 1960s LA teen anarchy overseen by stealth auteur Floyd Mutrux, is what some call a cult gem. Its lead character, New Bomb Turk (played by Robert Wuhl), inspired in its turn the name of a post-punk combo that achieved some mild distinction in the 1990s.

Grease 2 was Pfeiffer's first lead role. In a 1982 interview with Bob Lardine for the *New York Sunday News*, she said one thing that helped her clinch the lead role of Stephanie was the impassioned way she sang Linda Ronstadt's arrangement of the Buddy Holly song "That'll Be the Day." She'd later prove a more-than-credible lounge singer in Steve Kloves's 1989 romantic comedy-drama *The Fabulous Baker Boys*.

The first *Grease*, made in 1978, took the 1971 spoof-pastiche stage musical and made it into a somewhat straight-faced celebration of all things American-fifties, and was propelled to mega-hit status by the lead actors, John Travolta and Olivia Newton-John. (The picture came directly after 1977's *Saturday Night Fever*, which propelled Travolta to superstardom; *Fever* itself came directly after a supporting role as a lunkhead boyfriend in De Palma's *Carrie*.) For *Grease 2*, producer Allan Carr, knowing that the first film had inadvertently priced Travolta and Newton-John out of a follow-up, had a typically Barnumesque idea: the principal actors in *Grease 2* would be unknowns, the stars of tomorrow.

The male lead went to Maxwell Caulfield, a British-born performer who made his debut as a child actor in Joseph Losey's 1967 film *Accident*. Allan Carr's calculations about *Grease 2* proved wrong. But the flop did not attach a stigma to its performers. Pfeiffer went on to become Pfeiffer, and Caulfield negotiated a consistent and creditable career, in part by shifting to stage work.

"The casting director I met with was Alixe Gordin," Pfeiffer recalls of the not entirely auspicious beginning of her involvement with *Scarface*. "And she was lovely and brought me in and I happened to do a very good reading, which you never know how these things are going to go. And then she brought Brian in and I read for the two of them. It was a really long, arduous, stressful process. And at one point I was brought over to New York, to meet with Al.

"I remember there were a lot of actors being considered for different parts and it was kind of awkward. And, again, a lot of really seasoned, talented theater actors. And I was not terribly confident. And I was very intimidated. And we were kind of hanging out there all day, might have even been for a couple of days. And they would bring different people in and out to read scenes with Al. And I was terrible and I knew I was terrible.

"I think one of the most detrimental things to an actor, and really any creativity, is fear. And the longer the process went on, the more anxious I became and the worse I became. And this went on for a couple of months. And then ultimately, I believe Brian told me, and he was so sweet, he just said, 'It's just not going to work out.' And he really wanted it to work out. Because he and Marty saw something, some sort of chemistry between Al and I, which I was not getting. But then again, I was just too frightened to really be that aware of anything. But it still ended with, 'Sorry, it's just not going to work out.' And I'm like, 'I know, I know. I'm so sorry I let you down.' Anyways, but I was kind of relieved because it had been torture. While I was disappointed, I also was relieved not to be humiliated anymore."

But other actors were not working out either. Gordin circled back. "I don't know, a long time went by, I want to say a month. I got a call. They wanted to screen test me. 'Oh, no. Why?' I showed up on the day, and I think I did my own hair and makeup. I want to say, but I'm not sure, I brought my own wardrobe. Maybe not. They might have put me in something, but I just thought, 'There is no way. This is such a long shot I am going to get this part.' I showed up and I now thought I didn't really have anything to lose, so I wasn't really afraid. And I actually probably left my best performance in the screen test.

"And I was cast. I remember I was leaving town, I was going up to Northern California and feeling really good about myself. And this is really bad—but my friend drove me to the airport and we stopped and got a bottle of champagne and we sat in the parking lot at LAX and drank champagne out of coffee cups to celebrate that I had landed the role."

Once the shooting started, there was little reason to celebrate. While Pfeiffer felt a predictable kind of intimidation, she stresses that none of her collaborators actually tried to lord it over her. "Obviously starting with Al, who's iconic, and then the rest of the cast, who had such amazing bodies of work. I was young. I was twenty-three years old, and I was terrified.

I was terrified. I was just terrified every single day that I was going to fail. Because I had failed so miserably before. But Al was very kind and nice and patient with me, very supportive, as was Brian and Marty and everyone around me. It was just my own baggage really getting in my way, and my lack of experience and confidence."

In the Hawks film, Poppy, played by Karen Morley, is a relatively straightforward woman on the make. Pfeiffer hadn't seen the original picture until after she'd been cast, and she remembers thinking of Stone's script, "Well, this is a real departure from the original." Because there, Poppy is a simple opportunist. In the world of *Scarface*, the cocaine adds some complications. "Primarily, she's an addict," Pfeiffer says of Elvira. "And she likes pretty clothes, and she's well taken care of and protected. And I think underneath all of her bravado is a very scared, damaged individual. But somebody who has lived a life. She's smart and she knows how to survive and even leaves when she starts to really go downhill."

This intuition gave Pfeiffer a base on which to build the character, and to maintain it over the course of a shoot that continued at least a couple of months past what she'd thought it would be. "It was really long. And I was starving myself because I was playing a cocaine addict, and by the end of filming, the crew members were bringing me bagels. Everybody was really concerned about me. Like you said, I hadn't done a lot of films, so I didn't really know that this was maybe out of the ordinary. I don't really know what the original shooting schedule was. I can't remember, but I know that we went way, way, way over schedule. It's like building a house. You don't want to start building if you don't have really well-drawn-out and thought-through blueprints, plans. Otherwise, you know what's going to happen? It's going to go twice as long and cost twice as much money. And making a film is the same way. I've since been through other films where we've started without a finished script and you figure, 'You'll figure it out as you go along. And it's just going to take longer.' And you end up reshooting things and you end up spending a lot of time working things out on the set. And that's just kind of how it went here. Although in spite of the fact that Brian was very well-prepared." A significant factor in this was Pacino pulling Tony Montana this way and that. It's not something he ever gave up. Working with Pacino for a second time in 1991's *Frankie and Johnny*, Pfeiffer observed that while the overall atmosphere of the set was more relaxed, Pacino would work more or less the same way. "That's his creative process. And honestly, if you can get away with it, it's a lot more creative, to be able to continue to discover. And that is how creative brains work. And as frustrating as it can be for those around you… I think that he's always very in the moment, and not all actors work that way, but that is how he works. And if you're going to let him get away with it, he's going to do it. And by the way, a lot of us would love to be able to get away with that." Pfeiffer then gave me a couple of off-the-record demonstrations of how "I change my own mind all the time." She went on, "And I, like him, have really liked to do multiple takes, and even before working with him, I'm always wanting to do one more. But at a certain point when the director says, 'We really have it.' I'm like, 'Okay.' But I always want to do one more."

While Pacino was consistently supportive on set, he and Pfeiffer didn't form much of a bond in their off hours. In a 1991 interview with the *New York Times* to promote *Frankie and Johnny*, Pfeiffer said, "I remember Al and I had dinner one night. It was horrible. We were both so shy. We didn't have one thing to say to each other." Speaking of that last spring, Pfeiffer said, "It was also to do with the nature of our characters' relationship, and with his relationship with all of the male actors. It made a lot more sense for him to spend more time with them, not only for work, but there's more discovery they need to make with each other...and probably a lot more fun for him to be with. When we did *Frankie and Johnny*, I think we were much more relaxed. I was way more relaxed with him. And that just had to do with my confidence level. And I had a great time. We actually had fun and we laughed."

At one point I asked Pfeiffer: "What was a scene that you did where you felt you really just defined the character definitively? Do you think you had a through line where you were able to do that? You sound like you were insecure enough that you weren't necessarily going to give yourself a lot of compliments about the performance, but were there ever points in the shoot where you were thinking, 'Well, I'm in a good groove here,' or, 'This is going okay?'"

Without even pausing a beat, she responded: "Never. Not one day." She elaborated: "I was tortured every day. Every single day. Not, again, because of anyone on the set."

De Palma's direction had but one thing upon which to pivot, but it was a very definite thing. He could not allow Pfeiffer to drop Elvira's hard mask. "Brian was very funny. I was very relaxed filming with Brian. But I remember after almost every take, he would just come up to me and his only direction would be, 'You didn't smile, did you? You didn't smile on that take, did you?' And I think once, I did do one little tiny smile, but it's not even really a smile. It's when Tony and I are getting in a car. And what did he do? Did he take my hat off? He did something."

He did. It's a little after fifty minutes into the movie, and it actually comes after a pretty tense moment. Elvira is kitted out in an exquisite all-white outfit, complete with slightly floppy straw hat. They get into Tony's Cadillac—which Elvira has insisted that she is only riding in under protest—and do a few bumps together. After which Tony practically lunges at Elvira, attempting a kiss. She pushes him away with force and says, "Don't get confused, Tony. I don't fuck around with the help." Tony thinks it's hysterical, and delivers his next line. "Okay, if you want to play that way with me, I'll play that way with you." And he goofily puts on her hat. It's actually a very nice save for Tony. "He was being very playful and it was improvised and I wasn't expecting it. And actually it was a moment, a half a moment, and they did end up leaving that in the movie." She doesn't just smile as she brushes her hair. She laughs as she looks at Tony in the hat, beaming at her. "But I think that when I smiled, I just looked probably too sweet, maybe? I'm guessing in hindsight because I was so young, and still cherubic, even. And the way for him to keep the character contained is to just give me that simple parameter, don't smile.

"And I think I understood it. Not completely, but I do think I understood it. I wasn't really upset by it ever. I did feel very contained, but I just made that the character. And of course I hoped that it was good and I hoped that I was convincing. I didn't love myself in the film because I never do. I just seem to lack any sort of perspective on my work."

I continued to search for another instance in which Pfeiffer felt less than tortured while shooting. "I don't know I'd go so far as to say fun, but I enjoyed the scene where Tony is in the tub, yelling at the TV. And I was walking around: 'Can't you just stop saying fuck all the time?' And I remember maybe that was more toward the end of shooting, and I felt like I had a stronger foundation at that point. But I remember enjoying shooting that scene. I was moving around a lot in that scene. But I like that. I sort of thrive on movement and props, and it actually anchors me, more so than if I were just sitting in one place. Because that's kind of how life is. You're sort of doing something and thinking about something else and saying something else. And so I think it just gives you an opportunity to really create a behavior which makes things look and feel more real. And in the scene, the level of bickering makes Tony and Elvira come off as an old married couple."

Her first viewing of the movie was in New York, with a paying audience. "It was the only time really I saw the film, and there was a couple who had brought this baby, their child to the film, and I was so distracted by that. I wanted to turn around and say, 'Get your kid out of here. This is too violent for your child.' It was violent. And I personally kind of looked away during those parts." Nevertheless, one thing she appreciates most about the movie is the humor in Pacino's performance. "He's really funny, in the way he makes Tony so unaware and so full of himself."

Like almost everyone involved in the film, she's a little awestruck by its contemporary reputation. "It's become such a cult classic. God, I was in Georgia doing something, and I had this driver, and on the way back from where I had to be, he said, 'Oh, I just have to tell you, *Scarface* is one of my favorite films. I can quote every line in the movie.' And then he proceeded to quote every line in the movie to me. The whole way home. This is just recently. So that's always kind of fun. And that happens periodically."

Her next collaboration with Bregman came before her *Frankie and Johnny* reunion with Pacino. It was with writer/director/star Alan Alda for the film *Sweet Liberty*, in which she plays Faith, a film star with whom Alda's character becomes besotted. Asked about the movie, she took the cue to speak mostly of Bregman, and in the present tense at first, despite his having passed a few years back. "I'm so fond of Marty. He was kind of like a father to me. I think maybe he was to Al too, their relationship. But he does that. He's very parental, and he was very, very kind and a really, really good friend to me for a long, long time. When I was considering adopting my daughter as a single parent, I just wanted to check myself and make sure I was doing it for all the right reasons. And there were two people that I consulted with before I did, and one of them was Marty, and it was so secret. And it just really speaks to the level of trust that I had there. But he was a really, really kind man."

Pfeiffer now sees *Scarface* as a harrowing experience that produced a memorable film, and also steeled her for the subsequent ups and downs of her career. "Some time ago I had done a film which will go unnamed, working with a director who will also go unnamed. And it was really bad. It was a really bad experience. And I was talking to a friend of mine and he said, 'Well, the good news is it will never be that bad again.' And I would say having had the experience I had on *Scarface*, I'm not going to say that it was so bad, but it was hard. It was certainly hard. And I was young and I survived it, and I developed skills, survival skills, that I do think probably have carried me through. And I've had good experiences, I've had bad experiences, but I've never been that scared again. So that's a good thing."

8

MANNY

The first time Steven Bauer encountered Al Pacino in person, Pacino spat on him.

It would be about a year before Bauer, born in Havana in 1956 and christened Esteban Ernesto Echevarria Samson, would be cast in the role of Manolo Ribera, also known as Manny, in *Scarface.* So Bauer had no inkling he'd soon be Pacino's co-star and near-constant companion. Nevertheless, Pacino was, to Bauer and pretty much every other male actor of his generation, an idol and a model, and in the summer of 1981, the star was on the New York Stage in a revival of David Mamet's *American Buffalo.* The presenting venue was Circle in the Square, a venerable New York house, albeit its downtown branch (which in fact had predated the still-operating 50th Street location), on Bleecker Street in Manhattan's Greenwich Village.

"I sat almost in the second row. And the performance, what he projected—the fire was coming out of his mouth on stage. And so he spit on me."

His family emigrated from Cuba to Miami in 1960. He was almost immediately entranced by movies. Just as Tony Montana brags that he learned to speak "American" from tough guys like Humphrey Bogart and Jimmy Cagney, Bauer avers that Hollywood pictures "entertained me and engaged me and gave me language. I saw them as real life."

He was nicknamed "Rocky" at birth. "As in, 'the next Rocky Marciano.'" But the stage he chose was theatrical, not pugilistic. He pursued studies in theater at Miami Dade Community College and then the University of Miami. There he met Ray Liotta. They costarred in a collegiate production of Steinbeck's *Of Mice and Men*, with Liotta as the good-hearted, pragmatic migrant farmer George and Bauer as simple man-mountain Lennie; Bauer recalls a positive review in *The Miami Herald*. At the same time, he was working in a Miami-produced PBS show, *¿Que Pasa, U.S.A.?*, a bilingual sitcom. "It was a great bilingual learning tool, and it kind of made me a star overnight, at least in Miami. It was also shown in high schools all over the country." He knew staying in Miami wasn't going to get him into the larger world, though. "You had three choices. You could stay in Miami and do community theater...or you can go to New York and pound the pavement and try to find a place to live, and a job, and get pictures and send them, drop them at agents' offices and hope that they'll see you. Maybe they'll decide to run with you a little, send you in for auditions for off-Broadway shows or off-off-Broadway shows. That's what Ray did." Bauer chose the third option: Hollywood.

Where he studied with Stella Adler, who had been a big influence on Robert De Niro. "She was devastating to students who were not committed because she stood for the purity and the dignity of the art of acting." Bauer is such a naturalistic and appealing performer that one doesn't really see the work he puts into his performances; when speaking to him, one is soon aware of his thoughtfulness, and of just how seriously he takes acting. In that respect, he and Adler were a perfect fit. "She was tired of people looking down on actors. And so she insisted that anyone that she worked with, she trained, took the attitude that she did, which was always: I am this person. I am Queen Elizabeth, and this is my history. And my father was Henry the Eighth, and I do not walk like a modern girl. So if she ever saw someone doing that kind of contemporary movement on a stage in that context. Oh my God. She would destroy them."

In part as a result of his training, he became very picky despite his need to work. "Before I did *Scarface*, I turned down a lot of junk. To me, I should emphasize. It was junk to *me*. I wasn't interested in furthering my credits just for the sake of having credits. People will tell you, 'Get into a feature and once you're in a feature, you've made it.' Right. And I would say, 'Not any feature. If it's *Friday the 13th*, I don't want to do it.' Everybody thought I was crazy."

Along the way, he played with his name. His dad was a pilot, and his surname, Echevarria, confounded air traffic controllers in towers the world over. He considered calling himself Rocky Aria. Which has a ring to it. He adapted "Esteban" to Steven, and that felt good to him. After his father recounted his own experiences by way of giving him a form of permission, the actor took the name Bauer, after a maternal grandmother, a German Jew who had fled to Cuba to escape Nazi persecution.

In Hollywood he became romantically involved with Melanie Griffith, who was coming out of an intense period of personal crisis. "Melanie was already a veteran," he says of the excessive lifestyle one can indulge in Hollywood, "and she had to be pulled out of purgatory and disaster by people who cared about her. And when I met her she was just returning; but in a sense she had given up on trying, and the people who were helping her had given up… I had no preparation for meeting somebody that was so in need of help, in need of rescue." (Bauer relates all this by way of explaining how, in addition to helping Pacino with his accent, he also filled the actor in on the effects of cocaine abuse; like director De Palma, Pacino had never touched the drug.)

Bauer and Griffith threw in together and moved to New York to find work. "We got to do some scene work. We enrolled for classes with Stella there, made some really good friends. Then we ran out of money. The usual thing. I'm told, 'Go in for a soap opera.' And I was like, I don't know. They pay really well. But again—I don't want to be in a soap opera. So, I'm going stay here until I get a movie. And I don't. So we're going to move back to LA. Melanie leaves first because she had a really good audition coming up, a really good shot at something. And I stay in the apartment for another week or so, and the day I'm packing to go to the airport in the afternoon, my manager calls from LA and she says, 'Sit down. If you're standing, sit down. I know you have to leave today. What time?' I said, 'Five.' And he says 'They're casting a film. And your name came up. An agent that didn't sign you has recommended you to the main casting director. And she's an old-time New York casting director, casts big movies, *Sophie's Choice*. She found Kevin Kline for that.' Her name was Alixe Gordin. 'It's a movie about a Cuban refugee, a criminal. With his pal, they leave Cuba, and go to Miami and become drug kingpins. It's the drug trade. It's the rise and fall of the main character, Tony Montana. And guess who's playing Tony Montana? Al Pacino.' And I'm like, 'Uh, what?'"

Martin Bregman and Brian De Palma had decided, between them, that it would be a good thing to have a Cuban-American take the role of Manny. But Pacino had had another idea. One of his good friends was a young and unusually gifted New York actor named Jimmy Hayden. Jimmy, Bauer says, "had a bad heroin habit that he brought back from Vietnam. And he was a very unhappy guy. He was a great actor. And he actually did some really good roles on film." One, in fact, was in Sergio Leone's *Once Upon a Time in America*, which Hayden did not live to actually see. He died of a heroin overdose in November 1983, while acting in another production of *American Buffalo*. Pacino had continued to look after the actor. When I interviewed the actor William Forsythe in 2014, he remembered his *Once Upon a Time in America* colleague tenderly: James Hayden was a very special actor, a special actor, a special guy. "When the movie came out, because James Hayden and I were just the rookies of the cast, our names weren't on the poster, although our faces were. So when the movie came out, every poster I could find, I wrote James's and my name on the posters. Mostly for James."

As capable an actor as Hayden was, he wasn't right for the Manny role—among other things, physically. "He was an Irishman with blue, blue eyes," Bauer recalled, "and he dyed his hair black for the screen test." It did not convince. Pacino was then open to a new actor. One of the first things he said to Bauer when they met—after sizing up his costar and grinning from ear to ear at what he saw—was, "So you're a real Cuban? Then how come you're called Bauer?" And Bauer explained his name change.

Acquiring the role required a lot of callbacks, a lot of schedule changes—in a typical feast-or-famine scenario, Bauer had another movie role dangled in front of him as he was going through the *Scarface* process—but once that was done, he headed back to Los Angeles.

"I was living with Melanie in, in Malibu, in a little shack. Al, he wanted to know where I was living. And when I told him, he rented one of the big houses up on the beach, near our place. For a month or so. And he told me that he wanted me to come over for breakfast at nine or ten. And so I would drive my little car up, up about twenty blocks or something. And his assistants would greet me. And we started a ritual of meeting every morning and spending all day, until the afternoon, with him and the script, but not really reading scenes. We would talk in character, about anything in our lives, in Cuba, what we thought about coming to America, what we thought of ourselves and stuff like that."

To this day, Bauer says, he gets very defensive when people criticize Pacino's Cuban accent in the movie. In part because Bauer helped Pacino out with the accent, basing it on how his own father talked. He has little time for people getting tetchy about Pacino's presumption in playing a Cuban. "Nobody remembers this," Bauer says, while allowing it's not such a huge consideration, "but Tony isn't entirely Cuban anyway. In the interrogation room he says his father was 'a Yankee.' So that's part of it. He says his father took him to the movies growing up, that's how he learned English. That's a layer that Al was able to use, and use it to take the liberty of creating his own Cuban accent based on all the information he was getting. And be consistent about it, because it's consistent throughout the fucking film. He never wavers. He never falls out of that thing. Why, though? Because every single day, that's how we talked to each other."

And this continued throughout the shoot. During which Bauer was often called upon to be the bearer of bad news to director Brian De Palma. "After we did twenty-four takes or something, it would drive Brian crazy. I was with Al every take. And it would go from nine to ten to thirteen, and after every one Brian would say, 'Okay, how do you feel?' Not just to Al, but to me as well. Just to not make me feel small, to make me feel like my opinion counted. 'How do you guys feel about that last one?' And Al would look at me, and he would say with his eyes, 'What do you think?' I might say, 'It felt good, felt okay. I think the one before was stronger. Just more natural, I think.' And Al would say, 'Yeah, the one before is better. So let's do one more.' Brian would be standing there waiting with his eyes sort of rolling back in his head. Like: 'Oh my God. Now the both of them are doing this.' Literally I had to turn to Brian and say, 'Brian, one more. Can we do one more?' And he goes, 'Okay, okay.'

"And there was a guy on the set who was a really big guy. Really big guy. A prop guy. We had like several characters on the crew who, who felt nothing about, about imposing their personalities on the shoot. They had been around. And this one guy, he had picked up Al's accent. And sometimes when we'd get ready to do another take, he would blurt out, in that voice, 'I never been so embarrassed in my life.' And Al loved the way the word *embarrassed* came out of him. And we were dying to use it in the movie, just to roll around the word. The accent has become iconic because there was nothing like it in a movie performance before. It has its own thing. It has its own sense of humor about language. Where you're enjoying it, you're just chewing on it, rolling it around."

At the end of the day, Pacino needed to decompress. "We'd finish a scene, a serious scene. And we'd go back to his trailer; I'm a little more relaxed because my performance does not require me to be as intense as he. Where he has to be aggressive about everything. And we're in the trailer, and once he'd exhaled he'd turn to me and, still doing the accent, say, 'What would you say to a game of Uno?' And I'd just lose it. Because ten minutes earlier he was spitting and snarling."

Bauer's rapport with Mary Elizabeth Mastrantonio was almost as easy and instantaneous as his affinity with Pacino, although their first meeting was awkward. "I was asked to read at a final round of auditions for the role, and there was another actress there, someone I had known in school, and when we saw each other, she immediately put on this semi-conspiratorial air, like, 'We're going to be in this movie together!' And as soon as Marty Bregman saw her and I speaking, he pulled me aside. 'Listen to me. Leave her alone. Get away from her. See that girl over there? She's Gina. I want you to do the scene with her. In fact, I want you to ask her if you could rehearse the scene over in the hallway.'" This was Mastrantonio, whom De Palma had been set on since seeing her onstage. "We had excellent chemistry. And in what we shot, that chemistry was made more explicit." Bauer says that for the scene of Tony and Elvira's wedding, in addition to shots in which Manny and Gina look at each other with something more than extended family affection, there had been included a glimpse of the characters making love in the woods of Tony's new estate. In the editing, it was determined that this would be too on the nose, and this was the right call.

Other cuts, Bauer remembers, were made even before shooting started. "The first blow to poor Oliver Stone came as we were getting ready to shoot. Did you know that in one screenplay, there was a scene set in Mariel itself, before getting on the boat to Miami? It's a mosquito-infested hell. And at the docks there are hundreds of little boats, yachts, mid-size yachts, that have come from Miami to pick up their relatives. And we see Tony and Manny. They get put on different boats and vow to find each other when they get to Miami. Tony gets on his boat with a bunch of other people and it's overloaded.

"It's not that big a boat. And there's a woman with a child that Tony notices. Now the water is getting rough and the wind's blowing. And some people are like murmuring and saying, 'Oh my God, we're all gonna die.' And Tony is trying to just keep to himself. And the woman starts screaming, and the boy is overboard into the raging waters. And Tony Montana does not think twice. He dives overboard. Somehow he gets to the kid and grabs him and he swims back And everybody's like: 'What a hero. What a hero.'

"Now this would have changed the whole movie. Had we shot it. But we did not. Marty Bregman walks in one day and says, 'I have an announcement to make. I'm sorry to say that Thom Mount, the head of production at Universal, has cut the opening sequence.' Oliver almost lost it. 'How can he do that?' Marty says, 'Oliver, this is just the way of the world. It's too expensive. They don't want to go to Cuba. They don't want to shoot a boat on raging water. You want to talk to him? You can talk to him.'"

Stone told me he had never been banned from the set, although he allows that he was on occasion asked, politely, to leave for the day. Bauer remembers somewhat differently—and remembers that, when actually on set, Stone would have trouble getting information from people. "He would show up and he would say, 'Steve, Steve, come here, come over here.' And he would have a big manuscript, a *Scarface* script on him. He would say, 'Have you shot this scene? Have you shot this scene yet?' And I'd say, 'I think they've cut it.' And he'd say, 'Are you fucking kidding me?' And he would run to, to Brian and say, 'Brian, what happened to scene fifty?' And Brian says, 'Oliver, Oliver, Oliver, you can't just barge in here asking what, which scene is cut and which is not. We have to make the movie the way we feel. It has to be made. And there are scenes that we don't need.' And Oliver would just go nuts. It was funny; he would use me to get information because nobody else would talk to him. People would see him coming, they would put on their masks and crosses and stuff: 'God, here comes the fucking vampire.'"

Speaking of the experience now, Bauer sounds as if he could have gone on with Pacino forever, take after take after take. At the end of the shoot, he says, "I didn't actually collapse." But he did feel a certain separation anxiety, having been hooked up to the Pacino apparatus for so long: "I didn't have my own thoughts and responses of reactions to things. I sort of was guided through his lens, through his eyes, through the way he views acting. Which I trusted implicitly. It became central to my life, something I could always draw on."

★★★

Almost a decade after *Scarface*, De Palma cast Bauer in the role of "the other man" in his corkscrew thriller *Raising Cain*, opposite Lolita Davidovich and John Lithgow. "Here Brian was in his element, in his genre and, and he was very comfortable, and he loved being the sole commander of that ship. He enjoyed it thoroughly." Without the demands of a Pacino, things moved differently. But not casually. "Brian remained meticulous and demanded it of the actors. He expects the actors to be prepared and receptive so he doesn't have to say things twice. And he doesn't have to do more than five takes." Bauer found his role a puzzle at first. "Brian said, 'I want you in this. And I want you to just prepare yourself because I am going to make sure that you are an absolutely perfect man. That's your role: you're a perfect man. I have costumers and makeup and hair people, and they are going to make you perfect. They're going make you beautiful. That's what I need. I need you to be beautiful.'" As for costar Lithgow, who plays a killer with multiple personalities, Bauer said: "Lithgow is just, blazing, brilliant, brilliant. His portrayals were so creepy and, and original. It was just so great to be on the set with him. He'd just be so nice. He was his own sort of New Englander, a very proper guy. And then he would turn into Vlad the Impaler.

"But," Bauer laughs, remembering long days with Pacino, "he didn't stay in character."

9

UNWELCOME IN MIAMI, STRESSED AT UNIVERSAL

In 2008, Martin Bregman told Steve Persall of the *Tampa Bay Tribune*, "I've never really talked about this before. But we had to get out of (Miami) because someone was going to get hurt."

The location shoot for *Scarface* in Miami, Florida, starting in the fall of 1982, was supposed to be a lengthy one. The sweltering Miami sun is practically a character in the film. The tropical heat, the edge-of-melting feeling it brings—it's a defining atmosphere. Whether a tent under a bridge in Freedomtown where the boatlift refugees wait to be relocated or the private deck of an outdoor pool where a trophy wife waits to be courted (not that she thinks that's what she's doing), it's all Miami, and it contains the entirety of the world Tony Montana aspires to possess. Oliver Stone knew the territory, and he had gotten producer Martin Bregman and director Brian De Palma acquainted with it too.

But Bregman, he admitted in 2008, feared he might have

some issues well before he sent tons of equipment to Florida. Word of the film had reached the larger Cuban expatriate community, and in the winter of 1982, some of its representatives reached out to Bregman in New York. "The problem started when I had some Cuban expatriates visit me," Bregman told Persall. "They were from Union City, NJ, right across the river. They told me that it would be very unsafe for me, my family, and everybody involved in this enterprise to make this film. They said they were aware—and they used the word *aware*—that Castro was financing this film to embarrass the good Cuban community." A claim that, Bregman said, was "absolute stupidity."

According to Bregman, the very idea that Cuban expatriates were drug trafficking in the land that gave them freedom from Castro was inimical to the Union City guys. "They said over and over: 'There's no Cuban drug people. No Cubans are involved with that.'

"Now, I had just gotten back from Miami with Oliver Stone, and we spoke with nothing but Cubans, and they were all in the drug business. Not all Cubans, but the people we talked to, the big guys in the drug trade."

Meanwhile, in Miami, the city commissioner of Miami, Demetrio Perez Jr., didn't care about the revenue a major Hollywood film production could potentially pump into his town. In the summer of 1982, the *New York Times* reported that Perez, counter to the perspective of Florida Governor Bob Graham, who supported the *Scarface* production and indeed all potential big studio filmmaking in Florida, had sent a letter to Bregman requesting numerous changes to the *Scarface* script, and asking that a certain percentage of the movie's story devote itself to the activities of anti-Castro Cubans in Miami. Speaking to the *Times*, Perez said that a prior Al Pacino picture, Sidney Lumet's *Serpico*, also produced by Bregman, set off alarms in Perez's head, because its story—entirely fact-based, and accurately so, as it happened—"tried to affect the credibility of the New York City Police Department."

In 2008, Bregman told interviewers for the *Miami New Times* that Perez was "a very stupid man. And I told him that." He also recollected stating that the movie contained more corrupt Jews than corrupt Cubans, which may or may not have been strictly true. In any event, the script then contained, and the finished film contains, scenes of Tony's honest and hardworking mother bemoaning her son's chosen lifestyle. And this is in and of itself a gangster movie trope in general. (Although one can't be certain what James Cagney's creepily worshipped mom in *White Heat* thinks of her son's chosen line of work, but that movie's an exception in several notable ways.) As for Perez's stupidity, it kind of caught up with him in 2002 when he pleaded no contest to fraud charges related to the Little Havana apartments he owned and managed. The man was, plainly put, a slumlord. Yet a few years later he finagled a sweet bond issue to float some private charter schools, having greased a lot of palms in the Miami-Dade County commissioner's office. Perez died in March 2023.

In any event, at the time of Perez's protests, Bregman, then operating in Miami, was inclined to dig in his heels. In a syndicated column that ran on August 30, 1982, reporter Marilyn Beck revealed the tensions that the Miami objections were creating within the production entity itself. "Bregman reportedly decided last week that, despite protests by at least one leader of Miami's Cuban community over his remake of the 1932 gangster film, it will roll as scheduled this fall." Beck followed with a rather definitive quote from Ned Tanen, Universal's president: "Martin Bregman is not putting up the money for this feature. Universal is and Universal won't make the movie unless I can be assured there will be no problems. The last thing I need is to end up having militants chasing us around the block." And in September, with very little footage in the can, Bregman got a call from Tanen's boss, the top man at Universal, the talent agent turned studio mogul Lew Wasserman. "He said: 'I'm pulling the plug. Come back to L.A. I don't want to see anyone get hurt,'" Bregman told the *Tribune.* "Lew grew up in a tough neighborhood [in Cleveland, Ohio, the son of Russian immigrants], so if it spooked him, it was real. It's so stupid, because more and more money would've been spent [in Miami], and a lot of local residents who needed jobs would have been hired. But that's no way to get up in the morning, with a policeman sitting by your bed with an Uzi." Miami's Freedomtown would be simulated in Santa Monica. Tony's estate would be a combination of Santa Barbara and the Universal backlot. Nobody protested.

In a September 1983 interview with *Women's Wear Daily* by J.A. Trachtenberg, De Palma vented: "The pro-Castro groups threatened us, the anti-Castro groups threatened us, everybody threatened us. The threats were very specific. 'If you make this picture, you'll be dead.'" (In the same interview, De Palma allowed that his decision not to cast Nancy Allen as Elvira put a possibly fatal strain on his marriage: "I didn't cast her because she wasn't right for the part. I'm a director. I have to make choices.")

The retrenchment allowed De Palma to do some reshuffling of the production team. Specifically, he fired the production designer Leon Erickson. Erickson hadn't had much of an opportunity to put a thumbprint on the production because most of the scant footage the crew got in Miami, including the finale of the motel chainsaw scene in which Tony executes the Colombian drug trafficker who tried to burn him right in the middle of the street, was of preexisting exteriors. Erickson was an art director and production designer of considerable experience and relatively wide range. He began his career making do with the threadbare budgets of Roger Corman pictures such as *The Wild Angels* and *The Trip.* When he hired on with *Scarface,* he had *Star Wars* in his filmography, as well as, and this is the salient point, several Robert Altman pictures, including *McCabe & Mrs. Miller,* for which he oversaw the building of the entire pioneer Western town where the picture is set. But if Erickson had a style, it tended to realism, and realism isn't what De Palma was looking for. De Palma doesn't say much about Erickson except that he had trouble communicating with him. But the highly stylized sense of design Ferdinando Scarfiotti brought to his work on Paul Schrader's *American Gigolo* and *Cat People* spoke to De Palma, as did, of course, Scarfiotti's work on Bertolucci's *The Conformist*, which had captured the imaginations and hiring preferences of the so-called Hollywood movie brats—in the early 1970s. Francis Ford Coppola would tap Bertolucci's regular cinematographer, Vittorio Storaro, to film the 1979 *Apocalypse Now* based on Storaro's work on *The Conformist.*

De Palma anticipated that Scarfiotti would understand the hard-edged sheen he wanted for the movie. When Schrader worked with Scarfiotti, the designer practically sat at Schrader's side; every camera setup was signed off by Scarfiotti before "action" was uttered. That's in part because Schrader's background was as a writer, and he had come up in the Hollywood system that way. He was not first and foremost a "camera director," but Scarfiotti helped to make him one. De Palma was a camera director from stem to stern but saw in Scarfiotti someone with the facility to complement his own schemes and instincts. Both he and Scarfiotti, soon after the designer was hired, gave extensive notes to costume designer Patricia Norris. (As did Martin Bregman. Michelle Pfeiffer sometimes disappoints fans who ask her to name the designer of her iconic backless slip-dress. It was Norris who designed and made it, and in interviews, Norris gave all credit to Bregman, De Palma, and Scarfiotti for their specificity about costuming.) The grandiosity of Tony Montana's settings after he becomes Miami's drug kingpin are pure Scarfiotti, and in a sense pure anti-realism. They do indeed look like opera sets.

But Scarfiotti also was careful to design with the exigencies of film well in mind. In an interview with *American Cin-*

ematographer in 1983, the film's director of photography, John Alonzo, recalled his first look at the multi-mirrored interior of the Babylon Club, at which the movie's centerpiece scene occurs. He thought, "Oh my God! Where am I going to put the cameras? I'll be seeing myself." But Scarfiotti had put all the mirrors on gimbals so they could be positioned in such a way that they would not pick up the camera's reflection in a given shot. Scarfiotti's expanded version of Frank's office, with its Stygian black depth, proved another challenge for Alonzo. "I called it 'The Black Office'—black on black on black! I had to pour an enormous amount of light there, just to get an image! I had to disregard the [light] meters!" Working by eye was nerve wracking, and that wasn't all. Once the lights were up, Alonzo said, "I also had to keep actors away from the hotly-lit areas." They could literally have gotten burned.

Alfred Hitchcock was not infrequently heard to remark that shooting a picture was, to him, the least interesting aspect of moviemaking. The master director Robert Bresson, whose pictures were singular articulations of an aesthetic that represented his austere spiritual ethos, once stated, "My movie is born first in my head, dies on paper; is resuscitated by the living persons and real objects I use, which are killed on film but, placed in a certain order and projected onto a screen, come to life again like flowers in water." David Fincher recently described shooting as a "necessary evil." Brian De Palma doesn't complain about shooting in his interviews, but one suspects that, at the very least, he's not terribly sentimental about the process.

What Hitchcock wanted from actors was their star power and their ability to hit their marks and speak their lines credibly, more or less. Having worked out a picture in his head and on both the written page and in storyboards, he arranged his shoots with the expectation that a lot of what he hoped for would be lost. The object of the exercise was to not lose *too much*. This explains in a sense why he had limited patience for the needs of actors. It's not true that he didn't get along with them. He was so treasured by the film comedienne Carole Lombard that she was able to convince him to direct her in the 1941 *Mr. and Mrs. Smith*, a romantic comedy that was a little outside the master of suspense's wheelhouse. But the times changed, and decades later, Hitchcock found himself at least mildly exasperated by a Method-inflected actor like Paul Newman, who, during the shoot of 1966's *Torn Curtain*, was asking the director to walk him through all of his actions, and then refusing to, say, provide a neutral look that Hitchcock wanted for a sequence of shots, because he didn't believe the character would give such a look in the scene.

De Palma was, as we've mentioned, a "New Hollywood" player, one of the "guys with beards" taking over the industry, as William Holden's old-school director complains in Billy Wilder's *Fedora*. Hitchcock was a touchstone director for these fellows, but so was Elia Kazan, famously an "actor's director" whose alliance with Marlon Brando was echoed (and expanded, actually; Kazan and Brando did only three films together, after all) in the teaming of Martin Scorsese and Robert De Niro. These were not directors who could afford to be cavalier about actors, nor, in the cases of Scorsese and Coppola, did they want to be. But De Palma, despite having been the first director to bring De Niro into motion pictures, had not acquired much of a reputation as an actor's director. Working at the behest of Bregman and Pacino, however, he became one. Even before shooting, there was a sense that Pacino would be running the show in certain respects.

A lot of people, many who ought to know better, don't understand what an assistant director does. The word *assistant* suggests a coffee-grabber, which an assistant director is not; the fact that the position is a subordinate one suggests a mentor relationship, and at least in Western filmmaking, that's not entirely accurate either. The way that an assistant director is most like an assistant is that they're often required to keep superfluous people away from the director, which can be a full-time job in and of itself. But the main function of an AD is to prepare the ground for which the director to call "action."

Jerry Ziesmer, who died in 2021 at the age of eighty-two, was one of the most storied and seasoned of assistant directors in American movies. He started his career in the early '60s, acting in television shows; his first AD job was on the 1970 picture *Tell Me That You Love Me, Junie Moon*, for the terribly exacting—abusive—Otto Preminger, one of the great American directors whether you like it or not. One of his bigger claims to fame was as AD to Francis Ford Coppola on *Apocalypse Now*, a film on which many of the principal participants at one point or another temporarily lost their minds. Ziesmer was able to keep his head throughout, and also appeared in the film as an actor, looking vaguely sinister and taciturn as the guy who tells Martin Sheen's Corporal Willard to terminate Colonel Kurtz's command "with extreme prejudice."

When De Palma first met Ziesmer, in March 1982, with an eye to hiring him for *Scarface*, the director was unimpressed. Irritated with how things were going in the post-production stage of *Blow Out*, he was curt to the point of outright rudeness. As production manager Ray Hartwick did some cheerleading for Ziesmer, De Palma waved Hartwick off and blurted, "All right! He's hired. OK?"

This account is from Ziesmer's memoir *Ready When You Are, Mr. Coppola, Mr. Spielberg, Mr. Crowe*, an invaluable book for anyone interested in how the cinematic sausage is really made. His section on *Scarface* is not long, but it's substantial. He compares Pacino's perfectionism to that of Barbra Streisand's on the 1973 romantic drama *The Way We Were*, and observes that their practice was "artistically fulfilling, but as the saying goes, 'Even

Rembrandt stopped sometime.'" It was an open question as to whether a director could compel them to stop. Ziesmer recalls De Palma practically pleading "We got the shot" and Pacino, the immovable object, saying "I'm not sure. I want to go again."

The crew, according to Ziesmer, came up with novel ways of coping with all the waiting for Pacino. Card games, chess, and checkers were the standard diversions. There were raffles. There was a betting pool, with crew members guessing how many times "fuck" would be said by Pacino. John Alonzo apparently began bringing a ballet teacher to set, to train crew members to move equipment more quietly, to help the actors maintain concentration. Ziesmer recalled watching grips and electricians walking around the set with books balanced on their heads.

"At about that time the idea was conceived to have a funny hat contest..." Once publicity about the contest leaked, a meeting was called to explore methods of increasing efficiency on the set. A meeting attended by all except for Pacino.

Later, while shooting in the faux Bolivia afforded by the landscape of Montecito, Pacino sponsored a lavish party for cast and crew: "Al Pacino was a benevolent king," Ziesmer recalled. But running into another crew member some time later, and asking him why he hadn't attended the party, Ziesmer was told, after a long pause, "Because I can't be bought off that cheaply." Oliver Stone recalls De Palma's response, delivered with a chuckle, when the writer asked the director if he'd be attending the shoot's wrap party: "Fuck no. Do you think I wanna be around these people another day? I'm outta here."

For his part, Ziesmer, who had, we recall, also worked on *Apocalypse Now*, averred: "I endured tedious months with Al Pacino and Marlon Brando because eventually those actors gave us some of the best performances we have in film, and I wanted to be a small part of it."

"Brian was a cold man," Oliver Stone writes in *Chasing the*

Light, "like [*Midnight Express* director] Alan Parker—it comes with the territory—but he wasn't threatened by me and seemed to want me around. So did Bregman, who stayed very much in control of the film, sitting with Brian through every casting call. At one session I attended, I fought hard for Glenn Close to play the role of Al's mistress in *Scarface*, as she'd been great in the reading. I'd written the original Elvira role as an upper class New York girl I knew, slumming in South Beach with a gangster boss when Tony meets her."

Bregman dismissed Stone's idea with a disparaging comment on Close's looks. Stone is not the first person to comment on how Michelle Pfeiffer's own looks hewed to a type that Bregman liked, a type embodied to a certain extent by Cornelia Sharpe, who by this time was Bregman's wife.

Stone immediately caught on to the fact that there was a time to be seen by the lead actor, and a time not to. "Al was still, at the time, quicksilver of nature, turning on a dime, very sensitive to his environment, eyes, ears, skin on fire. If he saw a new face on the set, he'd react. He was just that way. At all costs I'd avoid his line of sight when he was in acting motion lest my concentration disrupt his own—somewhat like particle waves. Billy Wilder described this sensitivity in recounting how Greta Garbo banned him from *Ninotchka* for appearing in her sightline. It wouldn't be easy to direct Al, but De Palma seemed indifferent to that; he was never really an actor's director like Lumet, whom Pacino had wanted. De Palma, it seemed to me, was more interested in the 'big picture,' and in that vision actors were more or less an important part of the scenery."

Is that true? Maybe yes, and maybe no, but nevertheless, De Palma had to give Pacino his head, because at the end of the day, he was working for Bregman, and Bregman was making this movie at Al's behest. Was Lumet the kind of "actor's director" who could have pulled Pacino back? As a former actor himself, and a lover of actors, Lumet no doubt had a lot in the way of practical solutions for getting performances. But would talking things through with Pacino have eaten less time than Pacino's insistence on take after take would have? It's impossible to say.

In any event, De Palma did not represent to Stone any kind of directorial ideal. "De Palma was simply not the most energetic of human beings," he writes. "He was overweight, slow physically, wearing the same copy of a pressed khaki uniform that an engineer might, throughout the production. [...] But he was, no question, brilliant; he had vision, and he'd set up elaborate shots that would pay homage to this aesthetic but also take quite a bit of time for cinematographer John Alonzo to light."

In *The Devil's Candy*, her book on the making of *Bonfire of the Vanities*, Julie Salamon, who was and remained friendly with De Palma after writing a remarkably unsparing account, notes how De Palma tried to marshal his energy. "De Palma's naps were legendary. The demons that always woke him before dawn every morning also arrived in the middle of the night whenever he was making a movie. He needed the naps for both physical and mental stamina. Almost everyone who had worked with him had heard about the production manager on *Scarface* who had made the mistake of interrupting the director's nap. De Palma's face had been crimson when he came to the door. He didn't have to yell; the look in his glinting green eyes said it all. 'That'll be the last time you ever wake a sleeping giant,' the director said, and the production manager knew from the tone that he wasn't kidding." Her remark about demons is telling. In *The Devil's Candy*, and also in Susan Dworkin's book *Double De Palma*, about the less calamitous making of *Body Double*, De Palma's follow-up to *Scarface*, the director is always thinking. And no doubt he's thinking something similar to what Hitchcock was, which is how the hell he was going to get the vision in his head, the vision he worked on 24/7 during preproduction, onto the damn celluloid.

Patricia Hitchcock said of her father: "He hated location. Just hated it. He says, you don't get the right lights. You've got the noise. And you have to then come in and redub. If ever he could get away without location, he would." He wrote out the film via script revisions and extensive storyboards, but he also knew that putting that vision on film was not an automatic, mechanical process. Circumstances, human error, the desires of the casts, and other factors compelled Hitchcock to think on his feet, or from the director's chair. Bill Krohn's exemplary study *Hitchcock at Work* depicts the director doing what he had to do to get at least an approximation of what he wanted, and filming—contrary to the assertion that he would never shoot "coverage"—at least a small variety of shot options to choose from in editing. De Palma worked similarly. It was painstaking. It took time. His on-set style was not that of a conductor waving time and trying to impart his energy to the assembled. It was that of an artisan trying to crank something real out of a cumbersome machine.

And Pacino was a gear in that machine that would not run as anybody would have preferred. Stone: "[T]here was another issue that was more difficult to see, a large one, really, in its implications. Al had grown into the habit of not getting 'up to speed' until approximately the seventh take. Sometimes a scene would need twelve, fourteen, even twenty takes. But it was generally those first six lost takes that surprised me. No matter how fast a crew moves, you'd lose at least an hour or two of prime energy to get an acceptable take. If Capra or Ford, for example, had been the director, it would have been one, two, or three takes, sometimes more, but there was a rhythm to the shooting. Here, there was a lot of lethargy and delay, and because he was such a star at this time, basically we could not move ahead to the next piece of business until Al approved what he'd done. Given Al's questioning of everything—sometimes right, but sometimes unnecessary and born of insecurity—there was no way in hell this film could stay close to its already expensive budget.

"So given Brian's methodical but plodding energy levels, we'd only get three or four, maybe five pieces of business done each day." Stone would himself direct Pacino, "successfully and relatively quickly," he says, in *Any Given Sunday*, when he had adjusted his working practices, but this was Pacino on *Scarface*: "No one ever knocked on Al's door. It wouldn't have brought him out any sooner anyway; he was sticking to his pace. Even Bregman walked on eggshells around him. He was too dangerous to be confronted."

De Palma did enjoy staging and filming the shoot-'em-ups. John Alonzo used multiple cameras for the climax of the Babylon Club scene, in which Tony Montana avoids assassination. For these scenes, the only acting was the action. The actors on the receiving end of gunfire, and there were lot of them, had to be outfitted with exploding "blood" squibs that took three to four hours to put in place. Effects men Ken Pepiot and Stan Parks developed a synchronization method that allowed the cameras to capture every muzzle flash; each gun was wired to a control device (the wires would run down the actors' legs, which were rigged along with their gun squibs). Alonzo explained the gear in *American Cinematographer*: "The synchronizer prevents the gun from shooting unless the camera shutter is open. It's a little cumbersome, because now the actor has another wire coming down his leg, and he can't necessarily fire as fast as he'd like to. It becomes something of a technical problem for the actor, because he has to perform and act in sync with the weapon. For those shots where it was essential to get the flash, to see the gunfire, it was invaluable."

Oliver Stone found De Palma's constant upping of the ante with respect to violence, particularly in the movie's finale, distastefully anti-realistic. "I challenged Brian on several staging issues, wherein the realities of a shootout were unbelievable to a Vietnam combat vet." In any event, he couldn't fault the relish De Palma brought to bear on such sequences. "Brian, with his macabre, chuckling grin, enjoyed shooting it, as the script called for an enormous amount of gunfire, stabbings, and whatever other mayhem we came up with, such as the interior of the nightclub being totally destroyed by machine guns, mirrors shattering all over the place, and Tony's mansion being eradicated at the end of the movie." But in Stone's account, the fun eventually dissipated, because, well, squibs: "There were no significant digital effects available at that time, so because we had to use the firing devices called 'squibs' that could imitate gunfire audio-visually, the pace slackened; each squib had to be replaced if the take was redone, which was often the case, and if there were twenty to fifty shots in a violent scene, it was quite a bit of labor and debilitating to the tempo. Actors would sit in their dressing rooms for endless hours."

Given the above stories, which all make the shoot feel like some more or less extreme variant of Hell on Earth, I was a little surprised when I spoke to the film's executive producer, Lou Stroller, in the late summer of 2022, who described the shoot as a relatively normal large-scale production that went a little bit late, nothing to get too excited about.

Born in 1942, Stroller was not an inordinately movie-crazy kid, and he never considered a career in the industry until he witnessed a set and got the bug. "It was a funny thing. My father was in the retail men's clothing business, and that's what I always thought I was going to do. I had finished college, and I was waiting to go in the army at that time. I had to wait a few months, and I was working with my father. One morning, a friend of his was filming a commercial out at Kennedy Airport, which Far Rockaway is right behind. My father literally threw me out of the house for his friend who needed an errand, so I went, and that was it. I was bitten by the bug. Then I started sweeping floors and making coffee to get into the film industry.

"New York in those days was primarily commercials, and

that's what we all started doing. Luckily, I got friendly with the group that was the in group in New York making films. There were maybe three films a year that time in New York, and we all worked with each other and helped each other get a job. If we were busy, we'd recommend somebody. It was a small group, wonderful group."

Stroller got used to chaotic sets early on. One of his first credits is as the unit manager for the Mel Brooks classic *The Producers* (1967). Brooks, who'd come up as a writer and occasional performer on TV Golden Age sketch comedy shows, was a first-time feature director, and his leading man, the raucous Zero Mostel, was a handful. Stroller's unit manager responsibilities extended outside the set. "I was living in the Village, and Mel also lived in the Village. My job started out in the morning. I would go pick him up at his house with a taxicab. One day, I went one morning, and I was sitting outside with the cab, and he leaned out of the window, yelled down to me, 'I'll be out in ten minutes.' The cab driver didn't want to wait. I said to him, 'I'll take care of you. The meter is running, don't worry about it.' He said, 'No, no, no, I got other things to do.' He went and got a cop because I wouldn't get out of the cab. The cop came over to me and said, 'You got to get out of the cab. This guy's going to make a living.' The minute the cab pulled away, of course, Mel came down and said, 'Lou, where's the taxi?' He was a funny guy. Nice man."

Stroller worked with De Palma on *Sisters*, and *Carrie*, but has only spotty memories of those shoots. What he does recollect more vividly is being taken under Martin Bregman's wing, and working through Bregman with Alan Alda, on *The Seduction of Joe Tynan*. "I was the guy that was on the front lines with them, whoever 'they' might be, in all the good times and the bad times. Marty was instrumental in all my films, or most of my films, and he hooked me up with some wonderful people. It was always like family. I stay in touch with Alan. He's a wonderful human being, and we made five or six films together. He's a real person.

"I don't know if you know Jerry Schatzberg. He was another guy, a wonderful guy that I still stay in touch with. They're just some very special people that I've hooked up with over the years. I've done a lot of films. I did *The Rock* with Bay and Bruckheimer in those days. Those guys, they're in their own world. And even when I went out to LA, I was a New York guy. I lived in LA for thirty years, but they always considered me a New York guy. And there's always a little difference between New York and LA people." Bregman identified as a New York producer all his life and deplored the fear that got into good filmmakers after they'd gotten too accustomed to Hollywood itself. Once *Scarface* was set, through Bregman, Stroller's involvement was a given. He set up an office in Miami to coordinate the shoot.

"And things started to get a little bumpy right away. We pulled the film out of Miami and did the entire film except for, I think, ten days, in LA and Santa Barbara. The Cuban community was split—I know, because I was the one dealing with all of them. They were lovely, but there were two communities. There was a community of very well-to-do older Cubans who had come to live in the States, and they lived down there very nicely and lovely. The younger Cubans that lived there resented that a little bit. The new ones that were coming in Calle Ocho and everything else were not too happy with the Cubans that were already living there. Almost everybody was very nice to me and tried to help me get it going, but there were some internal things. I don't know what actually happened." Once the production returned to Miami—under stealth, so to speak, when all of the other photography had been done, and still, according to De Palma, accompanied by security people—things had settled down considerably.

"It went very smoothly down there. I mean, we got it all.

I had good relationships with everybody down there, and the Cuban community and everybody else were great. Working in Miami was a pleasure. We were there only there like eight, ten days, I think, a whole sequence.

"Everything was copacetic. We came in and out so fast, I think, that there was no time to get a head of steam going to protest our being there a second time. So, boom, in and out. Short and sweet and fast.

"And we had, I think, two days in New York. it was outside the UN, which was one sequence. The Bolivian stuff we shot in Santa Barbara was just to save us some money instead of traveling thousands of miles with a crew and everything else. We got the great look in Santa Barbara, the houses and stuff."

Still, there were the multiple takes and the going over schedule. I asked Stroller, "How were you able to keep the studio off your back, so to speak, while this is occurring?"

Stroller laughed. "Well, if I showed you my back right now, you'd understand I didn't keep the studio off my back. Not totally. No. Filming is not an exact science. Pacino is a brilliant actor, and Brian a brilliant director. It just takes time. It's not where you can say, 'Okay, we got that. Let's go.' I mean, when you do a TV commercial or you do a series episode, you got to move against the clock. Here, we scheduled ourselves out. I mean, in those days, if you went over ten days or two weeks, that was a lot. Now, you go over months, and the numbers are exponential in the course of things, but I think we did a pretty good job for the film that we did, in the amount of time that we took. Listen, you work with actors that you want to get a performance out of. Sometimes it takes more takes, sometimes it takes less takes, but I don't think we were so out of whack on that film.

"And Brian was wonderful. I mean he's always prepared, and he's great with the actors. We work with some brilliant people, John Alonzo, the cinematographer who's wonderful, and we got it taken care of. I think everybody was really happy with the way it went. We had a lot of tension from outside about the amount of violence was in the film and the vulgarity. The MPAA gave us a difficult time in getting an R rating because of all that stuff. But I thought all that material was realistic. You're dealing with drugs, and people dealing with drugs. It's not intellectual, elitist. You got to get down and dirty with them and be on their level. Oliver Stone was on board with that idea also. At their best, he and Brian and Al were like a team. Was there conflict? Yes. But you're dealing with intelligent people here, and everybody has opinions. Oliver was also just starting out at that point. At the beginning, we had a time where Oliver was saying that he wanted to go to dailies and Brian didn't want him there. Oliver kept bugging us. So, I went to Brian and I said, 'Brian, let him come to dailies. So, what's the big deal? It'll be fine.' So Brian finally relented, and we let Oliver come to dailies. Brian told him not to say anything to Al about them afterwards. However, the next day, Al came in with six pages of corrections that he watched. Oliver had poked them, and that was the last of Oliver going to dailies.

"Steven Bauer was lovely. He was very young and getting started. He looked up to Al, and it was great. The two of them were buddies, and then Michelle was a doll to work with. One funny story that I tell a lot now is about the stunt coordinator, a guy named Dick Ziker. 'Z-Man.' Brian and I were in dailies. Z-Man doubled for F. Murray Abraham, who played Otto, who ends up getting thrown out of a helicopter. It looked great. I'm sitting there with Brian. I said to Brian, 'It looks great.' Brian said, 'There's something bothering me. Let's watch it again.'

"We watched it again. He says, 'We've got to reshoot it.' I said, 'Why, Brian? Why are we going to reshoot it?' He says, 'No, I want his hands tied.' He didn't have his hands tied and it looks awkward. 'He should have his hands tied.' So, we put the whole thing back together. I had to call Ziker and tell him he had to do it again. He freaked out on me a little bit, but we went back and we reshot that with his hands tied." Such was the latitude that Bregman and Stroller allowed their director.

Stroller believed, and continues to believe, that it's the job of the producer to let the process happen and understand that as every member of the cast and crew comes together, what they bring to the table has to be considered. "Al is a brilliant actor and he has his things, and Brian is a brilliant director. We'd do the rehearsals, and everybody knew what we were going to do, what they wanted to do in each scene. When shooting, we do a few takes, and everybody has opinions and suggestions. As you're actually having other actors work against each other, you get suggestions. Brian is a wonderful director who knows what he wants but lets the actors bring things to the table; he'll see certain things and know he does or doesn't want them. So, it's just the process." Going over schedule wasn't due to a lack of preparation. "Everybody did their homework, and you came in and you worked. You do the pages, you do the shot list."

Steven Spielberg stopped by to say hello to his friend Brian during the filming of the final shootout. "It was quite an elaborate set, especially for its time," Stroller says. "This was the early days with everybody, and Steven was just one of the guys."

And as for many of the participants in the production, the *Scarface* payback in recognition remains, for Stroller, substantial. "I think it's a great movie. When it came out, we got… *chastised* is not the right word, but we got a bad mouth from the industry. Over the years, it's become a classic. People find out my profession, they ask, 'Well, what'd you do in movies?' You say everything. I did *The Rock*, I did this, I did that. Then I say *Scarface*, it's like a different ball game. That gets people excited."

10

A THOUSAND CUTS

It's possible that one reason Brian De Palma would, after *Scarface*, feel compelled to make a movie set in the milieu of pornography was because he spent so much of his working life surrounded by adult entertainment. For some time, De Palma edited his films in a suite of offices at 1600 Broadway, in Manhattan, directly across the street from the live adult entertainment emporium called the Pussycat. (The building was razed and replaced by the Crowne Plaza Hotel years later.)

"There were peepshows all over the place," Bill Pankow remembers. "A lot of times, on movies I worked on, guys, that's where they'd go for lunch hour. They'd get a roll of quarters and hang out."

Over the years, De Palma cultivated working relationships with a number of astute editors, including Paul Hirsch, the brother of *Greetings* and *Hi, Mom!* producer Charles Hirsch, who introduced Paul to De Palma. In Hirsch's excellent book, *A Long Time Ago in a Cutting Room Far, Far Away* (Hirsch also edited George Lucas's *Star Wars*, as the movie subsequently retitled *A New Hope* was known in 1977), he details a very active collaboration with De Palma—how they contrived the final jump scare in *Carrie* after seeing *Deliverance* and endeavoring to improve on that movie's iconic final shot, for instance. He also avers, "[S]plit screen can be interesting, but it's not emotionally affecting," and provides instances of pushing back at De Palma when he felt the effect was compromising a movie's gut impact. They worked together on and off into the early '80s; while *Dressed to Kill* brought future *Scarface* editor Jerry Greenberg into the De Palma circle, the director and Hirsch reunited for 1981's *Blow Out*, and it was an unhappy experience for Hirsch. He describes in his book how a structural flaw in De Palma's script meant that, were the film to be edited according to it, the villain would not actually show up until a good hour into the picture. Hirsch's strategy was to push particular scenes forward in the narrative. Like De Palma, he is pleased with the initially poorly received film's latter day reputation. But he concludes: "I learned an important lesson on *Blow Out*. A director deserves to have an editor who is solidly behind the project. My problems with the script should have made me turn the picture down. I unconsciously brought a negative attitude to the editing of the picture. This brought me into conflict with Brian and damaged our relationship somewhat." The relationship was repaired, as De Palma gave a generous blurb to Hirsch's book.

As for Bill Pankow, he was working with veteran editor Jerry Greenberg when Greenberg was hired to cut *Dressed to Kill*, and, he recounted to me, "[W]e were invited to use those editing rooms. They were all on the third floor; it was three rooms on the third floor. Two were adjacent to one another, and one in the corner looked right out over Broadway, and then the interior room, further down the hall, was used for backup equipment, because the Moviolas would often break, and things would happen. You'd have to have a spare one handy, otherwise you'd have to wait for the repairman to come over, so that was just a backroom that held equipment. So we had those two rooms, and one of them was in a corner kind of overlooking Broadway, and I remember, on *Dressed to Kill*, at some point when it was a discussion about the rating, Brian had an X sign—'X,' you know, like the rating, like they'd have in the movie theater, that he stuck in the window, and it was there for a long time."

The veteran editor Greenberg, who died in 2017 at age eighty-one, had apprenticed with the great Dede Allen. He was her assistant on *Bonnie and Clyde*, whose shocking final gun ambush was but one of that groundbreaking film's cutting coups. (Allen had also maintained facilities at 1600 Broadway.) Greenberg made a big splash with William Friedkin's *The French Connection*, whose still-iconic car chase scene remains awe-inspiring as far as both shooting and editing are concerned. The early '80s saw him shuttling between two seemingly very disparate directors: De Palma and Robert Benton. Benton, best known for his domestic drama *Kramer vs. Kramer*, had a considerably more serene shooting style than De Palma, but was not unconversant with genre and, like De Palma, is always acutely alert to what he's putting in the frame.

Pankow is credited as an associate editor on *Scarface*. The second main editor credited with Greenberg is David Ray, and *Scarface* was not only a big job, it was his first big credit. "I'd worked for Jerry as apprentice and assistant," he told me. "So he and I were close." Ray had been a sound editor on 1974's *The Taking of Pelham One Two Three* and assistant editor on Bob Fosse's 1979 *All That Jazz*, both overseen by Greenberg, both classics, and both quintessential Manhattan movies. "So by the time of *Scarface*, I'd had some experience as an editor. And the schedule was brutal. It was a long shoot. And we had to have it ready very soon after shooting ended. So Brian De Palma realized that he needed another pair of hands. He was one of the first people to hire me and trusted me. So, he brought me onto the film. And I'd never met Brian before. I knew a lot about him, and I knew Paul Hirsch, but I'd never actually met Brian. And they did the shoot in Miami first. And they had trouble there with the local population because it was a crime film, where Cubans were depicted as the criminals. And so there was a big political problem there. So they did what they had to, they used a couple of locations, which were important, because it had to look like Miami." In Ray's recollection, the abrupt ejection from Miami meant that scouting for Miami-like locations in Hollywood would take up some time, during which the production moved up to New York for the scenes set there, and for which locations had already been locked down. "So they spent a week in New York doing the New York sequences, which is where I met Brian for the first time.

"The whole chainsaw scene was shot very piecemeal as a result of the ejection from Miami. For the motel, they replicated the location, the interior and the stairway going up, on a set in Los Angeles. So the interior of the motel room was shot in Los Angeles. Brian wanted to figure out how to deal with the exterior once he'd shot the interior. And they replicated this location beautifully. But they were able to go back to Miami and shoot the exterior with a car driving up and all that stuff. I'm sure he had that all figured out. He was a director, as far as I can tell, who really planned things in advance. And it was always very deliberate. He wasn't a director that necessarily allowed for a lot of spontaneity."

Because of the tight deadlines, rather than use Ray as a second set of eyes and scissors to fine-tune material, Greenberg delegated entire scenes to Ray. There was a huge amount of footage to consider, because Al Pacino wanted a lot of takes, and he and producer Bregman wanted a lot of those takes printed. "I cut the scene in the bathtub, and I cut the scene in the restaurant towards the end," Ray recalls. "And you could have created any number of different characters for the different types of performances he gave you, some hysterical, some very calm. And you really had to go through his material and make choices. What is interesting, because we didn't have a lot of time afterwards to adjust these scenes if they weren't right, so we were sort of under a lot of pressure, and I was working for Jerry as much as I was working for Brian.

"Because Al's approaches were hugely varied. Particularly the scene in the bathtub. Sometimes he would do it very quietly. And other times he'd be very over-the-top. And I discussed it with Jerry, because we were worried that time is running out, and we wouldn't have time to figure out how to give everything a coherent flow. There were films, when I started working in the business, there would be a year between the first day of shooting and the film being released in the theater. So a lot of the editing was re-editing, reevaluating the scenes that you cut, looking for different performances. So, the way you put the scenes together, you'd know that would never be the way they would end up. You'd always be reevaluating and looking for a better line reading for this, or a better line—because when you'd first put a scene together, it's a little bit of guesswork. And we all worried because on *Scarface*, we knew there wasn't going to be a lot of time for doing that because of the release schedule and the fact that shooting had gone over the schedule. So we had to do a lot of extra guesswork, and mine was occupied with trying to get a middle ground in terms of where the movie and the performances were going. But because I knew a little bit about Brian, I knew Brian was not scared of going over the top a little bit, whereas other directors I worked for might have been squeamish.

"So I think that's how I approached it, by not allowing it to go *too* outrageously over the top. But this was not a subtle character who had deep psychological issues. It was a very up-front character. So I also didn't want to go too quiet, too self, too introspective. I think I didn't use a lot of his more introspective takes, to the best of my recollection. And this was the same in the restaurant scene, which was very much over the top."

While cutting scenes such at this, Ray noticed that Michelle Pfeiffer appeared to be, at times, at least a little thrown by what Pacino was putting out. "I felt very much for Michelle. I don't know what she'd done before. But it was the first time I'd become aware of her. I'd never seen her in anything. And to work with somebody like Pacino, who would all of a sudden throw something so huge at you. How do you deal with it? How do you deal when this anger comes out of this character? And I don't think there was that much rehearsal, in which he could try these different approaches; he would just spontaneously throw these things out. How do you, as an actor, deal with that, particularly if you're young and inexperienced? So yes, I felt very much for her, and I cut the restaurant scene, and I could see that she was not on a sure footing of how to deal with this man, both the character of Tony Montana, or the actor Pacino. As I said, Pacino would come out with these things with no warning at all. I mean, you knew the general trend of where the scene was going, 'cause you knew the script. But he would come from the dialogue very low, and just suddenly, there would be this burst of hostility, which he'd throw the other actors. I think Steven Bauer, he was cool with it. I think Mary Elizabeth Mastrantonio found it easier—just from looking at the dailies, I remember, she could handle that type of thing. I don't think that fazed her. She really was consistent, whereas Michelle was not consistent. But Mary Elizabeth, I think, sort of could take that sort of thing more easily."

"I think when you have actors like Pacino, who are very well-established, they will often do something to give you a different nuance," Bill Pankow told me. "The next take will be slightly different, or at the end they'll say, 'Well, let me do a take because I wanted to try this thing.' So there's often a lot of material that you can add on or use instead in the actors of that caliber, I guess. That's not always true with actors who don't have that same kind of cachet, because the directors and the studio always try to get everything done. And I didn't get that—I think in terms of when Jerry was editing, I think he was just trying to get to the essence of the character and the essence of the way Brian wanted to present him."

The film's centerpiece, the nightclub scene in which Tony escapes an assassination attempt, was a challenge on many levels, one being the actual workflow of analog moviemaking. When film was a physical process, the material, it follows, had to be shipped away a lot of the time. The wishes of *Scarface*'s lead actor held this process up. "You know how they worked in those days. They'd shoot the film, and they'd make one print of it," Ray says. "And then, the editors, they'd screen it that night in dailies, and then the editor was free to edit it. When they were shooting in Miami, they used the New York lab, so the material came straight to us. But when they were shooting in Los Angeles, and we were cutting in New York, Al Pacino wanted to see the dailies. And I guess he didn't have a lot of time, so they'd hold a lot of dailies back, sometimes for as much as a week. And we'd run out of stuff to cut, and we were just sitting on our hands waiting for new material. And then Al Pacino would come in on a weekend apparently, and spend both Saturday and Sunday watching, and then they'd send the stuff to us. But it meant that a whole week's material would come to us at once. And then we'd have to go to work on it. And with the nightclub sequences, Jerry and I just decided, you take this part, and I'll take that part, and we'll eventually put it together and see how it works."

Decades after the fact, Ray almost flinches when recalling the violence of *Scarface*. He understands that as an editor he has a firsthand knowledge that it's all film craft as opposed to real violence, but that's the magic of craft sometimes. "A lot of the scenes are a bit difficult to take. The chainsaw sequence I found very disturbing. Jerry cut that. And the only way I could get used to it was to take the actual reel into my own cutting room, and I'd run it down and look at the frames by themselves. And then I eventually got used to it. And then what was shocking started not to bother me at all. I guess just from being familiar with it." The chainsaw is never seen to touch skin, real or manufactured. Which Ray of course knows makes the scene more, not less, upsetting.

"I think if they actually showed an arm being cut off, it would have looked like a fake arm that you'd cut off. Which is why the controversy that happened about potentially getting the X rating turned into such a circular argument. They said to Brian, if you take off this, this, this, and this, okay, we'll give you an R rating, we won't give you an X rating. And I think he knew perfectly well, yes, I'll do it. And it's not going to make the slightest bit of difference. Because it's not what you see, it's what you *know* is going on. And that's what scares you, that's what shakes up the viewer. And untold genre horror movies rely on that phenomenon. And as I say, I've never talked to him about this. But I sense that Brian knew he could take these shots out and it wouldn't make a difference, and he could also then accuse them of being disingenuous."

"Brian was in Los Angeles. He wasn't around," Ray recalled when looking at the experience in its entirety. "So I took my instructions, a lot, from Jerry. I didn't know to what extent Jerry was in touch with Brian in this period. But looking back on it, he must have been in constant touch with Brian. I suspect at the end of the day, Brian would call Jerry and they'd discuss it, but Jerry would never tell me about this. It was very interesting. Once, I looked on while Jerry was cutting the scene at the end.

Tony Montana's being shot all the time, over and over. And I said, 'Is this really going to work? You know, it's obvious that he's dead. I mean, he's been fired at. There are bullet holes all over him. And he's not falling dead. He's continuing to fight.' Jerry looked at me and he said, 'That's because he's been dead all the time.' I thought, God, he's brilliant. 'Jerry, you really hit this. He's like a vampire. You know, he's indestructible. And that he's been dead for the second half of the movie.' I realized some time later, Jerry got that from Brian. He didn't invent that. But Jerry would never totally tell me how much of this was coming from Brian and how much of it was his own idea. And Jerry had wonderful ideas. Jerry was a genius. I think he was one of the greatest editors there's ever been. And certainly, he was very influential in my filmic education, as it were. But Brian was also a person I could really learn something from. I didn't get to know Brian very well on *Scarface*. I got to know him much better on *Bonfire*." *Bonfire of the Vanities*, the 1990 adaptation of Tom Wolfe's best-seller, was both a critical and a box office failure, and its very troubled making was chronicled in Julie Salamon's book *The Devil's Candy*. Salamon's account is frank, funny, and mortifying, and it would not exist had De Palma not given the journalist unprecedented access to pretty much every aspect of the production. To De Palma's credit, he didn't distance himself from this scrutiny even as the picture was falling apart.

Ray continues to believe that *Bonfire* has never been given a fair shake. "*Bonfire* was never a successful film. I have feelings about that, by the way. It has been highly criticized, but I learned a lot working on that. I have a lot of respect for him. He knows film and knows film history. And I took a lot away."

For Pankow, a formative part of the *Scarface* experience had to do with it being his first long work experience in Los Angeles, on a large studio mixing stage. "The thing that was unusual for me in that film, one thing, was that once we finished editing, all the sound work was done in Los Angeles—not the sound preparation, but the mixing. So the sound editors prepared everything in New York, and we moved our whole operation to LA. Unfortunately, David Ray and his assistant, they didn't come for very much over there. But the thing that was stunning to me was—as I mentioned, the sound studios that I was used to working in, the Brill Building, across the street from where we were, they were of a certain size, and they were not very big. The New York sound mixing studios were not particularly large compared to the ones in LA.

"So this was my first experience of going into a sound studio in LA to mix a movie, and I was overwhelmed. It was like the size of a movie theater. Down by the screen there's a full-sized pool table, a full-sized ping-pong table. Then there's a bunch of real estate before you get to the seats. And then behind the seats is the console where we were recording mixes. It was huge. But by the same token, in terms of our editing room—because we were still…well, we weren't editing much, but we had a lot of optical, visual effects coming in on film that had to be incorporated into the movie. So we had a small, tiny little editing room upstairs in this facility in LA. We had a very small room for Jerry and me to work in.

"Prior to this, I spent most of my time running—because in New York, obviously, you take a cab, or you get the subway. You're at the optical house in five minutes or ten minutes and then out, off to the mix. In LA you had to have a car and drive to all the different places that were doing optical effects for you, and then you had to bring them in and screen them. It was a tedious process, but there was a lot of a different kind of running around, trying to chase down these different houses because they were all over the place because LA is so spread out. That was one of the fun things for me, to see that kind of operation—suddenly see this big studio—and still to this day, I find it extremely impressive. I'm always impressed when I have to mix a film in LA; it's incredible because you get to hear it the way it's going to be in a movie theater.

"There was a hotel called Hollywood Regency; the whole sound crew was there. Eddie Beyer, Maurice Schell, and Jerry had his room. I was there. So it was a bunch of us that stayed at this one facility. I guess the studio obviously got a good deal to put up this whole crew that they brought out there. That was fun too, sort of socializing sometimes on the weekends, hanging around by the pool, and learning from other people there what to do in LA, or where to go to eat, or what to see. It was a very exciting time for me, that whole project."

This was the one period on *Scarface* that had a steady, well-delegated workflow. But there were challenges, relative to a lot of issues, including, of course, aesthetics. "Because Jerry was supervising the mixing, Brian would typically not spend a whole day in a mixing studio. Like the editing, he would get it all mixed and then we would call and say, 'Okay, the reel is done,' and he'd come back and review the reel and give his input. I was busy, as I said, going to the optical houses and all. Where the negative would get cut and then they'd start to make a print. They'd make a first answer print, so we could see it. I would go over it cut by cut to make sure it was accurate against the work print. That's what you always did on a film, you run the two things side by side in a synchronizer to make sure that the cuts were proper.

"Then, once you get past that, then they start to time it—to do the color timing. So John Alonzo, the DP, went in and timed the film the way he wanted it, as I recall, and then Brian saw it and he wasn't happy and it was because—he said, even though he wanted a tropical feeling—he thought it was all too red, everything was much too red. So we had to go back in there and re-time a lot of the reels at certain areas that Brian didn't want to have that red in there so strongly. Part of it came from the fact of the filmstock that it was being printed on. We had the work print on whatever it was, it was 100 percent color-accurate. But Alonzo printed it—I think it was on Fuji stock, which by nature has a more reddish cast to it, as I understand—I could be wrong. I'm pretty sure we did it differently. I don't know if we used a different stock, or it was just in the color timing process. In any event, I got sort of a baptism of fire in the sense that I was doing a lot of the things that a full-blown editor might do but that wasn't my official position. Jerry was kind enough to give me some of those responsibilities, and that helped me with my own career because I was learning everything along the way. There's a lot of things that I was charged with on that film which were new to me and exciting to learn from." It was the beginning of a long association with De Palma, during which Pankow got several courses in, naturally, dealing with the MPAA ratings board.

By the end of the process, with De Palma in some senses pretty much "over it," the rating process revved up. "There's always somebody in the studio side who is the liaison, who's getting that information from them, and then they give it to us, we work on it, show it to them, and then they have new stuff. So after two or three times of that, Brian just says, 'Well, forget it. You can't keep doing that.' They did the same thing with *Snake Eyes*, which was a Paramount picture. I don't know if you remember the film, but there's a scene where the secretary—he's a political guy, he gets shot, and Carla Gugino's sitting in front of him wearing a white outfit, and she just gets blood all over it, blood on the arm. I remember going back-and-forth with the ratings board over that several times to try to keep removing some blood on her sleeve." The 1998 movie was eventually granted an R rating.

Pankow's assessment of the director doesn't differ terribly from anyone else's. "He doesn't suffer fools gladly. He's very respectful of people's abilities and skills, and the position that he's brought them in to work with him on, but he doesn't really want to bullshit around. He's not a fan of small talk and chit-chat. When he comes to the editing room, we do our work, occasionally have lunch together, and then he's off to do whatever else he's doing—mostly reading and probably preparing other projects. He's very direct. He knows what he wants. If you give him something else, he'll consider your idea and either accept it or not, depending, but he doesn't like to bullshit around and tell stories, and drag things out. He's very direct and precise in his filmmaking and, in my interactions with him, socially."

Unlike De Palma, he has good things to say about filmmaking's shift from physical film to digital. Mainly having to do with the absence of the physical. "You can make so many alterations—so many iterations, I should say, and put them on the side, and then try something else, and you'd always have what you made before, which, in the film world, that was so hard to do and so expensive to do. The thing that bothered me, at least in the beginning, was that a lot of directors and a lot of producers just assumed that if you could execute it faster digitally, then you should be working faster. There's two different dynamics going on, for me—one is, you can't short-circuit the thought process. Whether you've got film in your hand or dailies on a disc or whatever, it takes time to consider, review, and think about how that's going to go together; that is no faster to me than it was when we would edit it on film.

"And now directors expect to hear more sound right away. And when I'm editing, I work a lot of times with the sound off. I cut my choices and I'm working the scene with no audio, and then eventually put back in layers, like the dialogue, fine-tune that, and put in some music, whatever. In the old school days, if the director was watching over your shoulder with a Moviola displaying picture, they weren't expecting to hear much sound. It was only when you reviewed it on the flatbed they expected a little more sophisticated audio. Now, if they're working over your shoulder, they'll expect audio, which at a certain point in the assembly is, to me, beside the point. And then there are some directors for whom having sound in there is too disconcerting. So yes, there's pluses and minuses. I mean, overall, I think it's a plus, but it's still a process."

Producer and musician Giorgio Moroder remains best known for his work with the American-born singer Donna Summer. Born in Northern Italy in 1940, besotted by rock and roll at an early age (apparently Paul Anka's swoony 1957 hit "Diana" was an inspiration), he took up guitar and began work as a touring musician before he was twenty. He relocated to Munich in 1968. In the early 1970s, he met Summer and concocted, with Pete Bellotte, the groundbreaking disco single "Love to Love You Baby," which, like Serge Gainsbourg and Jane Birkin's "Je t'aime, mois non plus" several years before, generated a lot of controversy over its breathy, orgasm-suggestive vocals—which also had the unwanted side effect of kind of camouflaging Summer's talent as a singer, which her subsequent work enabled her to exercise a little more. While "Love to Love You Baby" was recorded with a conventional lineup of backing musicians, the 1977 single "I Feel Love" was a triumph of minimalism, using a pulsating synthesizer riff, an artificial hi-hat, and a bass drum played by future superproducer Keith Forsey to create what experimental rock musician Brian Eno recognized at the time as the future of pop and dance music. Moroder didn't define himself by synthesizer music, though; a subsequent Summer hit, "On the Radio," from 1979, has a conventional, and conventionally pleasing, orchestral backing.

The soundtrack to *Scarface* is almost entirely synth-driven. A 2022 article in *Mixdown* magazine lists the giant array of electronic keyboards used; these are now, for better or worse, vintage instruments. They run the gamut from patch-cord-driven modules like the Serge synthesizer to polyphonic electro beasts like the Roland Jupiter 8 and the Yamaha CS-80. Early samplers like the Fairlight CMI are in there too, as is the LinnDrum drum machine. For all that, in terms of orchestrating and arranging, Moroder's full capabilities were brought to bear on the enterprise, as, for instance, on the song "Vamos a Bailar," in which organic percussion grooves along with drum machines and synth horns to create a credible approximation of Cuban pop music.

Prior to collaborating with Summer, Moroder contributed music to a couple of cheesy German softcore pictures, including 1972's *Sex Life in a Convent*. His first Hollywood score was for the alarming Turkish prison movie *Midnight Express*—written by Oliver Stone—for which the propulsive, fixed rhythms made by analog synthesizers generated entirely appropriate tension. Its "Chase" theme, an instrumental not too dissimilar to "I Feel Love" (and crafted deliberately to sound like that, at film director Alan Parker's request) but somewhat darker, became a dance floor hit and charted the world over.

In a commentary he recorded for his 1979 film *Hardcore*, Schrader described that film's score composer, Jack Nitzsche, experimenting with different sounds and instruments in his work with Schrader, how he used wineglasses filled to various portions and then manipulated by fingers, along with synthesizers creating a kind of atmospheric underscoring. Before synths, Nitzsche, the arranger and orchestrator who also scored Schrader's debut, *Blue Collar*, worked with a Mellotron, a keyboard that triggered snippets of prerecorded tapes to simulate not just flutes, violins, and so on, but environmental sounds. "And now we've moved to a place where there's very little difference anymore between music and sound effects. It's really almost become the same job." Nitzsche and Moroder were certainly pioneers in this trend, from one direction—music functioning as sound effect, atmosphere. Filmmaker David Lynch and his longtime audio collaborator

Alan Splet were pioneers from the other direction—sound effects becoming music, in a way.

It was because of Moroder's score for Schrader's *American Gigolo* that De Palma approached Moroder. De Palma and Schrader had a history—Schrader had scripted De Palma's 1976 film *Obsession*, and the way De Palma handled the script caused a rift between Schrader and De Palma that to this day hasn't fully been healed. (The critic and screenwriter Jay Cocks, who will figure later in this story, still feels kind of bad about the whole thing: he instigated a screening of Hitchcock's then rather difficult to see *Vertigo* at the Museum of Modern Art for them. "They had an IB Technicolor print off the books. And because I was the guy from *Time Magazine*, I arranged a screening and Brian and Paul and I watched that movie at one of those smaller screening rooms upstairs, the old MoMA. That definitely happened. But that's kind of where *Obsession* came from. I hadn't realized until recently that this had been the source of much angst between Brian and Paul.") De Palma nevertheless had an eye on what Schrader was doing and sensed that Moroder's tone for Schrader's movie was a good fit for *Scarface*—the whole sleek, disco-and-cocaine-infused moneyed Miami milieu.

Just as the lengthy shoot had created a crunch for the movie's picture editors, so it was with the music. Moroder did not get the time to work up demos as such; the movie didn't even get a temporary music track as most pictures work with during the latter phases of structuring the final product. Moroder occupied himself with not just the accompanying songs for nightclub scenes and such, but the musical leitmotifs for each character. "The theme for Tony had to reflect the character [...] and of course the character of the movie. And it has to be a little dangerous, a little suspenseful, but a little deep, too. And I think it reflects quite well that atmosphere that was in Miami," Moroder said in a video interview for a DVD supplement.

Using electronic instruments for the score not only saved

time and money—and it didn't always save that much, given the way synths at this time tended to break down, and computer-generated tone analyzers/generators crashed—their sonics were more attuned to the worlds Schrader and De Palma were building, very contemporary worlds. "Better a mellotron than real strings," the rock critic Robert Christgau wisecracked in the late '60s. The Mellotron's fallible sound at the time decorated psych-pop treats by pioneers from the Beatles to King Crimson. As refined and advanced as synths and "emulators" could get as the years went on, they would never sound exactly like the real thing, and smart musicians used that as a feature, not a bug. In Moroder's disco, and in his soundtrack, the simulated violins were strings on cocaine. The "fake" was aspirational. The pianist and composer Ethan Iverson said of Moroder's score, in an email to me, "Moroder takes the Italianate curves of Nino Rota's score for *The Godfather* and updates it with a drum-heavy disco production." The score looks backward and forward. It has grandeur on one end and chemically induced grandiosity on the other.

As Moroder's work began, he reached out to a longtime friend from Germany to assist him in arranging and elaborating on those themes.

Sylvester Levay was a Munich contemporary of Moroder's and a disco innovator in his own right. "I started very early to play piano, went to music high school, piano composition and clarinet. And that was back in former Yugoslavia on the Hungarian border. I'm actually born Hungarian," Levay told me. "Then I went to Germany in '63 and I joined a couple of bands. And then I met my partner with whom I'm still working with after fifty years writing musicals, thank God successfully." This would be Michael Kunze, who in the 1970s worked under the pseudonym Stephan Prager. "And then we had a world-wide hit together with a disco song called 'Fly, Robin, Fly' with Silver

Convention." This worldwide smash more or less codified a particularly creamy kind of string sound that became a Eurodisco staple. At the same time—because Silver Convention wasn't a gigging band as such, merely a label attached to Levay and some session players and singers—Levay was orchestrating for a variety of studio sessions, which is how he met Moroder. "And we became quite friendly. I'd written some songs for Donna Summer, with Giorgio producing. And then he somehow mentioned he's doing a film, asked whether I would be interested to do for him the recording, arranging and performing. And I said yes. And that was the movie *Flashdance*." Moroder also hired Levay to work on Schrader's *Cat People*.

"I actually remained in Los Angeles because my own wish was to do film scoring. I got a little door open in Hollywood and started to work by myself. But before I got onto that track full-time, I worked with Giorgio."

He mainly remembers the work with Jerry Greenberg. They collaborated closely on "spotting" the picture. That is, determining just where to put the music score and sound effects. "I spotted the movie with him in Universal Studios; Brian De Palma wasn't present at the spottings because he trusted Jerry. Jerry was a great man. A great man. And we had a wonderful relationship. It was a really smooth spotting with him. And it was a big movie and a long movie and a complicated movie. And just as Brian gave Jerry his trust, so too did Jerry give Giorgio and me *his* trust."

Once the determinations of where the music needed to be were made, Levay crafted Moroder's themes to fit the particular moment. He didn't think technically so much as emotionally. "I was actually more into the state of mind of the characters. We had source music in there, and I thought that was very good. I was also in the other studio working a lot with synthesizers. First of all with the first Minimoog and then the Roland family, building on these themes."

Levay, as everyone else on the picture, has strong memories of the chainsaw scene. "It was quite difficult but I did it. It was okay. But at first it was a little bit tough when the guys come into this other Latino guy and in the shower cut his hand off and arm and everything. Nowadays it's nothing, but at that time it was quite hard. It's a tough one because one should know, it's Brian De Palma. He's not afraid of anything, and he is a little bit out there. That's why he felt free to do that. But what the scene shows about Tony was important to me. This is a criminal story.

"He comes to the States, and he wants to become one of the greatest of these bandits. And he was so confident that there was no question about it, that he will do it right from the beginning. There was no humbleness or modesty. And in these extreme situations, I try to inhale the character and the behavior. Because at the beginning of my career, other, in other movies, I would just do some score and realize later on I should have concentrated more on the character and his emotion, be it angry, criminal, sad or so. And that became really actually my obsession.

"Generally, in all my creativity, if a scene is emotional, I tend to go to a minor key. I have to admit, maybe I have in there, a little bit European, Eastern European touch or so.

"But sometimes I do a major key for emotional scenes, which is very tough. You have to really be careful how you compose, because a major song is an up key. What's crucial when you're doing that is not to rely solely on the melody. It's in how you do the harmonic structure, because I think that in a song, underneath the melody be it sung or be it instrumentally played, the harmonic structure is very much what's getting under the skin of people.

"I never underestimate the audience. An audience in cinema or in theater, where I've been doing musicals now for thirty years, they don't know exactly, technically, what's wrong or what's right. They only feel it. They can tell you in this scene, 'I don't like this scene or the music.' They cannot pinpoint it, but they feel it. And I think this is a key for a composer who should be thinking of that.

"So generally also, when you compose, you have to think about the audience, not only of yourself, if you like it or not, you have to like it, but you have to think of the audience too, because at the end, that's where it has to work. What helped me work was knowing that Brian was also having some emotions in the picture, even if they are very elegantly hidden. But he did that. And sometimes I could feel *with* Tony.

"It took about four or five weeks. At that time I was living in Los Angeles and actually at Giorgio's in his home studios. So I had my apartment. I could get up, have breakfast and go right into the studio, and I'm working all day long. So it was linear work. And I think that we didn't have any particular problems. Jerry was popping by, which was very important to double-check whether are we going down on the right track. Giorgio didn't bug me. We talked over about things, and he had some themes he gave me and just do it. So he trusted me, which was for me very helpful because I could be free to create things and to set up things and so on."

Levay enjoyed both the electronic instruments and the twenty-four-track analog tape machine on which he worked. "I still learn every day something of the electronic instruments. Instruments have great possibilities, incredible energy, and sounds. They're still valid. In the beginning of the '80s, in New York, I bought a big ARP synthesizer, and it had lot of these faders and things. And at that time… Now maybe I wouldn't have the, how should I say?"

"Patience?" I suggested.

"Yes. But at that time, I was young and I was playing around with it, and it is really incredible. Hans Zimmer—" the German-born film composer whose work with Terrence Malick and Christopher Nolan, among others, is continuing to advance the film-score-as-overall-soundscape ideal "—who is a friend of mine, he's spending a lot of time on the analog synthesizer, where you have to plug in patch cords, that doesn't come with a lot of finished sounds. Here you create these raw sounds and tweak them. And he's getting incredible results out of these analog synthesizers."

11

HOW TO GET AN R RATING IN THE REAGAN ADMINISTRATION

As we have seen, throughout his career, Brian De Palma battled the MPAA ratings board with some frequency. His 1980 film *Dressed to Kill* had, in the estimation of some, pushed boundaries in both the sex and the violence categories. The scene in which a central character is slashed to death with a straight razor in an apartment elevator, while inspired by the shower scene in Hitchcock's *Psycho*, differed from the 1960 black-and-white film by showing the weapon cutting flesh, repeatedly and very bloodily. And the movie's opening sequence, depicting the sexual fantasy that character has while showering on the morning of her death, had a real "did I just see that?" effect on audiences.

In the fantasy, Angie Dickinson's Kate is replaced in certain shots by Victoria Johnson, a *Penthouse* Pet; and violence is a significant part of the fantasy—Kate is looking, in life, for something rougher than what her uninspired husband provides. So in the shower, we see a man come up behind Kate, caress and then grab her genital area. One feature that distinguishes "soft-core" pornography or erotica from "hardcore" is penetration, and one shot in the sequence was apt to give some viewers the impression that penetration indeed took place. It didn't. And the ratings board must have felt confident it didn't once it bestowed an R rating on the movie. Bill Pankow recalled the seemingly endless back-and-forth that went on regarding *Scarface* and, prior to that, *Dressed to Kill*. "The whole ratings thing was kind of exhausting. We'd be in the mixing studio and show the film to some of the studio executives and—you know, this story's classic, everybody knows about it—one just got up and said, 'Well, I'm not going to release an X-rated film,' and then there was a lot of discussions about it. Eventually it got sorted out, but it was like I said before about *Dressed to Kill*, take out the little bit of blood here, this much blood there, can you take out some *fuck*s? We had some *fuck*s. Two *fuck*s was an R, and then more than that was crazy."

The '70s and early '80s found the mainstream culture taking more interest in genuine pornography than had been permissible in polite society before; the phrase "porno chic" cropped up around this time. De Palma explored it to some extent in his *Scarface* follow-up, *Body Double*. In the summer of 1980, I worked as a production assistant on a relatively high-end "adult film" titled *A Girl's Best Friend*, which starred, among others, the soon-to-be-notorious Ron Jeremy. Jeremy was then, and would remain for some time, convinced that at some point in his career he could make the jump from porn into "legitimate" acting. In addition, he was at this time irritated that mainstream cinema was, to his mind, appropriating porn imagery, so to speak. In 2011 I recalled Jeremy's indignation thusly: "A buff and boisterous 27 years of age, he was crowing to whoever would listen that he had just acquired his SAG card, and also completed some extra work in the new Woody Allen picture, which, as was even then the case with Woody Allen pictures, was as yet untitled. (My calculations put it as *Stardust Memories*, and I don't believe Ron made the final cut.) Because porno chic really still was a thing, and because of what was being perceived as the 'new' or 'newish' permissiveness in mainstream film, Ron believed that the porn thing would soon no longer be a stigma and that he'd be able to make a relatively painless and strain-free entry into the Hollywood firmament. I remember him waxing particularly eloquent on this topic with then-*Playboy*-writer David Rensin, who was visiting the set for an article and who sat around quietly dictating his notes into a mini-cassette recorder. Ron, I remember, had just done a threesome scene with two blondes that had sufficiently discombobulated him that he emerged from the bedroom set with his Fruit of the Loom briefs on inside-out. Warming to his topic, Jeremy ultimately decried the hypocrisy of the ratings system. 'Did you see *Dressed to Kill*?' he asked Rensin. Of course he had; we'd all seen De Palma's *Dressed to Kill*, which had been released earlier that summer and was something of a *succès de scandale*. I think I had seen it two or three times, 'cause me and my boys were big De Palma fans. Ron wasn't quite so sanguine about the picture. 'I can't believe they gave that picture an R! It's total bullshit! I mean, come on. That shower scene in the beginning? I saw that finger go up there, you can't fool me. And they call US perverts.'"

Jeremy would continue to be called a pervert, and more. He is, as of this writing, committed to a California mental health facility after being found incompetent to stand trial on rape charges.

As for De Palma, the constant war with the ratings board exasperated him to the extent that he felt, as we've seen, compelled to announce to journalist Lynn Hirschberg that after he got the "dignity" that *Scarface* would confer upon him, he would deliberately make an X-rated Hollywood suspense picture.

But first he had to get the R rating for *Scarface*.

★ ★ ★

In Oliver Stone's memoir, he speaks of his NYU film *Last Year in Vietnam*, and the praise it elicited from one of his professors, Martin Scorsese. "Well—this is a filmmaker," Scorsese said to his class after Stone screened the picture. He does not mention *Street Scenes*, a 1970 documentary signed by the collective Cinetracts, overseen by Scorsese and featuring New York protest footage shot by Stone. *Street Scenes* is a difficult film to see—it pops up on YouTube every now and again, but legal reps, probably Scorsese-affiliated, whack it back down like, yes, a carnival mole. It's an interesting picture that doesn't finally give much indication of where Scorsese or Stone or any of the other participants will end up. It just demonstrates, as I've mentioned before, the extent to which filmmakers and academics of Scorsese's generation were influenced by both the politics of the era and the response of Jean-Luc Godard to conditions in France post May '68.

At the time the film was made, the most famous participant was the actor Verna Bloom. She appears in a scene in the latter portion of the film, in which Scorsese, actor Harvey Keitel, some camera people, and Bloom's husband, the critic and screenwriter Jay Cocks, sit in a hotel room in Washington, DC, and talk about What Is To Be Done, and more specifically, what actually can be done by individuals in their position. Jay takes a pragmatist's position, asking Verna if she'd be willing to drop out of an upcoming film commitment—she's due to leave for New Mexico soon to work with Peter Fonda on the film *The Hired Hand*—as part of a hypothetical general strike. He's not trying to put his wife on the spot so much as to impress upon everyone else in the room what the real-world consequences of radical action might be, particularly for people who aren't longstanding radicals to begin with.

Cocks, who wrote film reviews and features for *Time Magazine* (where he was also a music critic, and quite an astute one, too;

see his essay on Huey "Piano" Smith and his New Orleans context in the classic Greil-Marcus-edited anthology *Stranded*), had met Scorsese in 1968, the same year in which he'd met Stanley Kubrick. Kubrick was finishing *2001: A Space Odyssey*; Scorsese was teaching at NYU and polishing his first feature, *Who's That Knocking at My Door.* Cocks hit it off with both men—he remembers when Kubrick got a phone call from director Mike Nichols, who told him how he was going to use "Also sprach Zarathustra" in his film version of *Catch-22*, and how Kubrick rolled his eyes at the news, knowing that it was now open season for parodies of his film—and as he traveled with Bloom back and forth from East Coast to West, and began working as a screenwriter himself, the alliance with Scorsese grew. And it was through Scorsese that the writer met Brian De Palma.

When I first began working on this book, De Palma suggested that I talk to some people about specific topics. He said that I should speak to Jay about the ratings battle over *Scarface.* I presumed it was just something that De Palma had grown tired of discussing, and that Jay's recollections of the time would better serve me than De Palma's own. As it turned out, that wasn't the reason at all. The reason was that Cocks was actually instrumental in securing the R rating for *Scarface.* And they say critics don't make a difference.

I should mention that Jay is a friend, and that we have lunch near his Upper East Side residence once a month or so when he's in New York. Scheduling a formal interview was slightly tricky—his preference, and I guess when you come down to it my own as well, is to just hang out and talk movies and life, two topics on which Jay has a very special expertise. Eventually we did sit for a genuine Q and A, and his recollections of early days of friendship and collaboration with Scorsese and De

Palma aren't just added value to the *Scarface* story. They're essential context.

"Brian and I met in Malibu," he began. He told the story you saw in the first chapter of this book of the downhearted De Palma and Scorsese sitting on the curb outside of Warner Brothers' studios. Scorsese arranged to bring De Palma to a party that Cocks and Verna Bloom were hosting at a house in Malibu.

"And it was a beautiful Pacific Ocean Saturday. Marty said, 'Why don't I call Brian?' I said, 'Sure, I'd love to meet him.' And over comes Brian, and we had a bunch of people there at the time, John Cassavetes, and there were people with their young families, I think, and they had kids jumping in and out of the pool. It was a lot of fun, and Brian came over, and he immediately sized up this family situation and started doing his Sheridan Whiteside act. 'What are these little brat kids doing at an adult party?' And that was my first exposure to Brian, Verna's too. And you either go with it or you could say… You say something like, well, I think you've already overstayed your welcome by some parameters, but we went with it. And we've been friends ever since. So that's almost fifty years too, right?"

Jay's description of a dyspeptic De Palma performing a "Sheridan Whiteside act" is spot-on and hilarious but may require some explanation. Or at least a recommendation, which is that you go out and watch the 1942 movie *The Man Who Came to Dinner*, starring Monty Wooley, Bette Davis, Ann Dvorak, Grant Mitchell, Billie Burke, and Jimmy Durante, names that alas grow more obscure in the fullness of time and the relentless erasure of "old" movies perpetrated by social media culture heroes, blah blah blah. The movie is an adaptation of a play about obdurate, querulous, argumentative culture mandarin Sheridan Whiteside, who, after an accident lays him up in a wheelchair, is required to spend his convalescence in the home of just the kind of middle-American white bread folks he holds in overweening contempt. Whiteside, who can concoct a thousand-word multisyllabic harangue over a slightly torn cuticle, was patterned by playwrights George S. Kaufman and Moss Hart after their friend Alexander Woollcott, the roly-poly connoisseur who was one of those Algonquin Round Table types. (See also Dorothy Parker, and um, George S. Kaufman.) The role was so closely patterned after Woollcott that the man himself made a big splash playing it in California. In any event, I'd never heard anyone compare De Palma in indignant mode to Sheridan Whiteside, and honestly the analogy cannot be improved upon. (De Palma never rises to this level in the tribute film made by Noah Baumbach and Jake Paltrow, but get him on the subject of digital cinematography and he'll achieve that pitch, only with more sincerity.)

The Cocks-Bloom social circle at the time also included young Robert De Niro, who had acted for De Palma in the film *The Wedding Party*, shot in 1963 and released six years later, and in De Palma's *Greetings* and *Hi, Mom!* Cocks and Bloom would introduce Scorsese to De Niro some time after this, at a Christmas party in their New York residence. During his reminiscences, Jay paused and said, a little bemused by himself, "When you're throwing these names down—Marty, Bob, Verna—it makes people think like it's some David Selznick sort of thing… No. It was really more like a graduate student party in the fifth floor walk-up at that time."

Nevertheless: "We knew Bob because Bob had been in a couple plays that Jack Elton directed with Verna at Lincoln Center. I had done a script for Marty that was called, interestingly enough, *Gaga*. And it was about his friend Sally Gaga, who was a real person and was the model for the character of Johnny Boy in *Mean Streets*. Brian loved this script and took it to Ed Pressman. Marty had many concerns about it. I was concerned he didn't love it. It was a very broad kind of comedy, more in the vein of something that Brian would cotton to more than Marty, who was very afraid that it would be read as insulting to his background, to his family. Which, in fact, inadvertently, it was. It was funny sometimes, but it was patronizing and stereotypical. But it had basically a great idea.

"Sally Gaga got run out of town. This was true. And wound up somehow hiding out in Miami. Anyhow, Brian tried to get the script made, and then we started working together, and I was working with Marty, too. I said to Brian, 'Well, you've got to understand I can't review your movies now.'" De Palma was stuck in LA with a movie he'd more or less been thrown off of, and needed to work.

"So, we came up with a script for an episode of *Columbo.* And I still think had an incredible idea, and I can't remember whose idea it was initially and who added what to who. And Universal loved it. They actually, I believe, paid us for it. The ultimate act of love. And the notion was about a Truman-Capote-like character who is going to write the definitive narrative, nonfiction crime novel. The story of a murder and the murderer is never caught. But how does he know who the murderer is if the murderer is never caught? Because the murderer is himself. And he writes this at the peak of his literary powers.

"It's this brilliant book he's writing. It's going to be great, but of course he can't be published until after his death. But that's fine with him because that will ensure his immortality. The major question is, how does he choose a victim? So, being a writer who's not only very gifted but has a very wise eye for commerciality, he decides to kill a celebrity. How do you decide how to kill a celebrity? What celebrity? Well, he's got to decide on someone, and it's got to be kind of random. So he picks up the remote control of the TV and starts channel surfing and stops on Johnny Carson. So he decides he's going to kill Johnny Carson. And that's indeed what he does. And it's Columbo who brings him down.

"I still think this is an incredible idea. And Universal pretended to be very excited about it, but they had thematic concerns. And then Brian got a feature or had a chance to do a feature or something, so he couldn't do the thing anymore. So he brings Marty in. So Marty, Brian and I go have a meeting with a very bright guy named Dean Hargrove, who was one of the guys who created the omnibus mystery series of which *Columbo* was part. And he was very nice, but didn't know quite how to handle these film crazies in his office. We were very deferential film crazies. 'What do these guys want?' he was thinking, and then he went down the list of what you could do or can't do. And with each tick down this bullet list, Brian and Marty were getting more and more uncomfortable. Brian was obviously embarrassed because he didn't know any of this. And one of the strict truths was in the *Columbo* episodes, this Dean Hargrove said to Marty, 'I know you may find this troublesome, but there's no moving camera.' Marty, I think, could adapt himself to that. Reluctantly, but he could have done it and found a way around it, as could Brian. But then they got really cold feet. I think about the Johnny Carson thing. Now it obviously couldn't be Johnny Carson himself, but it was somebody like that. But it still spooked them.

"And then we heard that Peter Falk didn't like the script or had problems with the script, so it never got made. But that was my first collaboration with Brian. We've done stuff over the years, but I've never made a whole movie with Brian, which was very frustrating for us both. I worked a week on *Mission Impossible*; I had a great time. They really got their money's worth out of me, because we came up with the Chunnel sequence. And I came up with the idea of making the head of the mission into the bad guy. Which of course Brian loved. And then the other writers, including David Koepp, who's the credited screenwriter and had done such a great job on *Carlito's Way*, came on. We got some good stuff going there. We've worked very, very well together."

Cocks is credited with "Documentary" on *Sisters*, the movie De Palma went to New York to make after the bad experience on *Rabbit* and the implosion of the *Columbo* idea. The movie contains a film-within-a-film faux doc about the Siamese twins of the movie's title, one a sweet Margot Kidder and the other a murderous Margot Kidder (they have of course been separated surgically, and yes, there is a plot twist, which has been rather relentlessly recycled in doppelgänger-type movies but still feels fresh here). "I wrote the narration, and Brian called me up from the studio, very excited. The feeling was that it was great copy. I did some research, availing myself of the wonderful facilities of Time-Life, and got a bunch of stills together, wrote the narration, handed the stills, and roughed out a little script for Paul Hirsch. It was Paul and Brian who put it together. And that was it. I'm also in it." A waiting room cameo that one has to look very hard to find him in.

Cocks was also at the best-known rough cut screening in New Hollywood history. "Famously, Brian and I went to the rough cut of *Star Wars*, and he created havoc and in a very deliberate way. Because George was very demoralized after that screening. And most people, myself included, would've just gone, 'Oh, hey, listen, it's going to be okay. This is not really a problem. We can do this.' Brian takes the opposite approach. 'What is this fucking movie? What's the tractor beam? I don't understand.' He made George laugh. He was so over the top about it that he made him laugh. And that's very brilliant."

Was that Brian showing "tough love?"

"If Brian wanted to do the tough love thing, which he's done with me a number of times, he would damn well have done it. But I think he chose instinctively to do, again, the Sheridan Whiteside number, and make everybody laugh. I mean, it's a big risk, but it worked. And then we all went out and had a good time, and then the next day there was this session… Kids ask me if I wrote the crawl beginning 'A long time ago in a galaxy far, far away.' I'll say I don't remember. I don't think so. Brian says yes, Paul Hirsch says no. So, I don't know."

Actually, Hirsch, in his book, states that "Jay Cocks, Brian, and the Huycks [married writers Willard Huyck and Gloria Katz] rewrote the three paragraphs."

"I mean, it doesn't really matter that much. But that seems to be my major contribution to *Star Wars* country. It's inescapable. 'Oh, you wrote that?' 'No, I don't think so, but maybe. I don't know.'"

I said to Jay, "Well, when people go up to Nick Pileggi and say, 'That scene in *Goodfellas*, "How am I funny?" That's amazing.' And it is, but it's not from Nick's writing or even Henry Hill's life; it's based on something that Joe Pesci witnessed. But Nick takes the compliment."

Jay and Verna knew De Niro well. Though the above-mentioned Cocks-Bloom Christmas party was the first time Scorsese was formally introduced to the actor, they had seen each other around, in early days; as Jay put it, "Bob grew up in the West Village in a Bohemian environment as you know, and Marty grew up on Elizabeth Street, a half a mile and a world away." Cocks had also met Al Pacino, who was not part of their circle.

"I think I met Al around the time of *The Godfather.* Al was dating Jill Clayburgh, who was a dear girlfriend of Brian's. And Verna was great buddies with Johnny Cazale. And so between Jill and John and Verna, we all just kind of got to know Al. I never really knew Al the way I knew Bob. It's certainly not the way I knew Marty, but yes, that's how we met. Just through the association with the movie starting around the time of the *Godfather.* But we had been friendly with Bob for some time before we met Al. How Al and Bob met, I have no idea. Do you?"

"Not really."

"That's a good question.

"I don't remember the first time I saw *Scarface*, but I thought it was just astonishing. It really was just a challenge. It really rocked you back. It gave no quarter. It was unbelievable. And the word you used about it earlier, *operatic*, that was the thing that was just so recklessly great about it. But I knew that people were having trouble with the running time, and the excessiveness, the punitive excessiveness. And we talked and talked about what to do. I do remember other than some slight trims that I suggested—I don't even remember what they were, and I don't remember whether he made them or not—it was more like hand-holding from me and reassuring him this was a great film. I do remember going to a sneak preview of it in Boston on a Friday or Saturday night. And his audience was not happy.

"And one thing I do remember suggesting is that Brian dedicate the movie to Howard Hawks and Ben Hecht, so film critics wouldn't jump down his throat as they were forever doing about him at Hitchcock." As we shall see, with some critics this strategy backfired. "I do think that this may have disarmed people a little bit and stopped them from comparing it to the Hawks. This is exactly what Friedkin did with the very great *Sorcerer*, the remake of Clouzot's *The Wages of Fear*. He dedicates it to Clouzot, right? Anyway, they were not happy in Boston. Many people walking out, booing at the violence. And Brian was loath to change anything. Do you know how Brian goes to his screenings? Did he ever tell you this?

"I don't know another filmmaker who does this. He goes up to the screen. They put a chair there for him off in the corner. And he sits facing the audience. And that's the way I've seen him at all his public screenings. He just watches the audience. By the same token, though, Brian, he could care less that people get upset about this. What he was worried about was making it less upsetting. He did not want that, because he quite correctly knew that the muscle of the movie was in this confrontational, operatic quality of it. I was going to say it's over the top, but there is no top in that movie. So the censors, they gave it an X. Right. And Brian had to appeal."

Executive producer Lou Stroller, for his part, said that the most difficult part of making *Scarface* was the rating process. "The hardest time was getting it out there. We went before the MPAA, and we spoke to some psychiatrists. We spoke to all sorts of people to get opinions about the violence and the profanity to get an R rating, because they want to give us an X rating and we didn't want that." Nevertheless, as of October 30, 1983, X was the rating. The decision was sufficiently significant that *New York Times* film reporter Aljean Harmetz wrote on it in the paper of record, quoting a possibly sanguine Martin Bregman as stating, "We have been officially designated as a pornographic film. We'll accept the X rating and appeal." De Palma, also possibly gritting his teeth, said the ruling "was kind of good," adding, "If we win the appeal, the whole world can see what the board considers an X picture." He was bluffing. The head of theatrical distribution for Universal, Robert Rehme, had, Harmetz noted, "said that under no circumstances would Universal release *Scarface* with an X rating." This despite a Massachusetts theater chain owner telling Harmetz that such a film "should not be lumped in with *Debbie Does Dallas*." The film *had* to get an R.

"You get your rating, you appeal, then there's an appeals board, and I think they sustained the X, and then you get one last chance where you've got to show up and the filmmaker and some expert witnesses, so to speak, have to make speeches," Cocks recalls. "I think that that was the third tier. It may have been the second one, I'm not sure. But they screened the movie in Lorne Michaels's screening room at 1619 Broadway. Do you know that place?"

"Broadway Screening Room. Lovely room." Long since shut down, which is a shame, because it really *was* great—ample screen, comfortable seats, consistently excellent projection. You should have been there.

"That's it. They screened it there, and they were members of this MPAA, the Supreme Court of the MPAA or whatever they were. And everybody's watching the movie, and then we get up and make statements. And I got up and made this impassioned statement about how this is an antidrug movie. It's a movie that in every…"

Here Jay paused and chuckled. "You're going to lose all respect for me now, Glenn. I said, 'It's a movie that every American child should see. I have a son who's a friend of Brian. He's ten years old. I want him to see this movie right now. He will understand what's going on. This is vital. This is a vital social document that everybody must see.' I don't think I've ever spouted such a crock of overt shit in my life, but by God, I think that it worked or at least helped to turn the tide. They gave it an R—and he changed *nothing*."

The then First Lady, Nancy Reagan, had initiated her antidrug campaign only a few years earlier (best remembered now for the 'Just Say No' slogan that became one of living memory's favorite punchlines). It was much ridiculed at the time. But apparently it resonated with the ratings board.

And so, in the *Times*, Aljean Harmetz filed a follow-up, datelined November 9. "'I'm ecstatic,' said Mr. De Palma. Among the people he had marshaled on his side were Jay Cocks, former film critic for *Time Magazine*; Roger Ebert, film critic at the *Chicago Sun-Times*; Nick Navarro, a narcotics policeman in South Florida, and five psychiatrists."

12

A NIGHT AT THE OPERA: WATCHING *SCARFACE*

Killing Communists for Fun

The motion picture begins with—after the mighty Universal logo, of course, and its gold-and-blue colors under a Moroder chord sequence for synth and percussion—a text crawl. It is almost exactly what is specified in the November 22, 1982, revision of the script:

> In May 1980, Fidel Castro opened the harbor at Mariel, Cuba, with the apparent intention of letting some of his people join their relations in the United States. Within seventy-two hours, 3,000 U.S. boats were heading for Cuba. It soon became evident that Castro was forcing the boat owners to carry back with them not only their relations, but the dregs

of his jails. Of the 125,000 refugees that landed in Florida, an estimated 25,000 had criminal records.

Except, in the script, there is one more sentence: "This is the story of that minority—those they call 'Los Bandidos.'" Had that been included in the film, it might have saved a lot of trouble in a lot of ways, at the very least by underscoring the fact that this criminal element was a *minority.*

The crawl is followed by news footage of Castro making an impassioned speech on the matter, saying (in Spanish) of the Marieletos: "...they are unwilling to adapt to the spirit of our revolution... We don't want them! We don't need them!" According to an *NPR* report, the speech's official title was "Our Criminals Are Leaving to Their Allies in the U.S.," but Castro did not refer to the country's jails in the body of his presentation.

One of the real people who came into the United States via the Mariel boat lift was Reinaldo Arenas, the gay Cuban poet who was deemed undesirable—someone not adapting to the spirit of the revolution—on account of his sexuality. While he had sought to leave Cuba for years, it was only when Castro's government concocted the boatlift plan that he was afforded the opportunity. In his memoir *Before Night Falls*, he writes of his passage:

> Before we boarded the buses for the port of Mariel, [an] officer told us that we were all leaving "clean," that is, that no passport contained any criminal records, and that, therefore, when we arrived in the United States all we had to say was that we were exiles from the Peruvian embassy. There was, no doubt, a dirty and sinister game behind these procedures; the Revolutionary government purposefully intended to create enormous confusion so that authorities in the United States would not know who were the actual exiles and who were not. Before boarding the boats, we were

> sorted into categories and sent to empty warehouses; one for the insane, one for murderers and hard-core criminals, another for prostitutes and homosexuals, and one for young men who were agents of State Security to be infiltrated in the United States. The boats were filled with people taken from each of these different groups. [...] [T]he majority were people like myself; all they wanted was to live in a free world, to work and regain their lost humanity.

In any event, the text proved controversial enough that when the movie was revised for television screening, the opening was changed:

> In April 1980, Fidel Castro opened the harbor at Mariel, Cuba, allowing an estimated 125,000 people to emigrate to the United States. This group of refugees included a very small number of violent criminals released from Castro's jails. This movie is a fictitious account of one of those Mariel criminals who arrived in Miami that year.

What's very small? According to a researcher cited in the *NPR* report, only 350 of the Mariel refugees had "serious criminal backgrounds." Still, the Mariel boatlift and its fictionalization here arguably fed fuel to racist tropes about Latin America that Donald Trump seized on and amplified when he announced his candidacy for the US presidency in 2015. From an escalator in his horrible Fifth Avenue building, Trump Tower, he complained of the US border to Mexico, conjuring demons over what kinds of terrors Mexico was "sending" our way: "When Mexico sends its people, they're not sending the best. They're not sending you, they're sending people that have lots of problems and they're bringing those problems. They're bringing drugs, they're bringing crime. They're rapists and some, I assume, are good people, but I speak to border guards and they're telling us what we're getting." It is not even vaguely a stretch to infer that Trump has sat through *Scarface* multiple times.

The movie's opening credits are red on black, interspersed with newsreel footage of boats at sea. One of them has been christened "The Body Snatcher."

For our first proper shot, we have a typically bravura De Palma take. Tony is in an interrogation room. It's not specified if it's been set up by the Immigration and Naturalization Service, or by some law enforcement agency. In any event, the thick-waisted fellows grilling Tony—for quite some time we see only their midsections, not their faces—talk like movie tough guys, not bureaucrats. The camera circles the room counterclockwise, keeping Tony in close-up/medium close-up, as his interlocutors circle him, moving clockwise and counterclockwise more or less willy-nilly. The dialogue is expository while the visual is disorienting. It's a Brechtian effect, for the first and only time portraying Tony at the mercy of oppressive, faceless forces. Not that he appears to feel too oppressed himself. Tony gives their tough talk right back to them. While proudly admitting he learned English from famed Hollywood gangster portrayers like Humphrey Bogart and James Cagney—"they teach me to talk, I like those guys"—he insists he has no arrest record. One of the interrogators points out the scar on his face and sneers, "Where'd you get that beauty scar, tough guy? Eatin' pussy?" Tony insists it came from a childhood mishap. Grabbing Tony's hand and looking at a small tattoo between his thumb and index finger, one official notes that their office has been seeing more and more of such ink. "It's some kinda code these guys use in the camp. Pitchfork means an assassin or something." (A 1989 paper in the *American Journal of Forensic Medicine and Pathology*, by R. Martinez and C.V. Wetli, titled "Tattoos of the Marieletos," insists that "[i]n general, tattoos on Cuban refugees signify prior incarceration in Cuban prisons, usually do not reflect criminal specialization, and often reflect affiliation to Afro-Caribbean cults [especially Santeria, Palo Mayombe, and the Abakua Secret Society]. In addition, many tattoos reflect the values and attitudes of Cuban jail subculture.")

The tattoo never comes up again, and Tony indignantly insists, "I'm Tony Montana, and I'm a political prisoner from Cuba." When Tony leaves the office, one officer, named Harry, grouses, "That son of a bitch Castro is shitting all over us."

If the voices of two of the officers sound familiar, it's because, if you're a film person, they are. Dissatisfied with the voice performances of the actors playing the roles during the shoot, De Palma had their voices dubbed in by veteran character actors Charles Durning and Dennis Franz. Durning was nearly fifty when De Palma cast him as a building superintendent in 1970's *Hi, Mom!*; he played a bluff private detective in De Palma's *Sisters* two years later. The final shot of that movie depicts his character ever so close to discovering the clue that can break the movie's whole murder case right open, but strongly implies that this revelation will never happen. Durning presents a figure both ironic and poignant in this moment. The part got him noticed, and he was soon doing support work in big-ticket '70s pictures like *The Sting*.

Franz, about ten years Durning's junior, had a small part in De Palma's 1978 *The Fury* but became most beloved of De Palma fans in his *Dressed to Kill* role as tough-guy Detective Marino, who commands Nancy Allen's hooker character Liz to get her client "Ted" from "out of town" and get him "in town and in here" to fill in the details of a murder Liz witnessed with the john. Franz then played a sleazoid porn peddler and divorce detective in *Blow Out*; after *Scarface*, he'd do a turn as a wiseass director in *Body Double*. If De Palma had a repertory company, Franz would have been a key member. Franz would achieve his greatest fame in the cast of the '90s television drama *NYPD Blue*, as dyspeptic (few, if any, of the characters he's played could be called *easygoing*) Sergeant Sipowicz.

The scene ends in a standoff. But Tony must have done something right, because the film cuts to him on the bus to "Freedomtown," the Miami not-quite-structure in which boat lift refugees were temporarily housed. Tony's younger friend Manny recounts his own experience in interrogation, and we're treated to malaprop humor, with Manny having confused Tony's instruction to tell the authorities that he'd been in a sanitarium; instead, Manny told them that he worked in "sanitation," something of a non sequitur.

The song under this scene and the next is "Vamos a Bailar," sung by Maria Conchita, a Cuban-born singer and actress who would achieve screen stardom under the name Maria Conchita Alonso in the 1984 comedy *Moscow on the Hudson*, as the love interest of a fur-covered Russian immigrant played by Robin Williams.

Alonso was a well-known singer in Hispanic circles at the time and had been approached by Giorgio Moroder to do this song. While he's not associated with Latin music as such, Moroder was serving as a model film composer for the new Hollywood, invested in creating a full aural signature for the movie as opposed to just contributing musical themes to go under or over the action.

Stone's screenplay expands upon the Freedomtown experience. There are film screenings! Tony watches the aforementioned Humphrey Bogart in "a badly damaged 16 mm print" of *The Treasure of the Sierra Madre*. He philosophizes with Manny about the crazed Fred C. Dobbs character, telling his friend, "I'm never gonna be crazy like that." The completed film throws all this away, cutting to the ostensible chase: a quick ticket out of Freedomtown for the duo. After a title card, "One Month Later," there's a long Steadicam shot following the boys through camp—so far so De Palma—and the introduction of Emilio Rebenga. A Castro crony who fell out of favor with Fidel, he was responsible for the death of someone close to the party commissioning his death, the accomplishment of which will yield a green card and a hundred dollars for the assassins. Tony is not unimpressed by the offer but also puffs up his chest, asserting his atavism: "I kill Communists for fun." (In the script, Tony's reaction is a mere, "Hey, you're kidding, that's great!")

Emilio Rebenga, wearing a straw hat, white shirt, and loosely knotted black-and-white striped tie, and chain smoking, is a very, very nervous character. Tony and Manny scope him out, the camera making lateral moves in matching shots as Rebenga veers from right to left and Manny and Tony from left to right. The character is played by Roberto Contreras, a St. Louis-born actor with a lot of television work under his belt. He plays Rebenga in a ticcy style not dissimilar to that of William Finley, the performer who played very very nervous to perfection in De Palma films from *Murder a la Mod* through *The Fury* and beyond. (He was the title character in the splendid *Phantom of the Paradise*, and De Palma tapped him for a role in the director's final American studio picture, 2006's *The Black Dahlia*.)

Rebenga's assassination is staged during the real-life Freedomtown riot, triggered by an unannounced "shakedown inspection" of detainees. News reports place it on August 6, 1980, while the film gives the date as August 11. There's a fire in the tent, chaos all around. The reason Rebenga is so nervous, we have inferred, is because he believes he's a marked man. He walks through the clamor, friendless, trying not to be noticed, and is more or less steered into a doorway, hearing someone shouting his name over the chants of "Libertad!" As he goes through a doorway, he practically walks right into Tony's knife. His collapse is shown in an overhead shot; he hits the ground, rolls over, and we see blood spreading on his white shirt. The omniscient perspective is a De Palma signature, a statement that the universe is indifferent to this and all suffering.

When Manny and Tony get their discharge papers, De Palma

keeps the official portrait of President Jimmy Carter in the immigration office prominent in the frame.

Days in El Paraiso

Throughout *Scarface*, artistic representations of the ideal Miami stand in contrast to the actual town. Miami's an attractive city, but in the murals, it has a tranquil idyllic quality we don't really get in the film's story—its characters never have any moments of respite. Even when they're taking in the sun and "relaxing," Tony and Manny's gears are grinding, as we'll see. In any event, once they're out, the first thing we see is a Miami mural. Part of the outer decor of the Little Havana restaurant. The camera dollies back to show us that's not where Tony and Manny are working. Rather, they're operating a sandwich stand called El Paraiso and not enjoying it in the least. "I didn't come to the United States to break my fuckin' back," Tony grouses. Taking in the swanky customers pulling up to valet parking at Little Havana, Manny observes, "Look at those titties." The man seems to have his mind on precisely one thing. Or maybe a few things. "That's style, flash, pizzazz, and a little coke money don't hurt any." In the meantime, our duo has to tolerate their clothes smelling of onions.

But soon they'll be hearing, indirectly, from their sponsor, cocaine magnate Frank Lopez, who commissioned the Rebenga hit. Their next big job comes from a very coked-up associate of Frank's named Omar, played by F. Murray Abraham, who had a brief role opposite Pacino ten years before, in *Serpico*, and who would become something of a star in 1984 in *Amadeus*. Stone's script specifies Omar's pockmarked face, which Abraham possessed.

Tony asserts himself without pause. Does he see Omar's weakness through the guy's high? He reflexively refuses the first task he and Manny are offered—weed, five hundred bucks; Tony's like, "Do we look like baggage handlers?"—and the car's driver,

Waldo, says to Otto: "The Colombians!" with the enthusiasm of someone plotting to hand out a booby prize. "Do you know anything about cocaine?" Tony is willing to learn. Here the take is five thousand dollars, but the risk is more substantial: if they mismanage the cash/cocaine exchange, Frank will stuff their heads up their asses "faster than a rabbit gets fucked." Tony is game even as he hones his hostility: "I don't like fuckin Colombians." Throwing his apron at his boss, he declares, "I retire!"

Miami Chainsaw Massacre

"I'm not out in fifteen minutes, something's wrong. Room 9," Tony instructs Manny as they park across the street from the Sunray Apartments. (In a rare lighting mismatch, when Manny parks the car, their side of the road is in the shade; in subsequent cutaways, the whole scene is sundrenched.) They've driven past some pleasant-looking Miami deco structures to get there, but the Sunray is nothing special. Manny affects a "hanging loose" attitude as Tony and their buddy Angel head up to pick up the drugs.

Hector, "the Toad," is played by Al Israel, and he's grinning and friendly for about a minute, maybe. The woman sitting on the bed, Marta, "the Lizard," immediately gives one pause. Her deep-set eyes and rouged cheeks give her a vaguely undead look, which is augmented appropriately by a sneering lip. The actor is Barbara Perez. Hector introduces his "brother-in-law," as if this information is of any consequence. The you-got-the-goods/you-got-the-money exchange goes sour almost immediately, two more hoods with guns enter the picture, and Tony tells Hector, "Why don't you try sticking your head up your ass and see if it fits," his idea of a proven negotiating tactic. Stone's script has the TV on during this whole time; it specifies that the Lizard is glancing at "the news, not so ironically in Miami," being about "a drug-related triple-homicide"; but what's on the tube in the finished film is a risible episode of the William Shatner cop show *T.J. Hooker.*

In Stone's script, Angel's dismemberment by chainsaw while Manny and Chi-Chi wait, oblivious, in the car for the fifteen minutes to elapse is conveyed in straight cuts from interior to exterior. De Palma shoots and edits a little differently. Over the revving of the chainsaw, De Palma's camera moves off of Pacino's face to the circular window of the bathroom until the frame is filled with smoked glass. THEN he cuts to a reverse shot, directly outside the window. The camera, on a crane, pulls back and crosses the street, descending to the car. Where Manny is chatting up a blonde in a bikini.

Avid De Palma watchers of a certain age, such as my twenty-four-year-old self when I saw the movie for the first time in 1983, might have expected this contrast between the trauma in the bathroom and Manny's girl-crazy indolence to be presented in split screen. The cut from the circular smoked window in the bathroom to the outside is very quick, almost too quick to allow the viewer to register any relief, because there is no relief: we're not seeing slaughter, but the noise helps us imagine it. The camera swoops on to the action in the car. The comedically oblivious Manny is clearly more impressed with his own pickup lines than the blonde he's chatting up is. (Incidentally, Michelle Pfeiffer is the luckiest blonde to have participated in the movie. Tammy Lynn Leppert, who plays Manny's would-be pickup here, had a mental breakdown and disappeared a year after the film's shoot. One of the dancing extras in the Babylon Club was Lana Clarkson, who later got more substantial roles in B genre films, and was murdered by Phil Spector in 2003. Phil Spector, who was played in 2013 by…Al Pacino, in an HBO film directed by *Untouchables* screenwriter David Mamet.) The camera goes back up again, and once we are back at the window, we stiffen, knowing De Palma is going to take us back inside, and dreading what we're going to see there. There's a very good reason he doesn't use split screen here, and it speaks to the point that Paul Hirsch made about the effect sometimes blunting potential emotional impact. In most of his split screen scenes, he's showing us another person watching what's happening from a certain distance, a different angle. The point being to show how the watcher, the voyeur, is affected by what they see. That's not what's going on here, as Manny has no idea what's going on. What the cutting in the scene gives us, without any actual break in the linearity of the action, is a visual withholding of that action, and a sense of time slipping away while Manny's otherwise occupied. One wants to shout at the screen, "GET IN THERE!" A split screen version of the scene would not be nearly as potent.

Back in the bathroom, Hector instructs Tony: "Watch what happens to your friend." He looks away as Angel's own eyes widen. Blood spatters. Tony spits, "Coño." Downstairs, having struck out, Manny say to Chi-Chi, "Let's do it man," and they leave the car with no sense of urgency. But they're quick on their triggers once upstairs and all hell breaks loose.

Wanting to be sure he doesn't go anywhere, Hector and friends bind Tony to the water pipe rather than the curtain rod. Hector calls Tony "cara cicatriz," Spanish for "scar face," and tells Tony, "You can die too, it don't matter to me." The ensuing shootout has an overhead shot that has a similar feel to the cutaway ceiling shot after the massacre in Scorsese's *Taxi Driver.*

Here, to some extent, is relief. De Palma does not skimp in any way on the emotional gratification of vengeance. We are glad to see Marta and the two gunmen killed. Hector flies from the window of the motel room onto a balcony and jumps his way onto the street. Even as the sirens warn of the approach of the cops, Tony takes his time in executing Hector right on the street, ignoring witnesses. And it feels righteous.

In front of a beautiful Miami sunset, Tony stands at a pay

phone and tells Omar the good news. He still has the money he was supposed to use to pay off the Columbians. "And I got the ye-yo." So there. Proud of the job he pulled off, he tells Omar, "I'm taking it to Lopez myself."

This represents a highly improbable outcome. By all accounts, Tony should have died in that hotel room. What's extraordinary in his confrontation with the Colombians is, at first, his bullheaded stupidity. Except once we've processed it enough, it feels, actually, something like courage.

Informed that he's going to be killed, he just tells his would-be executioners to fuck off. Did Waldo and Omar set Tony up with the Colombians knowing that a burn was imminent? Sure feels that way. Faced with that burn, Tony sees a binary choice. He can't care in this situation whether he lives or dies. The only way he lives is by succeeding. If he dies, none of it mattered anyway. Killing Rebenga got his foot in the door in this business. That being the case, he is determined to keep rising.

So Tony prevails. And then defies Omar and takes the "ye-yo" to Lopez himself. Lopez likes Tony and sends him with Omar to see Sosa. Who kills Omar. Which puts Tony in the catbird seat with Lopez. After which, as much as Tony "likes" and "admires" Frank, he knows the guy has got to go. Because Tony won't be satisfied until he's in Frank's position.

But being in Frank's position puts him subservient to Sosa, which Tony doesn't like. You see how this goes. Tony lays it out for Manny a little later on.

Frank Lopez

Character actor Robert Loggia got into the movie business maybe one or two years year later than he ought to have. His gregarious big shot here is someone who might have been completely comfortable in a 1950s crime picture like Joseph E. Lewis's loopy noir *The Big Combo*, the flick in which Richard

Conte turns down Brian Donlevy's hearing aid before having him whacked—and the corresponding reverse shot shows the machine gun muzzles of Lee Van Cleef and Earl Holliman flaming up in complete silence.

As it happens, one of Loggia's earliest screen appearances was in George Stevens's cameo-studded Jesus tale, *The Greatest Story Ever Told*. In that 1965 picture, he plays a brown-bearded Joseph, stepdad of the Savior, and does little more than narrow his eyes sagely. Joseph's always a tough part for a screenwriter, never mind an actor.

Loggia is practically fourth billed in *Che!*, director Richard Fleischer's peculiar 1969 attempt at a life of Bolivian-born Cuban revolutionary Che Guevara. He plays Faustino Morales, a "lawyer" who's first seen as part of Castro's band of guerrillas. The movie is centered around various characters on the periphery of Che's life, who speak to the camera directly in their now-current positions. For instance, one is a schoolteacher at a place named for Che, whom the teacher still reveres. Morales is a lawyer, who addresses the screen in a three-piece suit from a well-appointed and book-lined office. The device of direct address was something Godard used quite a lot of the time, but it's not one that Fleischer really pulls off. In any event, Morales comments on Che's taste for executions thusly: "So…the physician burned his Hippocratic oath…and a latent martinet revealed himself."

Loggia also plays a lawyer in Blake Edwards's 1981 *SOB*. Herb Maskowitz is the steel-spined divorce attorney for Julie Andrews's Sally Miles, an "America's sweetheart" kind of movie star (akin to Andrews herself in the 1960s) who fears that ditching her falling-apart director husband will stain her wholesome reputation. (Edwards was, and would remain, Andrews's husband; the movie has no small autobiographical element.) Loggia had played comedic criminals for Edwards in several *Pink Panther* films. He played a reformed cat burglar in the cult TV series *T.H.E. Cat*, but Lopez, the part-Jewish cocaine magnate, was his first really serious bad guy role. (He played a bad, alcoholic father in *An Officer and a Gentleman*, but that's not quite the same thing.) The role of Lopez paved the way for a lot of mob-type guys, some of them at least partially comedic (John Huston's mafia black farce *Prizzi's Honor*, 1985; John Landis's blood-drenched vampires-meet-the-mob picture *Innocent Blood*, 1992). In 1992 he was sufficiently well-established as a tough guy to play himself in that role, in black jacket, black shirt, and black necktie, to extol the virtues of Minute Maid orange juice to a sufficiently awed American kid. In 1997 he topped all his prior tough guys as Mr. Eddy and/or Dick Lamont in David Lynch's *Lost Highway*, wherein he gives a schmuck who's been tailgating him a lesson in driving etiquette never to be forgotten.

Speaking of *Scarface* in 2011 to Joel Keller for the online publication *The AV Club*, Loggia recalled, "We rehearsed our *Scarface* to the nines. Long period of rehearsal, so that by the time we started to shoot, it was almost like doing a play. We all had a grand time doing it. It was a wonderful cast. We all got along well together, and that's it." Asked about whether Pacino remained in character even when cameras weren't rolling, he merely said, "I would not want to be under the veil of a character I'm playing for the entire shoot. You should have to bounce back and forth between illusion and reality," and implied that Pacino was fully capable of doing the same. He said between setups he'd either hang out on set or go to his trailer and meditate. He praised De Palma's attentiveness to the actors and their sense of what would be credible in a given scene. "Pacino came in with his arm in a sling and De Palma had him grab me and slam me down on the desk with the gun pointed between the eyes. So we had an argument, I suppose. I said, 'If the guy has a gun, that's the power. He doesn't need to wave the gun; he just needs to point the gun in a very relaxed fashion.'" De Palma was persuaded, and they ended up blocking the scene that way.

★★★

As Tony and Manny enter Frank's residence, a more stately than usual synth theme introduces itself. Inside the place, the viewer is now finally delivered from the grime of the tent city, the grease and onions of the sandwich stand, the blood-drenched linoleum of the motel room.

Frank Lopez's home is both loud and cool. The furnishings and colors are very late '70s modernist hangover. There's a variation of designer Eero Aarnio's clear plastic "bubble chair," one that sits on the floor rather than hanging from the ceiling, as the original model did. And a clear elevator, too!

Tony's wearing a green three-piece suit whose shirt has a very big collar, while extravagantly tan Frank hangs a little looser, a flashy gold necklace with Hebrew letters reading "life" on the end being his most prominent accessory.

Ushered in by Omar, Tony stands almost at attention when he's introduced, but soon begins to relax, putting his hand on his hip and pivoting from his waist as he looks around. He's impressed with these trappings. When Frank thanks him indirectly for murdering Rebenga, Tony reiterates: "That was fun!" Frank and Omar exchange looks that say, this guy's quite a character, huh? But Frank is genuinely impressed, thinks Tony has what it takes: "I need a guy with steel in his balls."

Soon he's discoursing on his abundant lifestyle, and how his wife, who has yet to make an entrance, is always either dressing or undressing. Tony takes a seat, as does Manny. While Manny sits up straight and leans in, attentive to Frank and Omar, Tony's body language here changes. He sits in almost a slump—he'll slump more and more as the movie progresses—not so much of a slump that he signals overt disrespect, but enough of one to suggest his mind is on other things.

When Michelle Pfeiffer's Elvira, in that iconic silk gown, steps into that clear elevator—and another musical motif that does not really turn out to be the "Love Theme from *Scarface*," but bears the title "Elvira" on the expanded motion picture soundtrack, begins—Tony is impressed further still. When the trophy wife gets out, she barely glances at the men and strides through the room as if she wishes she could teleport from it. But Frank won't have that.

In the Hawks *Scarface*, Poppy's motivation for going with Tony after Johnny Lovo is usurped seems nonexistent; it may as well be Darwinian. Once Johnny is no longer top dog, the trophy girlfriend goes with the newly established alpha male. This seems to be the case in this *Scarface* too, at least at first glance. But when Elvira and Tony are introduced, look at Pfeiffer's first reaction to him. Yes, later she'll use sarcasm to shut him down, several times, but when they meet there's an intrigue in her eyes that suggests just enough attraction to make the subsequent alliance a little more than a mere falling in with hierarchy.

Where to celebrate? The Babylon Club, a bit of an on-the-nose name. "Again?" Elvira asks. "Again." So Frank decrees. Frank, like so many of us, apparently enjoys going places where he can see people he doesn't like. In a bit of foreshadowing, not so much for Frank as for Tony, Elvira notes, "If anybody ever wanted to assassinate you, you wouldn't be too hard to find."

De Palma's camera swoops onto the dance floor. In this scene, the director's eye adheres to a conventional investigatory mode of views and reverse views. The music in the disco is a Giorgio Moroder/Debbie Harry collaboration, "Rush Rush," literally a cocaine anthem: "Rush, rush, who's got the ye-yo" goes the chorus. And the verses describe a desperate kind of hustler: "The son of a devil/he wants mine and more." But the song is not foregrounded; in the back of the sound mix, it's just part of the aural scenery.

Frank points out the other drug kingpins in the house, including "El Gordo"; his disdain for these players is plain. He calls the fat man a "haza," and asks Tony whether he knows what that is. It's the "Yiddish word for pig," he explains. Pigs being not uncommon in this business, leading to Frank's first piece of advice: "Lesson number one: don't underestimate the other guy's greed." He says those last three words in all-caps.

In a tired voice, Elvira articulates lesson number two: "Don't get high on your own supply." Frank notes that "not everybody follows the rules," and gives Elvira a mocking glance.

A waiter brings a bottle to the table: Dom Pérignon 1964. Omar pours. "Five hundred fifty dollars a bottle," Frank boasts. "For a bunch of fucking grapes." In conversation with the filmmaker Joseph Alexandre, he reminded me of the way Pacino's Tony processed his first real champagne experience, and how, as with so much of Pacino's acting, it comes down to the eyes. Tony's are wide open as they make the toast. Frank asks him how he likes it, and his eyes force a smile. "Oh, that's good Frank." Then he looks, very briefly, into the middle distance, as if asking himself, "Was I convincing just now?" When Frank mentions to Tony that he's got "something big next month," he and Omar crowd him on the settee as if they're trapping him. After Tony takes up Elvira's not even half-hearted invitation to dance, Frank asks Omar what he thinks of Tony, and Omar spits, "I think he's a fucking peasant."

Elvira and Tony's first dance is slyly funny. She can barely bring herself to look at him as he pokes her with questions. Rolling over her surname, Tony says, "Sound like a bird. Hancock." An exasperated Elvira sighs, "Look it doesn't really matter, all right."

Tony tries out his customary bluntness. "You got a look in your eyes like you haven't been fucked for a year." That crosses the line. She shuts him down definitively.

And yet, in the car home, Tony says, not without reason, "She like me." Manny doesn't credit his observation. "The eyes, chico, they never lie." Stone's line can be taken, many viewings in, as relating to Pacino's own distinctive film performing mode.

Ego in full peacock mode, Tony pronounces Frank soft. Manny feels obliged to rein him in. "Don't fuckin' go crazy on me." The scene ends with Tony once more stating what he wants, what he thinks he has got coming to him: "The world, chico. And everything in it." But…

Three Months Later

…as a red onscreen text tells us, and Manny and Tony are still talking the same shit, while wearing somewhat better clothes. This beach scene is one of the most famous in the film, featuring the notorious line, "This town like a great big pussy just waiting to get fucked."

"If I'd come here ten years ago I would have been a millionaire by this time," Tony marvels. Manny in the meanwhile can't stop looking at the extras in bikinis. Manny tries to demonstrate his pickup chops, which are just as bad as they were at the motel. And here involve some gross tongue humor.

Tony tries to amuse some children, instructing them to watch Manny blow it. The soft side of Montana is here, for the first and only time. Manny strikes out. There's another iconic bit of philosophical instruction. "In this country, you gotta make the money first. Then when you get the money, you get the power. Then when you get the power, then you get the woman." Notwithstanding the fact that many men without high incomes or substantial amounts of power have successfully chatted up women on beaches and at poolsides, Tony's ultimate point is: "That's why you gotta make your own moves." And they're still talking shit like this because, in three months of working for Frank, they still aren't making their own moves.

The adages animating the World According to Tony Montana derive, of course, from the Hawks *Scarface*. "This business is just waiting for some guy to come and run it right, and I got ideas," Paul Muni's Camonte tells George Raft's Guido, before calling his current boss soft and announcing, "Someday I'm gonna run the whole works." He finishes his spiel thusly: "Listen Little Boy. In this world there's only one law you gotta follow to keep out of trouble: do it first, do it yourself, and keep on doing it."

This kind of venal self-help palaver was the lingua franca of the 1930s gangster picture. Mervyn Leroy's 1931 *Little Caesar* opens with its protagonists Rico Bandela and Joe Massara sitting in an all-night diner having pulled off a minor job. Flush for the moment, they nevertheless bemoan their status as small-time, small-town crooks. Edward G. Robinson's Rico looks at a newspaper account of a party for successful big-city crook "Diamond" Pete Montana. "He don't have to waste his time on cheap gas stations. He's somebody. He's in the big town, doing things in a big way."

Massara, played by Douglas Fairbanks Jr., thinks the idea that Rico might someday achieve Montana's stature is mildly laughable. But he reconsiders, thinking about the good times the men who do things in a big way enjoy in the metropolis. He might want a taste of that, too, and then return to his first love, which as it happens, is dancing. Rico looks at him like he's nuts. "I don't want no dancin'. I figure on making OTHER people dance." He stabs the air with his table knife. The ultimate aim for Rico is to "be somebody. Have your own way or nothin'. BE somebody."

The extent to which Tony and Manny are still nobodies is underscored in the next scene, where they are dispatched to serve as Elvira's drivers after Frank gets "held up at the golf course." She balks at getting into Frank's canary-yellow Cadillac with zebra-striped seat upholstery, a kitschy new-money vehicle if ever there was. So to insist that he's NOT a nobody, instead of taking Elvira to the track, he takes her and Manny car shopping. For a

Porsche 928. Ignoring the salesperson's box-checking (machine gun turret costs extra!) he speaks of purchasing a tiger. "You're gonna drive around with a tiger in your passenger seat, Tony?" Elvira asks. A tiger will eventually materialize in Tony's collection of stuff. He instructs Manny to order the extras and pay for the car and renews his charm offensive on Elvira despite her insistence that she doesn't "fuck the help." Mildly puzzled by his implicit disloyalty to Frank, she calls him on it, and Tony replies in his best "I'm a simple man" fashion: "I like Frank. Only I like you better."

In Stone's script, this scene occurs later than it does here. First there's a scene of Tony, Manny, and accomplices doing some fancy smuggling moves coming in and out of Miami International Airport. And then, there's Tony's homecoming, which in the final edit is after the car-shopping scene.

De Palma's *Scarface* doesn't give us much real backstory on Tony. In the Hawks film, Tony Camonte is obliged to live out some of his backstory, having regular meals at home with his mother and sister.

Here we get a little of Montana's past in the flesh when Tony has Manny drive him to the modest house where his mother and sister, who got to Miami several years before him, live. If this scene feels more dutiful than anything else in the movie, that's because, well, it is. The mother's disapproval of Tony carries no real weight with him, and it doesn't really resonate in the movie, not even after Tony meets his doom. The true object of the scene doesn't become clear until its very end, when Manny gets a look at Gina.

Miriam Colon plays Tony's mother. The veteran actress was ninth-billed in Marlon Brando's sole directorial effort, the 1961 Western *One-Eyed Jacks*. In that picture, she plays a good-time-girl-cum-barmaid who answers to "Red." She greets Brando's would-be avenger Rio after he breaks out of prison, and Brando defends her honor by showing his revolver to a dirtbag who feels deprived of her attention. She is stalwart here in a perfunctory role, looking at Tony warily as he enters the house and bringing her not particularly effectual hammer down when Tony takes out a wad of bills and tells mother and sister Gina, the willowy and wide-eyed Mary Elizabeth Mastrantonio, that they don't have to labor at menial jobs anymore. (After Gina brags of being close to getting her cosmetology license, Tony sneers, "My kid sister don't have to work in no beauty parlor.")

"Who did you kill for this, Antonio?" Mama Montana asks point-blank, and Tony improvises a cover story about "working with an anti-Castro group." Stone's dialogue gets a bit pedantic here: "It's Cubans like you who are giving a bad name to our people."

Here Tony sits up straight, one of the few times he does so in the entire movie. But as his mother berates him, he recedes, retreats into toying with his cigar. He pulls up his slacks. Leans in to the table. And gets up and leaves. He bends over and picks up the money his mother has strewn onto the floor. "Okay, Mama."

Gina follows him to the car, where Manny makes the mistake of noticing her. Manny watches as Gina takes Tony's money, and pledges fealty to him: "You're my blood. Always."

Manny sounds almost innocent as he observes of Gina: "She's beautiful!" Tony's response is like a gunshot: "HEY! Stay away from her. She's not for you."

Cochabamba, Bolivia

Confident in his stride, wearing chinos and a light khaki jacket over a nearly see-through white shirt, Alejandro Sosa takes Omar and Tony on a tour of his cocaine refinery, boasting of its production capabilities.

The strikingly handsome Sosa speaks English with a light accent. It's a surprise to learn that Paul Shenar, the actor in the role, was born in Milwaukee, Wisconsin, and educated at that state's university. In a couple of years he would play Paolo Rocca in the Arnold Schwarzenegger action vehicle *Raw Deal*. For that film he used no accent, playing a high-level stooge to Sam Wanamaker's mob boss. The future ultra-conservative film director Robert Davi plays Shenar's lower-level stooge in the Schwarzenegger movie. In a few years, Davi will voice the character of Sosa in a *Scarface* video game.

In this movie, Sosa's stooge Alberto, "the Shadow," feels less like a flunky and more like a hired embodiment of death. Whisper-thin, and seemingly wary of attention, he walks like a ghost. He's played by Mark Margolis, a New York actor whose prior films included 1976's *The Opening of Misty Beethoven*, a prime example of the short-lived "porno chic" phenomenon of that decade. Directed by Radley Metzger, with an emphasis on visual stylishness hardly common in adult entertainment, it tells a variant of the *Pygmalion* tale in which a sexologist played by Jamie Gillis trains a Paris street hooker played by Constance Money in the finer arts of, well, you know. Like most pornos, *Misty Beethoven* is set in an ostensible erotic utopia in which sex is everywhere, including the first-class service on transatlantic air flights. Margolis plays a passenger who's not entirely happy with his experience: a flight attendant approaches him and says "Okay, let's see. We had one dinner, a brandy, two blowjobs and a headset." Putting down his magazine and looking mildly vexed, the actor responds, "Excuse me, but I had one blow job, and I haven't gotten my brandy yet." So next time somebody tries to tell you there are no "real" actors in porn, you can bring up this guy. (And also James Hong, beloved character actor recently featured in the multi-Oscar-awarded *Everything Everywhere All at Once*, in the incredibly creepy wannabe bio-thriller—featuring, of course, a "love serum"—*China Girl*, starring Annette Haven, with whom De Palma would consult on *Body Double*. And Aldo Ray in *Sweet Savage* [poor guy, dead drunk, needed booze money probably]. And Farley Granger in *Penetration*, except that doesn't count because it just intercuts stuff from a softcore giallo in which Granger starred with newly shot hardcore scenes featuring Harry Reems and Tina Russell. And so on. Anyway.)

Surrounded by sunglassed bodyguards, Sosa, Omar, and Tony talk cocaine while crunching on salad. The chatter includes lines like "We cut out the Colombians, we take risks on both sides." The ever-assertive Tony demonstrates that he's done his smuggling homework, particularly in terms of risk and reward. Omar once again gives the "I can't believe this guy" look. But Sosa sees Tony's point. And they're interrupted by a phone call.

The servers take away the salad plates as Omar upbraids Tony. A tense medium close-up of Sosa and Alberto silently consulting by the window breaks the steady, comfortable cutting pattern of the scene. Something bad is coming for someone.

That someone is Omar. Brisk without overtly showing his hand, Sosa suggests that Omar return immediately to Miami to consult with Frank about the new ideas that Tony's put on the table. "My associates can escort you to my chopper," which will take him to a plane which will take him to Florida. Uh-huh. But Tony will stay behind.

With Omar shuttled off, Sosa says, "I like you, Tony. There is no lying in you. Unfortunately I don't feel the same about the rest of your organization."

Not even a minute ago, Abraham's Omar was looking and demonstrably feeling very slick in his powder-blue suit. Sitting on the edge of the now-aloft chopper door with a rope around his neck, he's bloodied and scuffed up to a degree that would be alarming were we not aware that he's a dead duck already. Omar is a rat, apparently. And in a second he's a hung one.

Unflinching, Tony delivers another iconic line: "All I have in this world is my balls and my word, and I don't break 'em for no one. You understand?" Reflecting on Omar, who, you know, Tony never liked, he tells Sosa, "For all I know he had me set up and had my friend Angel Hernandez killed."

Sosa confides to Tony that he thinks Lopez's judgment stinks. He's handing Tony his rationale for usurping Lopez on a platter. Tony, not wanting to look too eager, assures the Bolivian that he'll "fix things" with Frank. Sosa, pleased, predicts that he and Tony can "do business together a long time." But: "I only tell you one time. Don't fuck me Tony. Don't you ever try to fuck me."

A blink-and-you-miss-it shot establishes Frank's legitimate business cover is a Mercedes dealership. Inside what looks to be a secret office—all black, save for another garish Dream Miami mural, all orange and yellow sunset tones silhouetting majestic palm trees—Frank is not amused by Tony's proposition. He doesn't have the five million that he can turn into twenty-five million with Sosa's Bolivian marching powder. "You can't lose money, no way," Tony insists.

Stone's script says: "The office is highly decorated with plaques, mementos, Cuban patriot flags, and lots of photographs, centering on JFK and RFK shaking the hand of Lopez, who now stares incredulously at Tony." As filmed, the office is sparsely furnished, with four framed pictures on a drawer behind Frank's desk: Robert F. Kennedy, Nixon and a man I can't identify, Agnew, Nixon again.

Gangsters trafficking in drugs often, in films and television shows, justify themselves by calling what they do "business." And certainly it is, and maybe it's really no different than "legitimate" business, but in scenarios such as this one, the level of mistrust on every side is arguably outsize. Here Lopez's temper flares, then Tony's does. Tony utters another immortal Montanaism: "Fuck the fuckin' Diaz brothers. Fuck 'em all. I bury those cockroaches." Frank tries to talk Tony down: "You want me to believe Omar was a stoolie because Sosa says so?"

Can this marriage be saved? No, it cannot. Here Tony is framed either in black or with the garish orange-and-black palm tree mural behind him, looking larger than life. We know that Frank's advice that Tony stay "low-key and quiet" is not even coming close to landing.

When Tony accosts Elvira at the side of her pool, some time has elapsed: she mentions that she's aware Montana is no longer working with Frank. Tony slides right in to the most cringe-inducing marriage proposal in dramatic cinema. "You like kids?" he asks. Elvira's response is arguably noncommittal. "Good, cause I like kids." Okay. His pitch to Elvira is not that he will treat her like a queen, make her happy, any of that. Rather, it is: "With the right woman, ain't no stoppin' me. I can go right to the top." It's mortifying, and for some reason, it elicits a response from Elvira that's the closest she ever gets in the movie to a state of vulnerability. Her hard veneer dropped for just an instant, she says, "What about Frank, Tony?" The answer will come as Frank moves against his former "help."

Nightclubbing

At the Babylon Club. Again? Again. The camera zooms in on Tony's eyes as he looks at an attractive woman in a glittery dress dancing with a slick male partner. The woman is his sister Gina. The song is Amy Holland and Giorgio Moroder's "She's on Fire," sung by Holland (fun fact: she is married to Steely Dan and Doobie Brothers singer Michael McDonald), and as was the case with Debbie Harry and Giorgio Moroder's "Rush Rush," it's here not mixed to get too much of your attention. She, Gina, is on fire, Tony disapproves in a more than protective brother way, and poor Manny has to come to a perfunctory defense of the slick third-tier drug trafficker schmuck who's soon going to be macking on Gina, and soon after that regretting that he ever did.

A guy we haven't seen before, a tall white middle-aged one, presents himself to Tony and asks, "Remember me?" And the viewer may ask, "Should I remember him?" But no. This is

Harris Yulin's first appearance of the movie as corrupt cop Mel Bernstein. Stone and De Palma trust the audience to infer they've crossed paths because a plainclothes narcotics cop is apt to encounter a drug kingpin. The pair has an easy mutual go-fuck-yourself attitude, and now Bernstein wants to talk actual business.

Yulin began as a New York stage actor, a few years ahead of Pacino; his film debut was in a rather free 1969 adaptation of the John Barth novel *The End of the Road*, in which he costarred with Stacy Keach, James Earl Jones, and Dorothy Tristan. Director Aram Avakian, brother of jazz impresario George Avakian and the editor of Coppola's 1966 *You're A Big Boy Now*—and of Marty Bregman and Richard Sarafian's *The Next Man*—cowrote the script with Terry Southern. Its "first-rate ingredients failed to make a first-rate dish," Barth himself has said of the movie, but others have been more forgiving. It's certainly a film of notable firsts—cinematographer Gordon Willis, later to put his distinctive stamp on *The Godfather* and almost define the look of maverick 1970s Hollywood, also made his feature debut here.

Ruminating on *Scarface* in 2017, Yulin told the online publication *The Purist*, "*Scarface* was so ubiquitous, so popular, that for many years, people would follow me down the street, reciting my lines. I always told them that they remembered it better than I did. I only saw it once, whereas I knew people who had seen it 200 times." His character, Bernstein, certainly has more than a few choice lines, including an offer to "bust" Tony's "wiseass spic balls." Except Bernstein prefers to do business.

Tony tells Manny to look after Gina. But it seems he can't keep his mind on the bribe Bernstein is demanding. The booth Tony perches in is ringed by Scarfiotti's long vertical mirrors, which gives the scene some De Palmaesque visual juice. Even as Tony seems distracted, he still sees all from his booth. As Bernstein lays out what he believes will be a steady and lucrative arrangement with Tony, he rather comedically sips from a tall glass of milk. "How do I know you're not the last cop I'm gonna have to grease?" Tony asks him, and predictably Mel shrugs that it's not his problem. He's quite amused to be providing Tony with some not entirely small discomfort. Oh, and: "By the way, I've got a vacation coming up, so I'm gonna take the wife to London, England. We never been there. So throw in a couple of round-trip tickets, first class."

In the meantime, Frank and Elvira have walked in. Truly, we are now in the realm of "mo money, mo problems." Seeing that Tony is growing increasingly glum, Bernstein tells him that "Every day above ground is a good day." Once he departs, Tony shakes it off and moves on his other project. He moves over to Frank and Elvira's booth; Frank is away for a minute, and Tony asks if Elvira has thought about his offer to father her children. Feeling feisty, Frank comes back and chides Tony: "Why don't you find your own girl?" Never not feisty, Tony says, "My own girl? That's what I'm doing." The dialogue again comes directly from the Hecht/Hawks *Scarface*, but in the earlier film, the exchange was between Muni's Camonte and the girl herself, Karen Morley's Poppy.

Tony's fleeting attention span notwithstanding, he's adding everything up: Frank "put that prick Bernstein on me." When he once more sees Gina out of the corner of his eye, we're back in zoom land. Tony's eyes in close-up, the guy's hand on her flank in close-up. Gina's date drags her into a room marked "Gentlemen" and then drags her into a stall. Tony's jaw is clenched. "My kid sister? In a toilet?"

The confrontation between brother and sister is a preview of what we'll see at the end of the movie, when both meet their dooms. In a long take, Tony gets rid of the date, brutally, and gives Gina a hard slap. Then Gina goads him: What's he gonna do to prevent her from moving as she wishes? Whatever it is:

"Oh yeah, oh yeah, do it now! I wanna see it!" They end at a standoff, and Manny is dispatched to take her home.

The lanky, jug-eared, perpetually sardonic Richard Belzer manifests here. He doesn't play himself, according to the end credits. Rather, he plays "M.C. at Babylon Club." This gig might not be the most cherry of engagements on which to land, as we'll soon see. His shtick to this crowd is not unpredictable: "Is that coke in your bra or are you just glad to see me?" (Belzer's own standup was considerably sharper.) The sound of his patter fades, and a foreboding Moroder motif comes in for a few seconds.

The standup comedian had only a handful of film roles prior to this, one of them in Pacino's *Author! Author!*, in which he played a mincing stage manager named Seth Shapiro. His big moment in that picture occurs while the play-within-a-movie, *English Without Tears*, by Pacino's playwright Ivan Travalian, is in rehearsals. Marveling at the facility of the show's leading lady, the brother accountants played by comedy legends Bob Elliott and Ray Goulding coo, "She's perfect!" and, "I smell money." Belzer, in the most trite effeminate voice imaginable, purrs, "She's divine. Simply…divine." Later, complimenting that leading lady on her coat, he asks whether the "peach divine" garment is "edible."

"Do you think he's bisexual?" Dyan Cannon asks Pacino as they exit the theater. "Don't be absurd. The man's never looked at a woman in his life." In case you were still wondering about the relative merits of *Author! Author!*

There's a nifty shot in Alfred Hitchcock's *Strangers on a Train* in which the director underscores one character's obsession with another. Farley Granger plays a tennis star, and Robert Walker plays Bruno, the spaced-out cat who wants to "trade murders" with him. Hitchcock puts Bruno in the audience for a tennis match; everyone around him is looking to the left, then the right, then the left, then the right, following the ball. But Bruno is staring straight at Granger's character.

Here, in the Babylon, De Palma's camera pans to the right as the crowd reacts with uproarious laughter to comedian Belzer. And then settles on two stone-faced guys at a single table. Tony, having had a lousy night, is alone in his booth, toying with a cigar, kind of wasted. Manny is driving Gina home, defending his friend: "Right now you happen to be the best thing in his life. The only thing that's any good, that's pure."

Back at the nightclub, Belzer introduces one of the film's more bizarre sights. "He's from Caracas, Venezuela, he's unlike anything you'll ever see in your life, so please give a warm Babylon welcome to the one and only… Octavio!"

This nightclub clown wears a big-eared papier-mâché mask and a fake pot belly and doesn't have much of an act. He dances "comically" first to Sinatra's "Strangers in the Night" and then, after a cutaway to Manny driving Gina home—wherein Gina makes the first suggestion that Manny take her out as an alternative to the unknown sleazebags who've been taking her out, an idea that does not sit well with Manny at all—to the Moroder song "Dance Dance Dance," sung by Beth Anderson. That song's chords are overtaken by more sinister Moroder synths as the two stone-faced guys get their machine guns ready.

Tony's frequent slump posture—here heightened by the fact that he's had maybe a little too much to drink—kind of saves his life here. As the two would-be assassins open fire, pretty much immediately ridding the world of Octavio, Tony is able to get under the table, get his own pistol ready, and return fire as he runs out of the Babylon.

But what of Octavio?

In 2015, a YouTube channel posted "Octavio's Last Stand," a brief sendup of the puzzling clown who meets his doom in the assassination attempt on Tony. After a couple of shots from the actual film, it cuts to a costume room where a balding middle-aged guy with no Venezuelan in his speech is on a phone, explaining his absence to his wife. "I hate this club too…but you said I wasn't working enough…it's today? I'll get her a gift on the way home." Uh-huh. Here poor Octavio is one of show-biz's losers, doomed to die on his daughter's birthday. (Never mind that even were he not doomed to die, he'd certainly not get home until the wee hours of the morning. Sometimes the comedic mind is so obsessed with sticking it to the objects of the lampoon that it forgoes all logic.) The plot of the skit turns on Richard Belzer "bumping" this clown, who then launches a rant at the club's manager, calling the Babylon "the trash bin to end all trash bins." But this guy is going to give them "the show of his life" and never return. He sings to himself—"Happy Birthday" to his daughter "Belinda"—and goes out and starts to "slay" the crowd, before he is himself slain. Once the sketch starts doing more frequent intercutting with footage from the actual movie, the parody looks ever more threadbare. There are no end credits, and with good reason, I reckon.

In a testament to visual illiteracy, credulity, and several other defects of the human condition, shortly after this video was posted, a Reddit user with the name "Zorro Means Fox" posted a lengthy observation about the limp, inept satire, taking it for an actual deleted scene from *Scarface*. The post builds up a nice head of indignation: "But the fact is, this is a truly shitty scene in a wildly overrated movie. It's hammy, saccharine, terribly shot, horribly acted, and obviously symbolic." What a world.

Back in the real world, the real world which you and I inhabit and the real world of the movie, that is, Tony Montana runs out of the Babylon Club into the pouring rain, into his Porsche, and off to plot his revenge. He will not return to the Babylon Club for the rest of the picture. This scene is the literal centerpiece of *Scarface*, starting at an hour and seventeen minutes in and ending after the ninety minute mark. The next scene is its coda, one that puts Tony Montana ALMOST at the apex he has long sought—and will never quite get to.

Shooting Shit

Manny, having dispatched Gina home safely (in a physical if not existential sense), is in bed with a blonde conquest when he gets the call from Tony, who is then seen laying out to a couple of generically sloppy-looking henchman his method of certifying what he already actually knows: that Frank Lopez sent the machine gunners to kill him.

The elimination of Lopez and Bernstein is the scene for which they rebuilt Lopez's office. If you're paying close attention, the garish palm tree mural is a visual link to the prior scene in the Benz dealership, but the overall layout is different from what we first saw. In any event, the framed Nixon photos aren't present. But Bernstein is. As is a bodyguard named Ernie. And an uncapped bottle of Jack Daniel's whiskey.

As the scene plays out, you can understand why Pacino in particular wanted the extra space. The position he takes relative to Frank is across a long table. He's slumped, again, in a wheeled chair; when he walked in, he weaved like a drunk, and slurred his words more than usual. As is often the case with Tony, it's half authentic, and half playing possum. When he decides to act, it's as if an adrenaline rush seizes him and wipes out all the intoxication and divided attention.

When the phone call Tony's instructed his guys to make comes, Tony lets the penny drop. Loggia's physical acting here is particularly good. He leans over the table, puts his hands on it, and slides to his left toward Tony, as if trying to approach a dangerous animal. In the meantime, Tony repeats Frank's definition of a "haza" to his old boss, speaks of cockroaches and of men who don't keep their word. We see a particularly hideous metallic sculpture at the far end of the room. As Frank gets closer, Tony backs up further in his wheeled chair. When

Frank prostrates himself before Tony and begins to beg for his life, Tony points his automatic down at the back of his lowered head and says, "I won't kill you." Instead he tells Manny to do it. "Chute this piece of chit." Manny does it with a sadistic grin that reminds us that, as amiable and common-sense a criminal as he's capable of being, Manny is himself a sociopathic murderer.

But Tony will take care of Bernstein himself, in spite of the corrupt law-enforcement rep's half declaration, half question. "You can't shoot a cop?" Tony Montana can. And does. The late film writer Jim Gabriel calls Yulin's words before dying "the finest expulsive 'fuck you' in the history of American cinema." A big claim especially when this movie itself contains an unusually large number of *fuck-you*s. But he's not wrong.

Steven Bauer endured a lot of anxiety while shooting this scene. "I was a nervous wreck for three days that we shot that scene. I have to stand there. And thank God I had a post to lean on. I'd ask Brian the stupid questions. I'd say, 'Where do you want me to, where do I go?' Brian says, 'Just go wherever Manny. Just go somewhere. I'll tell you if I don't like it.' And so I go, I lean on this post. 'Just stay; once you're there, stay there. And you're gonna be there a long time.' And Bob Loggia is toe to toe with Al and it's so, so powerful. His performance, his personality was so great. And so when Al comes in, Al has to be like a wild bull. Frank is a snake, but he's no slouch.

"I mean, Tony's justified when he walks in; the scene was written so beautifully by Oliver. But the scene took forever to map out. Because Al was testing things, testing whether he wanted to be on the chair and roll it around, like move around in the chair, whether it was possibly too comedic and would distract from his intent, or whether it was just a proper amount of black humor as he is rolling around in the chair. And it's not just funny because while he's doing this, Tony is torturing Frank by extending this thing. Trapping him into the phone call and the lie and all that stuff, which is beautifully written. Brian was very loyal to the script there because he loved it also."

The office had been rebuilt to accommodate everything Pacino had in mind for the way Tony toys with Frank, and cinematographer John Alonzo was up against it, trying to light what's pretty much an all-black room. "There were so many technical problems with the scene that I remember. We finished the first day, the whole day, and we hadn't even gotten to Al sitting down yet. So I knew that I needed to be absolutely disciplined. Because I knew that even though I'd be standing around leaning on the post, when we got to the end of the scene, I would be the one who had to shoot Frank. Bob was so, so willing to just lay it all out. That scene is just amazing to me. It was amazing. And every time he did it, I was just in awe. But while having to stay in character. That was another factor working on me: I'm looking at these two great actors and I'm in such admiration of them and I have to remain Manny throughout, obviously. And Al was all the time working on what he was going to do. Brian was trying not to betray any impatience, but it was so tense in the room because Al didn't wanna be rushed into making the decision about what he's doing with the gun after he taps it on the table. When does he actually pull the trigger back? He and Brian had a disagreement about that. I stayed out of Al's way because I saw that he had a lot of things that he had not decided yet. And he wanted the time."

The expansion of the office allowed Tony/Al to keep rolling his chair back, to draw out his torture of Frank. "Draw it the fuck out," Bauer laughs. "And then when it is just like, nobody can take it anymore, then Al stands up." And makes Frank beg some more, before reassuring him, "I'm not gonna kill you, Frank." And then walking away, and ordering Manny to kill him. Here Bauer digresses a bit. "When they were casting me in the movie, when they were all sort of decided that I was perfect, then one day before the final call, Marty and Brian,

I guess, they got a message to my manager, and my manager calls me and says, 'They love you for this role, but they are not yet certain that you can show the killer inside you.'" They sent Bauer to a consultant who told him, "You are a prince, and we have to find the frog in you." Bauer then had a frog to call on to allow himself to shoot Frank. But he needed more. Some of what he needed he found in the chewing gum he worked on in character during the scene. What clinched things for him in performing the scene—you see that he doesn't hesitate once Tony gives him the order—Bauer got from his dad. "Now, we had rehearsed with the gun, and where it can be pointed, and where it can't be pointed. Right. And Bob was a trouper. He would say, 'It's okay. You can shoot me right in the chest.' But Brian wants to check on that. It feels like a real gun, but it doesn't have live ammo, but still, what might be in there to provide the muzzle flash effect could be injurious. Brian consults with the armorer: 'If he shoots him from that close, is his face gonna be in any danger?' And the armorer said, 'No, no, absolutely not. But he should keep the gun low.' So I had that to think about, because it feels like a real gun. Anyway. I had spoken to my father about doing the scene. And my dad said, 'You have to create for yourself a reason why you hate that man so much that it's easy for you to shoot him. To shoot him point-blank, without a thought. I think that you need to verbally express your hatred. Say something, call him names.'" Without consulting anyone, Bauer chose, while chewing gum furiously, to mutter imprecations: "I'm like, you motherfucker, fuck you. You know? But in Spanish. In order to able to pull the trigger. He goes down. I'm standing there for a minute. And if you watch the movie, my mouth is going full speed on that gum." Bauer laughs. "I'm chewing, chewing, chewing. Because I was still so nervous."

The scene ends on a mordantly funny note. Manny—"I had to put the gum aside for this," Bauer recalls—asks of the still-standing bodyguard, "What about Ernie?" The camera dollies in to the nervous fellow. Pacino's manner slyly makes Tony's display of largesse almost Shakespearean. "You want a job, Ernie?" Considering the alternative, he absolutely does. Manny grins, and Ernie takes a long, relieved swig from that bottle of Jack.

The World Is Yours

Someone's sliding the silk sheets off of Elvira. "Where's Frank?" she asks when she sees Tony sitting on the bed. "What you think? Come on. Get your stuff. You're coming with me." Simple as that. Waiting on Frank's balcony, Tony sees the blimp telling him, in lights: "The World Is Yours." It's an advertisement for the now-defunct Pan American Airlines. That airline was the main rival of TWA—now also defunct—which was founded by the 1930s *Scarface* producer, Howard Hughes. Whole books have been written about the rivalry between Hughes and Pan Am founder Juan Trippe, and the relationship figures in Martin Scorsese's film about Hughes, *The Aviator*, in which Trippe is played by Alec Baldwin and Hughes by Leonardo DiCaprio. In the Hawks film, the message was on a Cooks' Tours billboard across from Tony Camonte's penthouse apartment.

We Need A Montage

Paul Engemann was born (in 1957) into the music business. His father, Karl, was a vice president of Capitol Records. In his late teens, he put singing aside to fulfill a Mormon-church stint as a youth missionary. In 1975, with his sister Shawn and a party going by the name "Christopher," he released a single on Casablanca Records called "For Your Love." Regrettably not a version of the Yardbirds hit, the cheesy AND treacly ballad, with sweet harmonies and saturated strings, sounded like a *Grease* reject. By the time Engemann met up with Giorgio Moroder, he'd honed his voice to a proficient anonymous gritty tenor. A voice you could not pick out of a lineup so to speak, completely consonant with those of the singers of movie tunes such as "Eye of the Tiger" (David Bickler, in the group Survivor, for 1982's *Rocky III*) or "St. Elmo's Fire (Man in Motion)" (John Parr, for, yes, *St. Elmo's Fire*). The voice that, accompanying an uncharacteristic passage-of-time De Palma montage, tells us in a new way of the Montana ethos.

The song "Scarface (Push It to the Limit)," written by Moroder with his longtime collaborator, the British songwriter and producer Pete Bellotte, begins over a shot of a cash-counting machine shuffling through a large stack of bills. Money's brought into a bank in duffel bags. A shot of a building informs us that Tony's cover business is travel rather than automobile dealing. Gina and her cosmetology degree don't work in a salon—Gina has her own salon, bought with Tony's drug money. (Mama Montana isn't around for the grand opening. On the other hand, the ribbon-cutting is yet another occasion for Gina and Manny to exchange meaningful looks.) Tony and Sosa have a few laughs on the phone. "You've reached the top, but you still gotta learn how to keep it," Paul Engemann warns over a propulsive/anthemic disco beat.

It is here that the movie seems most like an advertisement for itself and an announcement of a certain inauthenticity. It's Brechtian carried all the way to Baudrillard, perhaps. But there's also the chance that I'm reading too much into it. When I asked Sylvester Levay, Moroder's collaborator on the score, whether singer Engemann was deliberately chosen over a "name" artist (you may recall that in *American Gigolo*, Paul Schrader's 1980 film, also scored by Moroder, the theme song "Call Me" was sung by Debbie Harry of Blondie, then a popular singer and something of a style icon—the same Debbie Harry whose "Rush Rush" is relegated to a disco floor scene in this movie) because of his relatively generic quality, Levay said, no; Moroder just liked his singing and thought he was right for the song.

In any event, to what limit is Tony pushing it? Well, his wedding to Elvira is upstaged by what Frederick Forrest in *Apocalypse Now* would call "THE FUCKING TIGER." Yes, Tony has gone and done it; after the *I-dos* (during which Manny and Gina exchange ANOTHER meaningful look) Tony takes the wedding guests down a hill and shows them his new pet, who is never seen again. (Which is too bad. Imagine if the thing had gotten loose during the movie's final shootout? As it happens, the tiger is heard during that scene, growling as some of Tony's guards prepare for the siege of the estate.) The cash-duffel-bags-to-the-bank shot is reprised, this time with maybe quadruple the number of bag carries, a sight gag that would not look out of place in a John Landis comedy like *Trading Places*. The song fades on a bit of a downer: Elvira doing a couple of lines at her vanity table. As if to conclude by saying, "These were the good times. Now we are obliged to get real."

Who Do I Trust?

So here is the limit we've been talking about: business is TOO good. Tony's banker Jerry, trying hard to be easygoing, is trying to explain to Tony why he's got to raise his rates again. Where Frank had sentimental/political souvenirs in his office, the biggest feature of Montana's is the bank of black-and-white TV screens behind the kingpin, each fed from a different security camera. Dennis Halahan, a competent but not particularly distinctive actor, plays the blow-dried, bland banker, named Jerry in Stone's script but never referred to as that here. (Fun fact: In 1983, the year of this film's release, Halohan wed Loretta Swit, who was Alan Alda's costar in the sitcom *M*A*S*H*; the couple divorced in 1995.) He's toeing a line he has to hold to, but he's understandably nervous at how Tony is balking at his limits. "The more cash you bring me, the more I gotta rinse," he protests. "The IRS is coming down heavy on South Florida."

While Tony's non-lizard brain may understand the situation, when it comes to his getting what's his, the bank is just another fence. Because of course it is. The movie's operatic mien is dominated by Tony's personality and bolstered by the scenes of violence, but the observations on the criminality of capitalism are bubbling under these exchanges. When the banker leaves, he instructs Tony to "Say hello to the Princess for me, she's beautiful."

When he's gone, Tony calls the guy a "WASP prick" and a "smiley motherfucker." Manny responds that Tony should "talk to this Jewish guy." Tony is not enthused. He mentions "Mob guys" and "guineas" and notes that he doesn't trust them. Then he does a couple of bumps and asks Manny why it took three days to rig one of the security cameras.

So now Tony is breaking the "don't get high on your own supply" rule. And his preoccupation with security is starting to verge on the paranoid. Although this is, we have seen and shall see, a business in which one literally can't be too careful. And one in which being too careful paradoxically doesn't guarantee a thing. Tony mentions that "the Diaz Brothers" could come to get him at any time. The Diaz Brothers, whom we never meet, are now a running joke with these guys.

The gold of the hot tub is garish, almost comical, as are the suds in which Tony Montana luxuriates, cigar in mouth. The tube TV in a wood console looks quaint to our eyes, now accustomed to flat-panel displays. There's a commercial on the box. A slick spokesperson says in sincere "let's make lots of money" tones: "Miami's changing. You can see it everywhere. New construction. New jobs. Growth that's financed by Florida Security Trust. We've been putting your money to work for seventy-five years. Building a more prosperous Miami. Count on us being here tomorrow."

Like so many commercial watchers, Tony affects an "I'm not buying" attitude. With concrete reason: Florida Security Trust is the institution messing with his money. "Yeah, that's because for seventy-five years you been fucking everybody." Looking at this now, we can conjure visions of once-close relatives hypnotized by Fox News, yelling back at the TV that's yelling at them. At the time of the film's release, Tony more directly resembled television sitcom reactionary Archie Bunker incarnated as a Cuban drug lord. I will not take up the question "If Tony Montana had lived, would he have gone MAGA?" But I doubt he'd vote for Bernie Sanders. Actually I doubt he would vote, ever.

Manny hovers over the tub, and Elvira fixes her face. Tony expounds. "There's no laws anymore… You know what capitalism is? Getting fucked." He doesn't mean it in the sense that today's fiery young leftists do, obviously. When Elvira notes Tony's tiresomeness, he calls her a bubblehead. Tells her to lay off the blow. She responds, "Nothing exceeds like excess." Hoping to steer Tony away from picking a full-on fight, Manny talks him down, getting his eye on the ball. The TV provides a little stealth exposition/context, calling the cocaine trade in the US a "one hundred billion a year business," the number that so startled Marty Bregman.

The conversation grows increasingly inane; there's more malaprop humor in the "sanitation/sanitarium" tradition, centered around the idiom "fingers in the dyke." But Elvira can't leave well enough alone: perhaps anticipating American mothers whose teenage sons have just come home from seeing the film *Scarface*, she exclaims, "Can't you stop saying *fuck* all the time?" She walks out, and soon Manny does too, leaving Tony to shout at, well, no one:

"Who put this thing together? Me! That's who! Who do I trust? Me!" Public Enemy rapper Flavor Flav would take up this mantra in the jam "Welcome to the Terrordome," from the group's 1990 album *Fear of a Black Planet*, which also features "Fight the Power," which was the opening credits song for Spike Lee's 1989 *Do the Right Thing.*

Tony is left alone in the tub, muttering, "I don't need him. I don't need her. I don't need anybody."

Getting Burned

In the counting room, one of the supposed crew is idly talking cinema, asking no one in particular whether they've seen *Burn*, the 1969 Gillo Pontecorvo film starring Marlon Brando. Italian-born Pontecorvo's fiction filmography is not big. His 1957 *The Wide Blue Road*, a portrait of Italian fishermen starring Yves Montand and Alida Valli, was in a neo-realist mode. His concentration camp portrayal, *Capo*, starring Susan Strasberg, the daughter of Al Pacino's mentor and friend Lee, was the famous subject of some very pointed French critical disapprobation we needn't go into here, focused on the ideological underpinnings of a moving camera shot. He became an international sensation with 1966's almost-documentary style *The Battle of Algiers*. By turns rousing and disturbing, propelled by one of Ennio Morricone's most nerve-jangling scores (which Morricone would reprise to no small extent for his score for De Palma's *The Untouchables* in 1987), it depicted Algerian freedom fighters and French colonial torturers with a fiery indignation that roused bourgeois foreign film audiences in the States to a degree that anticipated what reactionary writer Tom Wolfe would term "radical chic."

There's a scene in which a café bombing kills a score of people who look just like the New York filmgoers who cheered it, prompting the film critic Andrew Sarris to write: "All right, you say you believe in indiscriminate violence. Then squeeze Robert Redford, Paul Newman, Jane Fonda, Jeanne Moreau, Catherine Deneuve, Marcello Mastroianni, Laurence Olivier, Vanessa Redgrave, Jean-Paul Belmondo, Peter Finch, George C. Scott, and Diana Rigg into a crowded café in Algiers. Then let the bomb go off five minutes after the picture starts and show all our cameo stars as shattered corpses. Is it still an occasion for cheering? I think not."

The movie made Pontecorvo a star, at around the same time that American superstar Marlon Brando was in the midst of a political awakening that would culminate in his famous refusal to accept the Best Actor Oscar he earned for *The Godfather.* The "Ugly American" Brando played in the 1963 film of the same name didn't realize how destructive he was; for Pontecorvo, he played a more consciously devious British agent provocateur stirring shit in a Portuguese colony; Pontecorvo and scenarists Franco Solinas and Giorgio Arlorio gave this character the name William Walker, after a real-life mid-nineteenth-century figure who meddled in Nicaragua. (Years later, Alex Cox would make a provocative picture about a more reality-based version of the character, called *Walker.*) While the picture was critically well-received, it was no *Algiers*, and as far as Brando was concerned, it mostly advanced the idea that he was difficult and unfriendly to Hollywood, issues that were thrown in Coppola's path when he tried to cast the actor as Don Corleone.

In any event, this fellow in the counting room brags of his friendship with Brando, as Tony and Seidelbaum, the "Jewish guy" Manny had mentioned, fail to agree on an accurate count despite the supposed infallibility of the machine they're using.

De Palma's camera creeps up the wall and settles on a wall clock with numbers on its face, except for 12; that part is missing. The time moves in a dissolve from 11:06 p.m. to 1:32 a.m. Someone jokes, "Two hundred thousand more and we ought to take a leak."

And then: "FREEZE."

It's Tony's first bust. Everyone here's a cop, and the hole in the clock has a camera looking through it, recording everything. Seidelbaum explains this to Tony and instructs him to "Say 'HI, honey'" to the camera. (Shades of "Bye bye, dickhead" in Henry Hill's bust in Scorsese's *Goodfellas* a few years after this film.) One of the narcs indignantly says to Tony, "You make a real Cuban throw up." Tony is all bluster, as is customary, harking back to classic Hollywood gangster talk: "You got nothing on me." They got nothing, and Tony's got lawyers.

Reality Check

Despite Tony's boast about having the best lawyer, said lawyer, Sheffield (Michael Alldredge, like banker portrayer Holahan primarily a television actor at this time) has bad news for Tony, which is that he's not going to get out of this fix without doing some time. Not for conspiracy, but for tax evasion. It's all a matter of spreading some money around. More than the hundreds of thousands of dollars Tony is putting on the table? "With that kind of money," Tony insists, "you can buy the Supreme Court." Boy, that line not only hasn't dated at all, it's actually gained resonance. Throw in a couple of lavish vacations and you're golden, Tony.

But some wheels can't be greased. Sheffield notes that the narc cameras recorded Tony in the presence of over one million in cash. It's "hard to convince a jury you found it in a taxicab."

More bad news: Sosa has summoned Tony to Bolivia, alone. After the exchange of pleasantries, including the awkward question "When are you going to have another Tony to take your place?" (Sosa's own wife is only a few months from delivering what Sosa likely hopes will be another Alexander), Tony is introduced to some very big shots. A captain of industry: "Pedro Quinn, Andes Sugar Corporation." A military executive: "Edward Strasser, Commander, First Army Corps." (Stone here reached into a grab bag of movie names and picked that of an antagonist from *Casablanca*.) A Bolivian government man: "Ariel Bleyer, Ministry of the Interior." And finally, looking very blond and WASPish—this guy and a slightly less severe Elvira could pose for the brochure for a very restricted US country club—Gregg Henry as "Charles Woodson from Washington."

Here Sidney Lumet's desire to explicitly state that the US cocaine trade was in some way sanctioned by the US gets a little implicit fulfillment. When Sosa fires up the projection TV and shows clips of a Bolivian whistleblower giving interviews naming Sosa and a high government official as cocaine traffickers,

De Palma includes a dolly-in close-up of Henry (who would go on to play the Gavin Elster stand-in in De Palma's subsequent film, *Body Double*) contorting his face in hatred as the activist (he's named Matos in the script but never called anything but "he" or "him" in the movie) speaks.

What's this got to do with him, Tony would like to know. Well, Sosa explains, for one thing, this "problem" affects them all. He dangles his carrot: help out with this and you'll have to cough up your back taxes and a big fine, but you'll do no time.

"He's scheduled for *60 Minutes* next," Sosa says with disgust as he switches off the TV. "You remember Alberto, don't you?" Sosa asks; Tony is in his usual slump on the sofa and indicates that yes he does and no he's not impressed. Alberto is an "expert in the disposal business" but "he doesn't speak English too well." Nor can he navigate the streets of New York, where this target is to be eliminated.

Truth to tell, this request is a little farfetched. Tony Montana is Sosa's US connection and a big earner for him. That Sosa wants to treat him as a henchman doesn't make a whole lot of sense. But by this point the movie has built up a sufficient head of steam that the good viewer should not be in a state where they're parsing the action to this particular extent. Tony's downfall has to come, and this setup, while arguably not ideal, will prove cinematically effective and thus emotionally effective.

The Last Supper

At a swank Miami restaurant, just the three of them, Tony, Elvira, and Manny. It's like Manny is their chaperone or something; we've not seen Tony and Elvira actually alone since Tony brought her away from Frank's place.

Tony has been considerate enough of Manny, his best friend and right-hand man, to insulate him from Sosa. And Manny is wary of Sosa; noticing Tony's deflation since his return from

Bolivia, he asks about the trip, and Tony mutters that it's "a lot of bullshit."

"Politics," he adds.

Again, it's interesting that Tony doesn't want to confide in Manny about this. And right now he's half in the bag, more slumped than usual—he's taking something very hard. What is it? The potential jail time? The prospect of having to help Alberto? He's falling apart. He half-heartedly tells Manny that he's in charge while Tony attends to this business in New York. And Manny doesn't like it.

"You're the one who got me into this mess in the first place. With that fucking Seidelbaum," Tony spits. Okay then. That's it. Just the idea of having had to endure a bust in the first place is inimical to Tony. And then learning this isn't something he can immediately wriggle out of and shake off…it's reversed his entire attitude. What's the good of the money, the power, the woman, if *this* is where it lands you? And so a hammered Montana, raising himself in his chair a little and then sinking right back down into it, slack-jawed, begins to reflect on his, and everybody's, existential quandary.

"Is this what it's all about, man? Eating? Drinking? Fucking? Sucking? Snorting? Then what? Tell me. Then what?" Mere minutes ago, Tony Montana was pushing it to the limit. Now his red-wine-and-cocaine-addled brain is electric with images of "tits with hair on them" and "a liver with spots on it." Tony then imprudently decides to poke the blonde bear seated to his right. "Got a fucking junkie for a wife… Wakes up with a Quaalude… Her womb is so polluted I can't even have a fucking little baby with her."

And that cuts it for Elvira, who throws her water at him. For the second time in the movie, Pfeiffer can give the character a little vulnerability; even as she tries to counter Tony's insults, she looks genuinely hurt. This arrangement—you can't really call it a marriage—was supposed to have rules, though Tony's never been a rules guy. But he's crossed a final line here with her.

Before she walks out on him she says, as if realizing it for the first time, "We're not winners, we're losers." Pfeiffer's beautiful face looks truly hollowed out here as she widens her eyes. When she leaves, Tony mutters that once she takes another 'lude "she gonna love me again." But as it happens, and this is easy to miss in all the hubbub that follows, she doesn't love him again, she doesn't come back, and she doesn't call. One hopes she got some assets together and cleaned up after clearing out. One never knows. (Nor, really, ought one speculate over the future of characters who end when the movie ends.) But she doesn't come back. It's over for her.

Now Tony is self-conscious about all the proper swells who are looking at him and acknowledges that he's a performer. He explains both himself and, in a way, the eternal appeal of the gangster movie: "You need people like me so you can point your fucking fingers and say, 'That's the bad guy.' So? What that make you? Good? You're not good. You just know how to hide." Having dropped that kernel of truth, he descends into absurdity. "Me, I always tell the truth. Even when I lie." He's a clown now. He approaches a tuxedoed guy with menace, halts, does a head-tilt double take, and turns around, comically. It's slapstick. His exit line is rightly famous: "Say good night to the bad guy."

Diplomatic Immunity

New York City at night. A white four-door Citroën DS, a car that reminds one of moody French horror movies from the early '60s perhaps (this particular model was discontinued in 1975), backs into an empty space on the street. Tony's target, looking pleased with his parking karma, gets out and goes into a nearby building.

Tony looks on from his car; Alberto, dressed like a mechanic, rigs the car bomb. Next morning: a high-angle look at the glittering Manhattan morning skyline descends to show Tony at a pay phone, telling Manny that everything is ducky. The location is Tudor City Place and East 41st Street; you can see Grand Central Station down the street. The light of day illuminates Tony's ride, a brown station wagon with Budweiser cans and Chinese food containers strewn on the top of the dashboard. Tony's hyped up; no sooner has he gotten back in the driver's seat than he wants to leave and call Manny again.

Apparently it's not enough to just off this whistleblower; Sosa has specified that it be done in front of the United Nations, where this guy is going to give a speech. Again, the logic here is a little questionable. If the cocaine interests want to deflect the attention this guy is shining on them, why would they blow him up in front of the United Nations? Yes, it is a bold move, but it also says, more or less, "Come and get us!" Terrorist acts are done to bring radical attention to a cause. What kind of "cause" is drug trafficking? Well, never mind, as Tony is not going to let the assassination happen.

Because the whistleblower is going to bring his wife and kids to the United Nations to watch his speech, as one does.

"No fucking way. That's it." It's weird to see Tony suddenly grow a conscience, but hey—as we learned at that beach scene so long ago, where Tony sat with a few tots and laughed at Manny trying to pick up girls, Tony likes kids. And as with the case of Sosa sending his big earner to run an errand for him, it ultimately doesn't matter why Tony won't go through with the errand. Tony has to end. The narrative just needs the pretext to bring about this end. The car pursuit with its occasional use of rear-projection effects may look a little wobbly to hypercritical contemporary eyes, but the cutting patterns bring the tensions to the proper boil as Margolis's Alberto stays stoically clenched and focused while Tony loses it more and more. "You fucking vulture," Tony calls Alberto; then he says to himself, "This is so fucking bad. This is so fucking bad." And then he explodes, pulls a gun, and blows Alberto's brains out. And here he begins what he'll do more than once again before the movie ends: he talks to the corpse. "You wouldn't listen. You stupid fuck, look at you now."

From another phone booth, this one at the 60th Pan Am Metroport, an airport shuttle for the very comfortably well-off in a hurry, Tony learns that things have gone off at home, too. The bodyguard nicknamed "Nick the Pig"—who Elvira called her "only friend" before walking out on Tony (she was being sarcastic, they weren't close), tells Tony that Manny's been gone the past couple of days. Also, Tony's mom called, looking for Gina. Hmm. Elvira has not called.

For the first time we get a look at the foyer of Tony's mansion, and boy is it ridiculous.

There's enough red fabric on the walls and floors to furnish three or four separate productions of the Zeffirelli version of Mozart's *Don Giovanni*. Twin marble staircases with gold-ornamented banisters, and at the top of the steps, a balcony and the door to Tony's office. We know his office with its multiple security screens and big black desk. Stone's script has Tony spooning coke onto his desk from a vial. Not enough. Here there's a lidded black box filled with the stuff, and Tony scoops some out with his fingers, then pours a bunch on the desk. Soon large plastic bags of the stuff will be torn open and emptied, a miniature mountain range of marching powder.

The coke first gives Tony the confidence to try to snow a pissed-off Sosa, calling from Bolivia. Too bad it can't give him any convincing words. "We had a little problem." The cutaways to Sosa are from a low angle as the drug lord paces; his angry energy and the camera position provide an electric current of long-distance menace. And now we realize, maybe, that Sosa treated Tony as a functionary because he saw him as a functionary: "I told you, YOU FUCKING LITTLE MONKEY, NOT

TO FUCK ME." That's right, he did. Tony tries to appear unperturbed: Sosa wants to go to war? "We take you to war, okay?"

Domestic Disturbance

Mama Montana *is* still around, and still not pleased with her son. Despite her anxiety about Gina being missing, she can't help but needle Tony; describing Gina's recent behavior, she recounts her daughter talking back to her, saying, "*Mira*, shut up. Mind your own business." Without even a pregnant pause, she adds: "Exactly like you do to me." The camera dollies into mom's modest living room, an appropriate kind of creep, as this mother is practically signing her daughter's death warrant.

On his way to the Coconut Grove address his mother gave him, on his way to being coked out of his skull, an elegiac Moroder synth march begins on the soundtrack. Montana's snow-white Rolls Royce halts in front of a house just as white, with doors so high that this could be the entrance to Hell. And so it is.

Manny grins, improbably, on opening the door. He says his friend's name. From the floor above, onto a balcony strides Gina, belting a bathrobe. All those stolen glances, that only the film viewer had been privileged to, have borne fruit; but not for long.

Tony gut-shoots his best friend; Gina screams a silent "no" and begins running down the stairs. The blood and the stairs and Gina's dishabille notwithstanding—although, come to think of it, Cesca's own preproduction code dishabille in the Hawks *Scarface* was pretty racy—this scene hews closely to its original. Although without the coin-flipping. Tony stands impassive as the hysterical, now bloodied-up Gina tells him, "We got married just yesterday. We were gonna surprise you." Well, they sure did surprise him. How would he have taken the surprise in a different circumstance? Not well, we can infer. Maybe he would have waited a bit before killing anybody?

Gina almost claws Tony as Nick leads her out. Tony stands

over Manny's corpse, silently, but soon he'll start speaking to his dead friend again.

Going to War

How much time has gone by since the phone call to Sosa? A half-hour? An hour? Two? In any event, Sosa's soldiers are already going over the wall of Montana's mansion as Tony's Rolls brings him and Gina home. The Tony who pronounced himself ready to go to war could now use a nap, although he's too pharmaceutically wired to sleep, of course.

Ernie and Chi Chi, ever trusty, have taken care of Gina. That is, they've filled her with tranquilizers and squirreled her away in a remote portion of the mansion. Plastic bags of coke are on the desk. The banks of screens showing the security feeds reveal a stream of figures infiltrating. Everywhere.

Tony slumps into his desk chair, and the camera dollies in to the desk, with one pile of coke taking the shape of a snow-covered mountaintop, kind of resembling the logo for Paramount Pictures, which did not produce this film. Tony just stares at the copious amount of powder. He goes onto his balcony for some air. Outside, Ernie talks to one of the other security guys in Spanish, tells him to keep his eyes open. Back in his office, Tony tells himself, "We gotta get organized here," and again collapses in his chair. He begins, as in New York, to grow some kind of conscience. "How the fuck I do that, Manny." One thinks of Macbeth and Banquo.

Screenwriter Oliver Stone had some objections to the staging of the movie's finale. He didn't see why De Palma had SO MANY Sosa guys coming to kill Tony. But the rationale is in the pudding. The beautifully staged and shot takes of these anonymous men swarming onto Tony's property and spreading mayhem are their own justification. You can see De Palma stretching, having fun, really letting loose on some elaborate action. When a producer gives you production value, use it. Now as magisterial as Tony Montana imagines himself being,

De Palma says, "I'll show YOU 'cry havoc and let slip the dogs of war,' fucker. Get a load of this!" This Montana employee gets garroted, this one gets his throat slit in the pool, hey, there's another one down, thrown on his side and knifed in the chest.

And Tony can only mutter "Manolo" and bury his face in coke.

Then Gina shows up. And in a way, here is perhaps the most undistilled De Palmaesque scene in the movie. Because up until now, this has been a picture that's almost surgically removed the sex from the sex-and-violence equation of the '80s R-rated thriller. The 1980s R-rated thriller that De Palma himself helped to define in the 1970s. Gina, her robe open, walks into Tony's office, bringing in not merely sex, but incest. (Which was part of the twist of De Palma's *Obsession*.)

Mastrantonio shows us a Gina who, having lost everything, speaks the truth of madness.

Her smile is sick, diabolical. "Is this what you want, Tony?" The viewer sees her lavender panties as her robe flaps. As does Tony, who seems to think he's hallucinating. "So you want me, Tony, huh?"

His reaction is fascinating. His eyes say, "I do?" And Pacino makes you think he could be on the point of saying "You know? Yeah, I fucking do!" But Tony's in no position to. So instead his mouth says, "What you talking about?"

And Gina raises a revolver and starts shooting at him. This kind of sobers him up. She grazes his knee, which sobers him up further.

The screenwriter Leigh Brackett worked for Howard Hawks on his 1942 adaptation of Raymond Chandler's classic detective novel *The Big Sleep*. Decades later, she wrote the screenplay for Robert Altman's 1973 adaptation of Chandler's *The Long Goodbye*. In an interview, Brackett, herself a crime novelist, exalted that Hollywood's new freedoms allowed her to contrive what even Chandler himself didn't dare: giving villain Terry Lennox the ending he deserved. (Spoiler alert: Elliott Gould's Marlowe tracks down his former friend in Mexico and kills him. "You killed my cat" is Marlowe's farewell to the unctuous creep.) The guys behind the 1983 *Scarface* clearly took no small pleasure in making what was subtext in the Hawks film into extremely blatant text. In a scene where every turn is designed to go over the top and then reset the top higher so as to go over it again, Gina yelling, "Fuck me, Tony, come on and just fuck me!" is quite the top to go over.

As delighted as Oliver Stone and De Palma might have been to present the moviegoer with "FUCK ME, TONY," one person who did not want to go along with the incest theme was Al Pacino. Early on in the production, during script readings, Pacino balked at the idea that Tony would have the hots for his sister, Steven Bauer says. "Brian and Al had a major difference of opinion about the relationship between Tony and his sister and the reason Tony gets crazy when he sees her with other men. Brian was implying that there was something weird, that Tony has a weird thing for his sister. And Al just wouldn't have it. He just wouldn't have it. He said, 'It doesn't ring true for me. I think it's a cheat. I think it's too vulgar. Too, too vulgar.'

"And Brian was adamant about it. 'I think it has to be there.' He and Al came to a compromise in which Tony responds as innocent. To say, 'What are you talking about? What the hell? No. Is that what you think?' It's funny, in Al's mind, where he drew the line—Tony is guilty of many things, but not incest. Not incest!" Eventually Pacino had to have realized that De Palma could give Tony incestuous desires for Gina without Pacino ever performing such an idea himself. As in the cutting from Tony's eyes to Gina's provocative dancing in the nightclub scene. It's called, in film theory, the Kuleshov effect, after a Soviet filmmaker who found that a man with a neutral expression on his face could, to an audience, look hungry if the filmmaker cut to a plate of food, lascivious if he cut to a scantily clad woman, and so on. The language of film could accomplish what an actor might find too distasteful to try to get across.

In any event, it's almost as if the machine gun fire that almost cuts Gina in half, and puts an end to her demands, is a form of deus ex machina. Tony, under his desk, kneecaps the balcony-climbing assassin and throws him down to ground level. Then the realization that his sister is dead overtakes him.

Outside, we are introduced to a man the script calls "The Skull." Cool as death, he wears wraparound dark glasses and carries a shotgun with which he kills Nick the Pig. Tony cries over Gina's bloody corpse. "Don't be mad at me," he begs. It's sad, but it's not quite poignant. His behavior plays, properly, as a form of coke psychosis. But he says he loves Manny, and he loves her too. A first time for everything.

We note that poor little Chi Chi gets off a few shots before he gets it in the back trying to get into Tony's office. The long-haired Sosa dirtbag and some confederates get in front of Tony's office door, now decorated in Chi Chi's blood. And now it's "Say hello to my little friend" time.

"You wait here, okay?" Tony says to Gina as he goes to the weapons cabinet. It's absurd, but by now we are as far gone in a way as Tony is. The scene *only* plays due to the overabundance of lunacy and its violent manifestations. De Palma has really modulated the heat; we're now comfortable with it. We can now believe that Tony's rage, combined with copious amounts of probably pretty pure cocaine, have at least temporarily made him superhuman. Lending further credibility to the vintage gangster movie times ten dialogue Stone gives Montana here: "Whores! Cowards! You think you can kill me with lousy bullets, huh?"

The gun with which Montana launches his final salvo is not one found in nature. Rather, it's an armorer/prop department confection; according to an article on the *Forbes* website, it's "a Colt AR-15 tarted up with a fake grenade launcher." The grenade launcher blows off the door, the AR-15 shoots like a machine gun, and you can see how even with blanks the muzzle flash could make things hot enough to sear your palm but good.

Endless mooks with guns fall as endless squibs of blood explode under their costumes. Tony replaces magazine after magazine. Sosa's guys shoot everywhere, chipping away at the gold ornamentation on Tony's banisters. As he calls his assailants "maricons," we see The Skull, having climbed up the balcony into Tony's office, coming up from behind, implacable. Some of the bullets hitting Tony are starting to cause him pain. But he half boasts, half marvels, "I'm still standing, huh?"

Some have discussed this remarkable scene as unprecedented, but that's not entirely true. Consider Akira Kurosawa's 1957 *Throne of Blood*, in which Toshiro Mifune's warlord Washizu faces, head on, an entire army of archers and withstands a literal shower of flying arrows before one lucky shot gets him right through the neck.

In Ken Tucker's book *Scarface Nation*, Patricia Norris recalls that she needed to make about nine separate black suits for Pacino, because he kept getting shot up, and the suits kept coming apart.

And then, finally, The Skull's shotgun—De Palma gives us a close-up of its two barrels—ends everything, pushes Tony off the balcony and into the small pool that holds the pillar with a globe encircled by the neon words "The World Is Yours" on top of it.

His mission accomplished, The Skull, played by Geno Silva, descends the stairs. Save for a couple of stray Sosa henchmen still reeling in the foyer, he's the last living figure in the movie. A text comes up: "This film is dedicated to HOWARD HAWKS and BEN HECHT."

Stone's script ends this way: "[O]ur camera now distancing itself from the body in the pool, panning past the dream villa, past the shambles and the wealth, past the hitters pillaging and looting and drawing that obscene word 'Chivato' in blood on the outside walls, past the stacks of cash blowing across the floor like leaves in autumn, with the looters running after it across the busted door with the tropic wind blowing down Coconut Grove—to the Miami skyline across Biscayne Bay."

13

SHOCK AND HORROR: THE REACTION

Martin Bregman's second son, Michael Bregman, got a kind of sneak preview of *Scarface* through what some would now call the nepo-baby method: he took a summer job as an editorial assistant on the movie. "I didn't have much going on," he recalls of his late adolescence. "I hung out in Central Park. I was a skateboarder. It's like I was in Central Park every single day. I just hung out with kids and, you know, there were kids who lived on Fifth Avenue and there were kids who lived in the South Bronx and, uh, you know, it was just like a mix. I'd bring those guys to the editing room late at night. I'd been hanging out in editing rooms since I was like fourteen, thirteen years old. And I was bringing them to the editing room at night at like nine, ten o'clock at night, drinking beers and smoking weed, watching the cut footage. Because, like, it was the greatest thing in the world. They loved it. And I remember mentioning it to my dad, like offhand like, oh yeah, no, the movie is great. All my friends love it. And he said, 'You what?' And I explained what I was doing and he said, 'Are you fucking crazy?' He ordered me, 'Don't bring anybody here.' Plus the fact I'm showing it on the work print! I mean, this one copy, you know, this is the work print. If the building burns down, we gotta start from scratch.

"We're on the picture, one sprocket at each side and, you know, a single piece of tape on the back side. I mean, it was like that. No music, no mix, no nothing, just dialogue. Even like that, though, showing it that raw, my buddies were like, wow!"

Oddly and hilariously enough, *Author! Author!*, the comedy that Pacino starred in right before embarking on *Scarface*, ends with its playwright character Ivan, surrounded by his loving and up-way-too-late children, retrieving a hot-off-the-presses copy of the *New York Times* containing a rave review of his play, which had premiered that evening.

The *New York Times* film critic Vincent Canby, a refined, literate, and astute writer who could be a little stuffy on occasion, turned out to be one of the few mainstream critics who actually got the movie, calling it "the most stylish and provocative—and maybe the most vicious—serious film about the American underworld since Francis Ford Coppola's *The Godfather.* In almost every way, though, the two films are memorably different." He called the film a "relentlessly bitter, satirical tale of greed, in which all supposedly decent emotions are sent up for the possible ways in which they can be perverted." Pacino's performance is of such "mounting intensity that one half-expects him to self-destruct before the film's finale." He got a kick out of the movie's absurdist touches: "Mr. De Palma pushes *Scarface* very close to the brink of parody when, near the end, the strung-out Tony plays his Gotterdammerung with a large, humiliating clump of cocaine stuck to the end of his nose. It's like watching a Macbeth who is unaware that his pants have split." And Canby noted the film's high level of violence but appeared unbothered by it. The film, he wrote, includes "dismemberments, hangings, knifings and comparatively conventional shootings by small arms and large. Be warned." (*Variety*, the trade publication that was then the show business Bible, called the picture a "grandiose modern morality play" and predicted, "Strong b.o. seems in store.")

Were the A-listers who attended the simultaneous bicoastal preview screenings of the movie warned? Possibly not. An account of both events in *People Magazine* kicks off, "Kurt Vonnegut walked out after 30 minutes, muttering 'It's too gory for me.'" Author John Irving felt similarly and voted with his feet. Model Cheryl Tiegs apparently stuck it out and weighed in: "It makes you never want to hear the word 'cocaine' again." Perhaps not surprisingly, high-strung actor and future social media nightmare James Woods told *People*'s reporters, "Personally, I'm all for any movie whose lead character keeps a grenade launcher in his living room."

Television comedy goddess Lucille Ball objected to the language, praising the performances but saying, "we got awfully sick of that word." Joan Collins was more philosophical: "I hear there are 183 'fucks' in the movie, which is more than most people get in a lifetime." (There is an apocryphal story that the pop-punk band Blink-182, upon being told in the early 1990s that they had to change their name from just "Blink" lest they be sued by another combo of that name, chose the numerical suffix 182 after their count of the *fuck*s uttered in *Scarface*, but it's actually more likely that the number was chosen at random. Even I, while writing a whole damn book about the movie, have better things to do than keep a tally of how many times that word is uttered in the picture. More to the point, forty years and Martin Scorsese's *Goodfellas*—to name but one subsequent movie with a lot of "language" in it—after, the word doesn't have nearly the same power as it did in 1983.) The singer Cher, who has always known what's what, said of the movie, "It was a great example of how the American dream can really go to shit."

The astute and seminal critic Andrew Sarris is, more than any other English-language writer, responsible for bringing the term *auteur* into common film parlance. He nevertheless tended to mistrust the "movie brats" whose consciousness of the likes of Hawks and Ford were in part derived from Sarris's writings. He'd gone sour on De Palma with *Dressed to Kill.* In the *Village Voice*, he and a younger critic faced off over that movie, as I've mentioned, with Sarris dismissing it as a *Psycho* ripoff and J. Hoberman praising the picture as a dazzling variant on Hitchcock themes that made the latent content in Hitchcock's Hollywood films utterly and messily and galvanizingly explicit. Sarris kicked off his *Scarface* review by saying the picture was "so much more an event than a movie, and so much more a disaster than an outrage." He used the notice less as an opportunity to take apart the film than to ruminate on the enthusiasms and practices of De Palma and his movie brat buddies: "De Palma's true stylistic inspiration is not the classical cinema of Hitchcock and Hawks, but the frenzied baroque of Welles and Kazan, all the way up to the mannerist fluorescence of Coppola in *The Godfather.* It is interesting that Scorsese, Coppola, Lucas and De Palma did not tune into Hitchcock until *Vertigo*, Hawks until *Rio Bravo*, and Ford until *The Searchers*, each a '50s film that stretches its director's classical style to new and uncommon virtuosities of visual expressiveness in the service of a comparatively sketchy scenario." Before launching this meditation—which goes on for much of the rest of the review, citing Robert Warshow's essay "The Gangster As Tragic Hero," Sarris dismisses De Palma's film as "...about 20 minutes worth of action and two and a half hours of middle-brow attitudinizing." If you know your Sarris, you know that "middle-brow" is one of the worst insults he can bestow.

De Palma had long been championed by *The New Yorker*'s critic Pauline Kael, but she was brought up short by the picture; her essay is a consistently evocative model of what publicists today call a "mixed negative" review. In terms of evocative: "And Frank's henchman, Omar, an anxious pockmarked creep who has a big laugh for his boss's jokes, is played by the whirlwind F. Murray Abraham;"—Kael, as ever here, shows her keen eye for character actors and their roles—"he manages to look like a shark here, and every time he appears in a scene, the energy level jumps." (One recalls Kael's similarly prescient praise of Morgan Freeman in the otherwise underwhelming 1987 *Street Smart*, which helped boost that then-relatively-obscure actor's career.)

Kael notices the lack of split-screen, the linear approach to time, the lack of diopter shots. "De Palma may have felt that he could stretch himself by using a straightforward approach—something he has never been very good at. But what happens is simply that he's stripped of his gifts. His originality doesn't function on this crude, ritualized melodrama; he's working against his talent." The word *ritualized* stands out here—Kael is closer than she knows to getting what De Palma is doing. In any event, she certainly didn't like what she thought he was doing, and liked Pacino's performance less: "After a while, Pacino is a lump at the center of the movie." The title of Kael's review was "A De Palma Movie for People Who Don't Like De Palma Movies."

David Denby, in *New York Magazine*, found a moral failing in the movie's method. During the chainsaw scene, he complains, "The entire emphasis is on Tony—and on Al Pacino—his courage, his defiance, his willingness to suffer. We have no desire to see Angel's limbs sawed off, but perhaps if we had seen his face we would have known if he appealed to Tony to cave in and save both their lives or had died willingly." This seems to misapprehend the nature of the transaction taking place in the motel room, and after all, the movie is titled *Scarface* and not

Angel. Denby concludes that the picture was "empty and bullying, a sadly overblown B movie."

Joseph Gelmis in *Newsday* ended his review by quoting Elvira's observation that Tony's constant repetition of *fuck* is "boring." He adds: "It's true. He is boring. And the movie is boring." In *Time*, Richard Corliss called the movie "a serious, often hilarious peek under the rock where nightmares strut in $800 suits and Armageddon lies around the next twist of treason." He concluded: "The only X this movie deserves is the one in explosive."

The columnist and reviewer Rex Reed took the occasion of the movie's release to wax indignant, as was, and remained, his wont. "Brian De Palma's gutbusting remake of Howard Hawks' 1932 gangster melodrama *Scarface* sets out to accomplish only one thing—disgust, sicken and horrify the audience with a rampage of violence, bloodshed and carnage." Wrapping up, he says, "The violence is endless, the four-letter-words take the place of English, the actors work vigorously, the decadence and perversion drown everything in viscous grunge. When it's over, you feel mugged, debased, like you've eaten a bad clam." It's not a Reed review before a "they don't make 'em like they used to" grace note, so for his coda, he sings, "Where's Jimmy Cagney, now that we need him?" (As Reed well knew, Cagney was in his early eighties and long-retired, although he emerged on the big screen after a twenty-year absence to acquit himself well in Milos Forman's *Ragtime*, playing a seemingly fair-minded lawman who turns out to be a gargoyle after all.)

In *The New Republic*, Stanley Kaufmann took a higher tone in expressing his indignation, decrying the movie's "facile, flashy cynicism." In his *o tempora, o mores* kicker, he wrote: "This film is dedicated to Howard Hawks and Ben Hecht. I haven't seen a more hopeless attempt as aggrandizement through dedication since William Friedkin adapted his sorry *Sorcerer* from *The Wages of Fear* and dedicated his distortion to Henri-Georges Clouzot, who directed the original." Kaufmann died in 2013, the year Friedkin published his memoir *The Friedkin Connection*, for which occasion he hosted several screenings of a restored *Sorcerer*, which was beginning to enjoy a revised reputation as a latter-day classic.

After the reviews, the think pieces. Published a few days after his *Scarface* review, Vincent Canby wondered "How Should We React to Violence." His lead paragraph, a kind of boilerplate "let's consider some questions" contraption, suggests he really didn't have much enthusiasm for the assignment: "Does the new *Scarface* deserve to be rated 'X' for violence? Is an 'R' rating too lenient for *Star 80*? Should any movie that contains a single usage of one particular four-letter word—the word that the humorist Jean Shepard describes as 'the queen-mother of dirty words'—deserve an automatic 'R'? Will we ever see the day when it will be possible to give an 'X' on principle to all of Clint Eastwood's *Dirty Harry* movies, including the new *Sudden Impact*?" Canby cites a few examples of the inconsistent rulings of the ratings board, citing a particularly grisly bit in the PG-rated picture *Nate and Hayes*. As for the violence in *Scarface*, he insists that its "bleak, harrowing relentlessness is one of the conscious points of an intelligent, highly exploitable if, for some, offensive film." And he concludes: "Who should or shouldn't be able to see these movies, as well as *Scarface*, *Star 80* and, for that matter, *The Osterman Weekend*? [Canby was very much cheesed off by *The Osterman Weekend*.] It's a question that the members of the motion picture industry and concerned members of the public have been wrestling with for more than half a century, but it's an unequal match. Because no 10 people are likely to agree on any kind of formula for more than five minutes, it's the question that wins."

Speaking of "highly exploitable," two days after Canby's piece appeared in the *Times*, the *New York Post* expressed its no doubt sincere shock and horror over a stabbing during a screening of

Scarface in Manhattan, at the RKO National Theater in Times Square. A random miscreant "shot out of his seat" and began picking on moviegoers at random, eventually wounding three moviegoers whom the *Post* reported to be in stable condition. (The paper did not follow up on how they were doing.)

"The manager of the theater, who refused to give his name"—note the passive-aggressive tone of condemnation in that detail—"confirmed the incident. 'I have no comment. I can tell you that what happened was an isolated incident,' he said.

"Despite some mental health experts' claims that violence in films can be a harmless release for human aggression *Scarface* is not the first movie that appears to have triggered violence in viewers." Because everyone knows that Times Square in the early 1980s was otherwise pretty much the safest place in the world to watch a motion picture.

In the *Village Voice*, Enrique Fernandez enumerated his complaints, rather than objections, in an engaging piece called "Scarface Died for My Sins," in which he said of the title character, "I don't see Tony Montana. I see Al Pacino acting." Fernandez had actually met Martin Bregman and had twice gotten close to acting as a consultant on the movie. He writes of feeling that Stone's script lacked any Cuban spirit, as it manifested on the island itself and in Miami. "Back when I read the screenplay I felt that little of it flowed from the experience of Mariel or Cuban Miami. Something about the Tony Montana character struck me as false," Fernandez writes; his derivation from the stiff "...old world peasant" played by Paul Muni was "nothing at all like one of the hard men of the Caribbean, all of whom, and particularly the baddest, know how to party. This guy was a bumpkin, not a bandido. I tried to explain this to the filmmakers, but I didn't succeed because I didn't know what to call the missing factor.

"Now I know, but it's too late. The movie's been made. What's missing is salsa."

In the *New York Daily News*, Miguel Perez took a more pious tone, one that echoes in contemporary discourse over such topics as representation: "There are many Cuban-Americans who could have been the subject of a good film, like those who fought and died in Vietnam or those who still struggle to liberate their homeland from communism, or those who now enjoy liberty after spending 20 years in a Cuban political prison, or those who just work very hard to reach the goal line before the strongest competitors." Perez then cites three-time New York Marathon winner Alberto Salazar: "No one seems to be worried about how he entered the country and whether he has a scar on his face."

Salazar eventually became a running coach. In 2021 he was banned from the sport for life after the United States Center for SafeSport found he had sexually assaulted an athlete.

14

"ME!": HIP-HOP MAKES TONY MONTANA AN ICON

As a box office proposition, *Scarface* proved a minor disappointment for Universal. Its stated budget was $25 million. On its opening weekend, it took in a little under $5 million, opening in about 1,000 houses. It ultimately grossed $45 million in the US and Canada and an additional $20 million overseas. In 1984, the spectacular grosses of *Beverly Hills Cop* would set the bar for blockbuster box office at $100 million. Which $65 million is not. Relative to all the risk and hassle the movie provided for Universal executives, from the Miami expulsion to the ratings board woes, the studio was probably not eager to reteam with the movie's principals anytime soon. De Palma's next project, *Body Double*, was set up at Columbia. Pacino signed to do *Revolution* with director Hugh Hudson and producer Irwin Winkler. The large-scale movie was distributed by a triad of Columbia, Warner, and Cannon, and was such a disaster that Pacino dropped out of filmmaking for a while to concentrate on stage work. Martin Bregman did stick with Universal, only this time supervising a sane and modestly budgeted project for his sane former client Alan Alda, *Sweet Liberty*, in which Michelle Pfeiffer would play a charming but ultimately at least slightly devious film star.

Scarface had a second life on video, as some movies tend to do, and it became an iconographic film after its narrative and ethos were embraced by hip-hop artists. The rapper known as Scarface released his first twelve-inch in 1988. In 1990, on the track "Welcome to the Terrordome" on the album *Fear of a Black Planet*, Flavor Flav, the raucous "hype man" to Chuck D's righteous teacher, repeats Tony Montana's "Who put this together? Me! Who do I trust? Me!" spiel from the film. Twenty years after the movie's release, Def Jam Records released a compilation album and CD, *Def Jam Presents Music Inspired by* Scarface. The front cover announced that it was being released "In association with the release of the *Scarface* Anniversary Edition From Universal Home Video." As such, the album jacket and CD booklet are decorated with stills from the film, and the rap tracks—one of which, we shall see, actually predates the release of the movie—are interspersed with snatches of dialogue from the movie's soundtrack. Which in itself is very frequently sampled by rappers.

Universal had even bigger tie-in plans. And here's a good example of why, when it's possible, the people executives now call "content creators" ought to do due diligence to be contractually able to protect what executives and lawyers and now way too many people call "intellectual property." The studio was keen on re-releasing the picture with Giorgio Moroder's score replaced by hip-hop hits. Bregman and Pacino did not think this was such a bad idea, reportedly, but Brian De Palma rightly did. He told the *Los Angeles Times*, "[N]o one changes the scores on movies by Marty Scorsese, John Ford, David Lean. If this is the 'masterpiece' you say, leave it alone. I fought them tooth and nail and was the odd man out, not an unusual place for me. I have final cut, so that stopped them dead."

Kevin Liles, one of the producers of the Def Jam anthology, and then the president of Def Jam, saw the issue differently. "Hip-hop, as Chuck D says, is the 'CNN of the ghetto.' Incorporating it into a classic like this would convey the current reality. The message, unfortunately, is as relevant today as when the movie emerged. I'll be the first up to bat to rescore the film, which touched such a nerve in the 'hood. Though Montana is Latino, all those kids identify with his job in the burger shop, idolizing guys with the big Benz and flashy women. Music is the soul of any movie, and a new soundtrack would increase its power." But, as De Palma said, he had veto power, and he used it. In any event, in 2003 the aforementioned Anniversary Edition on home video had a preorder of over 2 million units, surpassing sales of every other title in Universal's catalog at the time, including the likes of *Jaws* and *Back to the Future.*

Speaking today, De Palma remains bemused by the craze that *Scarface* became, but he's generally philosophical about the second life that movies acquire. "I was surprised, because I'm not a big hip-hop fan. People would tell me this. And it wasn't just one time, it was many times that Universal wanted to re-release this movie with a hip-hop score, and I wouldn't let them do it. Also, Scarface appeared as a video game character with some of the music from the original *Scarface.*"

Indeed he did. Three years after the Def Jam compilation went to market, *Scarface: The World Is Yours* was released by Radical Entertainment. It changes the ending of the movie to allow Tony to live and rebuild his empire. Also among the living in the supposed sequel are Manny and Frank Lopez. Steven Bauer and Robert Loggia actually lent their voice talents to the game. In terms of action and gameplay, it tried to do the extremely popular *Grand Theft Auto* games one better, and was praised by reviewers for its ambition.

"You can't predict these things," De Palma continued when I spoke with him. "You know, who would imagine we'd be talking about *Scarface* after so many years, and there'd be people with posters of *Scarface* in their bedrooms. It's always amazing to me. But when it came out, it wasn't well-liked. There were a lot of negative reviews, and people were disturbed by it. It did okay financially, but not a big hit. But as I've discovered with my movies, they live on. I mean, there was no bigger disaster than *Blow Out*, and now people talk about it as if it's the best film I ever made."

I spoke to my friend Harry Allen about *Scarface*'s influence on hip-hop. Allen went to college with Chuck Ridenhour at Adelphi. Ridenhour, taking the name Chuck D, would form the ensemble Public Enemy and designate Allen, who wrote about music for the *Village Voice*, which is where I first met him, Public Enemy's own "Media Assassin."

"I'm aware of *Scarface*," he told me. "I'm a little too old, I think, to have been profoundly affected by it. I was thinking about why this film has captivated hip-hop artists. The conclusion I came to is that it's, first of all, a very entertaining film. It's a very entertaining film, and it's entertaining in a way that to a young person will be utterly captivating. Now, when you're talking about the hip-hop generation, the most influential and the most substantive portion of it, the central artist in that coterie of artists would be Nas. Nas was born in 1973, which means that when *Scarface* was released, he was ten. I was twenty when *Scarface* was released. Grandmaster Flash would have been around twenty-five or close to thirty. So you have this group of artists like in Flash's generation who would have been around thirty when it was released, and people like me or like Run from RUN D.M.C. who would have been around twenty. We're not going to really be captivated by this movie in the same way that someone who is ten years old, who either sneaks into the movies or sees it shortly after it comes out on videotape, sees it. It slightly escaped my generation, and went to that one that's represented by Nas and artists like that who were born in the very early seventies, right?"

Grandmaster Flash and Melle Mel, as it happened, were inhabiting the same real world that *Scarface* was addressing. Their single "White Lines (Don't Do It)," a detailed anti-cocaine number, was released in October 1983, just a couple of months before the release of *Scarface*.

I fed Harry one of my pet theories: "I think one thing that definitely appealed to artists like Nas and Jay-Z is a combination of the extravagance of the criminality and its attendant lifestyle, but also the fatalism. *Scarface* doesn't really function as a cautionary tale despite the fact that Tony Montana is killed in an awfully grisly manner. The appeal comes from a fantastic baseline, a philosophy that says we're all going to die anyway. But the admirers of Tony Montana and characters like him think: before I do die, I want to get to the top of something. And when I go out, I want it to be in a blaze of glory, having conquered a world. I wonder if you feel that idea, in and of itself has appeal relative to the bravado and the braggadocio that is so often part of hip-hop narratives."

Harry corrected me. Certainly the narrative of *Scarface* did function as a cautionary tale for a lot of hip-hop artists. They took the "rules" that Frank Lopez laid out—in particularly the rule that Tony Montana winds up violating so egregiously, "Don't get high on your own supply"—and elaborated on them, as in Notorious B.I.G.'s "Ten Crack Commandments," from his posthumous album *Life After Death*, and also included on the Def Jam compilation of music "inspired by" *Scarface*. "I been in this game for years, it made me an animal," the rapper states. "I wrote me a manual." To paraphrase, the Commandments are: 1: Don't reveal your cash holdings to anyone. 2: Don't reveal your plans to anyone. 3: "Never trust nobody." Which is akin to Lopez's directive to never underestimate the rival drug dealer's greed. 4: Don't get high on your own supply. Biggie allows that the listener may have "heard this before." 5: Don't sell in your own neighborhood. Bring the drug blight somewhere else. Commandment 6, also familiar in bodegas, where the owners often put the message on hand-lettered signs: "no credit." 7: Don't get your family involved. Here Biggie throws in a homophobic simile, about money and blood not mixing "like two dicks and no bitch." 8: Don't carry the goods in any quantity. Let the guys who accompany you, the gun carriers, keep the supply. So you can't be charged with possession. Commandment 9 is pretty much don't even say hello to a cop, lest you attract suspicion that you're a rat. Commandment 10 is "a strong word called 'consignment,'" and if you're unfamiliar with the concept, as many are, you have no business selling drugs. Or anything.

"I think the cautionary aspect comes through in many components of the movie and particularly in Stone's script. It's filled with these pithy quotes that have become part of the lingo. And I think the people who were influenced by the film were very aware of all the instances in which Tony is caught slipping, when he's drunk. And the way he becomes delusional once he starts, sticking his face into the mountain of cocaine on his desk.

"*Scarface* is a film about a character that has resonance for people who were raised in neighborhoods where drug dealers have high status and visibility, where drug dealers are success stories. To see one portrayed in the film, where the character's success is enormous, it's gigantic, it's overwhelming, that resonates. Believe it or not, it made me think of *Willy Wonka*! The scale of it, the largeness of his power, how it is displayed and rendered in the film. And Pacino's performance is commensurate to that scale. A lot of people talk about his performance in that film as though it's a bad performance, and I just disagree.

"Pacino's performance is very, very compelling, and the character of Tony Montana is a very dynamic character. He makes things happen. Things don't just happen to him, and he really is a self-made man. I think if you're a person who's grown up the way that a lot of the hip-hop artists who connected to this film did, those are very important and compelling qualities, aspirational kind of qualities.

"Tony Montana, like them, comes from an impoverished upbringing. He comes in on the Mariel boatlift. Most rappers are the descendants of people who were boatlifted with hostility. Not recently, but hundreds of years ago…but still. Tony has an unrepressed ambition. I was thinking about that shot where he and Manny are dishwashers looking across the street to the Babylon Club. From that hole in the wall where they're working for. And I was thinking like, would you ever put a place like this across the street from a place like that? It doesn't seem too realistic from an urban zoning perspective, but it puts the goal right in front of Tony and Manny. It makes sense cinematically. And it's a powerful kind of image of their longing, looking at that place and thinking one day, I'm gonna be big enough to go to a place like that, maybe even own it.

"Another salient feature of Tony's character is that he's utterly cold, and that doesn't mean unemotional, but that means he's really able to keep his emotions in check when he needs to and be present, while showing nothing in his eyes. When you think of the chainsaw scene, for example, when Angel is carved up. His reaction there is very contained considering that his friend is being turned, you know, into, basically a cow, right in front of him. It's really something that you see all throughout the film, that ice-water-in-the-veins quality of his. And that's something you see in the personality of many hip-hop artists. What rappers are often known for is being able to detect insincerity or other forms of pretense in people. If you're around Nas, he's a very quiet but observant guy. I think a scene that really brings it home to me is the first time Tony meets Omar, when they're gonna hire him and Manny to take the marijuana off the boat. And Tony's not impressed. He knows who this guy is. He sees through Omar in a way that Manny doesn't. Manny's like, 'Yeah, great. We're gonna make some money.' And Tony's like, what are you talking about? And he's ready to really go head-to-head with this guy. And Omar sees something in Tony and says, 'Okay, I got a better job for you.'"

Now it may, of course, be the case that Omar is irritated by Tony and wants to set him up to be burned. Nevertheless, Tony and Manny find themselves on a sort of proving ground despite Omar's motivations. Which were put into action by the mere fact of Tony having Omar's number. "The ability to see people and quickly size them up is something that, if you've grown up in a place like many hip-hop artists do, is a life-or-death kind of quality that you want to develop," Allen says. "It's something you don't develop at your peril. I think seeing that in Tony Montana made him very, very relatable.

"I would say, last, he's unflinchingly real. There's that scene in Bolivia where Sosa says, 'I like you, Tony. There's no lying in you.' When Tony says that even when he lies, he's telling the truth, there's something to that. I think all of these qualities make an utterly compelling protagonist, an ideal one. And these qualities are especially compelling when delivered in this extremely cinematic way. *The Godfather* had been out for a while, and Pacino, of course, is in that as well. But it wasn't a movie about drug dealing. It was a movie about the Mafia, and Coppola's style was more stately. De Palma is from the Department of Blood. In his movies, red is not just a primary color, it's the primary color. That's the *Willy Wonka* quality of it, the exaggeration. I remember watching the film and just being amazed that you went deeper and deeper into his world, how much more outrageous it became.

"Does Tony Montana fail because he's stupid? I don't think so. I think he fails because he's human. When you live by your wits, watching someone else fail, there's always a question of you misdiagnosing why they fail. And often the way people diagnose that is, 'That person was stupid, and I'm gonna be smart and that's how I will avoid the failure.' But what a lot of people don't often realize is that actually that person was human, and that it's very difficult, once you get into a certain position of success, to avoid being undone. By the things that the human heart is undone by once you're in that position. So it's not really a matter of 'smart.' It's a matter of the heart, so to speak. And sometimes it's hard to understand that. Some things cannot be resisted. It's like in George Romero's *Dawn of the Dead*, when one of the characters has gotten infected, and he's going to die, and he promises, 'I'm not coming back. I'm not coming back,' pledging this to his friend that he won't become this undead creature. And of course he comes back. And he has to be taken out immediately. It's this heartbreaking fallibility in our humanity. And that's what makes these stories tragic."

Another thing the movie supplies is a kind of narrative factory for hip-hop artists. One song on the *Scarface* compilation, "Mr. Scarface," by the rap artist who in fact dubbed himself Scarface, sees its first-person narrator get into the game of "slangin' cane," break out of prison, massacre some rivals, and more over the course of over two dozen verses. I mentioned this idea to Harry.

"Oh, absolutely. Well, you know, Brad [Brad Terrence Jordan, the birth name of the rapper Scarface] has, you know, made an entire discography inhabiting that character to one degree or another. And yes, I think the narrative—you know, it's a very linear film. It's very easy, it's not like other De Palma films that play with time, and it's a straight climb to the top. And then. Is it a fall off a cliff, you know, or off a mountaintop? Because of that, it's an ideal kit for, kind of like, building your own. You can build entire narrative scenes around segments of the movie's action. It's become kind of an understood myth in the sense that one can draw on it the same way one can draw on the, the story of Christ or *Little Red Riding Hood.* Or any other story that becomes very well-known. In the mythology of human beings, I think certainly for hip-hop artists, *Scarface* is one. It's lore. So if you said you just start to talk about certain things in a certain way, and you're pulling from *Scarface*, people will get that and allow you to flesh out whatever you're saying in advance. When you're pulling from myth, you don't have to spell out certain things in advance, you know what I'm saying?"

15

SPIRITUAL SEQUELS: *THE UNTOUCHABLES* AND *CARLITO'S WAY*

Having made a picture in 1983 that updated a 1932 picture wherein the fictional protagonist was overtly based on Al Capone, Brian De Palma found himself, four years later, making a fictionalized account of the fall of the real-life Al Capone. His approach to *The Untouchables* betrays no particular amusement over that fact.

Watching the movie back-to-back with *Scarface* suggests a paradox. *The Untouchables* is stylistically much more a "De Palma" picture than *Scarface* was. Based on a television program and featuring among its set pieces a blatant recycling, with sprinkles on top, of an iconic silent movie scene (accompanied by a self-plagiarizing score from Ennio Morricone, maestro to epic radicals Sergio Leone and Gillo Pontecorvo), it's a meta-movie that nevertheless does a lot more overt crowd pleasing than *Scarface*. It is no accident. By the mid-'80s, despite "working a lot," as he told interviewers Noah Baumbach and Jake Paltrow in the terrific 2015 documentary *De Palma*, he needed a hit.

After *Scarface*, he had gone ahead and made the picture he had been threatening to, sort of: *Body Double*, a phantasmagorical riff on voyeurism, murder, and porn. It was not an X-rated picture, but it got close enough, and was greeted by howls of the usual outrage. It no doubt engendered some resentment among studio execs who were financing De Palma's kinky jollies to little return on investment. Sex doesn't always sell. The reaction to *Body Double* led to Columbia Pictures and De Palma agreeing to terminate what had been a three-picture deal.

De Palma doesn't come off as disingenuous when he tells Baumbach and Paltrow, "After the disaster of *Body Double* you start thinking about what you're doing, and why are you getting these kind of reactions, and I thought, I gotta do something completely different." He made a music video for Bruce Springsteen. He made a modestly budgeted gangster comedy with Danny De Vito and the then-viable Joe Piscopo called *Wise Guys*. "It was a cute little comedy, it got some very good reviews." Indeed, after you settle into its slightly cheesy tone, it's an agreeable film, better than its outlier reputation suggests. But it received little support, and De Palma was frustrated at how the film fared, blaming it on the fact that it wasn't sponsored by a major studio.

The Untouchables, which was being produced by Art Linson, was. The studio was Paramount, now being run by Ned Tanen, who had been at Universal for *Scarface*. Linson had overseen scrappy productions for maverick directors like Floyd Mutrux and Jonathan Demme and then hit the big time with *Fast Times at Ridgemont High*. In his frank and funny book *A Pound of Flesh*, Linson admits he never liked the source material for his movie—a black-and-white serial drama starring stolid Robert

Stack as Prohibition mob nemesis Elliot Ness, who was in fact a real person whom fiction subsequently twisted into a different shape—but was crazy about the cops and robbers narratives of special agents versus bootleggers, specifically "Scarface" Capone.

Before De Palma came on board, Linson had his heart set on recruiting Pulitzer Prize–winning playwright David Mamet, who'd been nominated for a Best Adapted Screenplay Oscar for 1982's *The Verdict*, to come up with a script. His pitch was, "Dave, don't you think that the best career move for somebody who just won the Pulitzer Prize would be to adapt an old television series like *The Untouchables* for a *shitload* of money?" To which Mamet replied, "Yes, I think so." That was, apparently, as smooth as things went with Mamet. Linson notes that Mamet hated doing rewrites, and that when De Palma was recruited, the director had a good number of plot point and structure questions. He also wanted more Capone, and that in its turn led to a series of considerations that made a great deal of difference to the movie.

The more De Palma wanted, the more hostile Mamet became. Linson recalls flying to the set of *House of Games*, Mamet's film directing debut, and begging for even a suggestion. The suggestion was this: "Tell that greasy bastard that if he gets into trouble, to use that scene from *Carrie* where the hand comes out of the coffin and grabs Ness by the throat." Mamet attended a preview of the film, and according to Linson, sank in his seat when a scene that did not have his imprimatur came on screen. "Be a good sport. You are bought and paid for," Linson told him.

By contrast, De Palma came to the project relatively brimming with enthusiasm. After taking note of De Palma's initially intimidating bearing, producer Linson warmed to him, and they became good friends and collaborators. Linson would produce De Palma's ambitious 1989 *Casualties of War* (written by David Rabe, an esteemed playwright—he got a Tony award and not a Pulitzer, if you want to pick nits, but still—who took De Palma seriously) as well as De Palma's last Hollywood studio picture, 2006's *The Black Dahlia*. (One should note that Linson maintained good relations with Mamet as well, producing 1997's *The Edge*, which Mamet wrote, and 2004's *Spartan*, which Mamet wrote and directed and contains one or two genre flourishes you might not expect from a guy who apparently held *Carrie* in such disdain.)

He had some specific ideas about casting; for the Irish cop Malone, who instructs Elliott Ness in how to uphold the law while kinda-sorta breaking it, he very much wanted Sean Connery. De Palma, at arguably the height of his ability to accurately forecast mass audience response, said that the shock value of killing off Sean Connery would be spectacular. He did not predict that if he killed off Sean Connery in a movie, Connery would win a Best Supporting Actor Oscar for his work, although that did indeed happen.

"I wanted to use Don Johnson," for Ness, De Palma told Baumbach and Paltrow, because of the actor's popularity on the television series *Miami Vice*. But Kevin Costner was more or less locked in. De Palma called his friend Steven Spielberg, who'd directed Costner in an episode of the television anthology series *Amazing Stories*, and got reassurance. But as he prepped the movie in Chicago, something nagged at him. The British actor Bob Hoskins had been hired to play Al Capone; despite Hoskin's intense work playing tough guys in films like *Mona Lisa* and *The Long Good Friday*, this choice didn't sit well with De Palma. "We've got this movie, it's like a sophisticated English playhouse theater," he says in *De Palma*. "We need an American gangster actor."

While Robert De Niro was still a year or so away from the release of the picture that would set him firmly as a movie star, 1988's *Midnight Run*, he now had a great deal of Hollywood clout. Getting him on board *The Untouchables* did not involve a sentimental journey as such. "Bobby takes a long time to decide to do things," De Palma says in the documentary. "You go out to dinner with him, you talk about the script. It took many, many weeks until he said, 'Yeah, I think I can make this work.' The last thing Bobby said to me is 'It's gonna be expensive.' And it was extremely expensive."

This put a ball in Linson's court that he wasn't necessarily expecting, but De Palma was ready to explain his insistence. In Linson's book, the producer recounts De Palma addressing Ned Tanen, who had flipped out not only over the dismissal of Bob Hoskins but the cost of hiring De Niro. De Palma's argument was that if he didn't get his way, the movie just wouldn't work: "[A]nd I cannot afford to make a movie that will not work." Tanen okayed the switch. The movie's budget went up from $18 million to $22.5 million. De Niro, unlike Pacino, likes to build his characters from the outside in, demanding authenticity in every aspect of the character's garb and accessories—he used the prop director's actual cash to bet during a gambling scene in *Goodfellas* a couple of years after this. For *The Untouchables*, De Palma remembers, "He wore the kind of silk underwear that Al Capone wore. You never saw it, but he had it on."

The calculations, including what it took to bring in De Niro, paid off in handsome grosses both domestic and international.

De Palma used the leverage of having a big hit under his belt to make *Casualties of War*, a harrowing Vietnam film he had been developing with David Rabe for years. It was critically well-received but too harsh a meal for mass audiences. As for his next film, *Bonfire of the Vanities*, there's an entire book you can read, a very good one, by Julie Salamon, about its development, production, critical lambasting and box office failure. As he had done with Susan Dworkin on the set of *Body Double* (a movie that has endured despite its critical and box office drubbings and is a latter-day "personal" De Palma film par excellence because of its ostensible absurdities rather than in spite of them), he gave Salamon, with whom he was friendly, unprecedented access to the process. Her portrayal of De Palma is not unsympathetic. But the fact of the film's boondoggle-resembling failure was unavoidable, and the failure was at least in part due to certain decisions that De Palma had to own. His next picture was a tricksy thriller, *Raising Cain*, reuniting him with *Scarface* actor Steven Bauer. Another De Palma picture that went from critic-befuddling failure to fan favorite (thanks in part to a revised cut that originated with one of the film's admirers and stuck to De Palma's initial intentions and was approved by De Palma for inclusion on a home video edition of the movie), it left De Palma once again in the position to search for a commercially viable project.

Fortunately Martin Bregman and Al Pacino were keen to get the band back together.

Carlito's Way is a far more simpatico kind of tragedy than *Scarface*, and the movie adaptation of Edwin Torres's crime fiction begins with its protagonist shot and pretty sure that he's about to die. The rest of the movie is an argument persuading us to care about the man and his death and understand the way it matters. Carlito is a criminal, for sure; his downfall in this story begins just as he gets out of prison. But he's a man with a lot of heart who happens to be a product of his environment, the crime-ridden streets of Spanish Harlem.

Edwin Torres is a product of the same streets, but a man who ended up on the enforcement side of the law, as a defense lawyer, then a DA, then a New York State Supreme Court Judge. His books make you understand the plight of his outlaw character Carlito. (In real life, as a trial judge, Torres was not as lenient as Torres the artist was; one of the most-quoted pronouncements he made from the bench was, "Your parole officer hasn't been born yet.") Hearing his life story from him gives one an even richer understanding of the air of crime that can get into the lungs of so many.

I visited Torres, then 92, on a hot July afternoon and found him and his wonderful wife, Victoria, lunching on chicken soup. Above the table where they sat were three movie posters: One for *Carlito's Way*, another for *Carlito's Way: Rise To Power*, the direct-to-video prequel directed by Martin Bregman's son Michael, and one for *Q&A*, the Sidney Lumet–scripted and –directed policier taken from Torres's second novel, a real eyebrow-raiser of where-the-bodies-are-buried-in-law-enforcement crime writing.

Victoria, he tells me, was the person who pushed him to write his first novel. (He wrote all his novels while a lawyer with the New York City attorney's office. Once he was appointed a judge, he says, he got a case of writer's block. Maybe.) They had gone to the movies and seen a crime drama starring Anthony Quinn. "Sounds like *Across 110th Street*," I said. "Could have been," Torres replied. Looking at Quinn's filmography, I'd say it had to have been. The movie has been praised for its brutal ostensible realism, but Torres didn't buy it. "So write your own," Victoria urged him, and the result was *Carlito's Way*.

When the book was published, both Torres and Al Pacino were regulars at the McBurney YMCA on 23rd Street in Manhattan. Michael Bregman told me that he thinks Torres presented the book to Pacino at the gym. Torres doesn't recollect doing that, only that he was acquainted with Pacino from the gym and that Pacino knew the book and it interested him. It took almost twenty years for it to happen. Pacino had, in the late '80s, tried to make it happen with producer Elliott Kastner, with Marlon Brando set to costar, perhaps as Carlito's crooked lawyer. Pacino backed out and was sued by Kastner. And a few months after the suit was filed, according to Pacino biographer Andrew Yule, the production was back in play, overseen by the man who could always make such things happen for Pacino, Martin Bregman.

Carlito's Way is the movie that it is largely because the Bregmans especially—by now Martin's son Michael was in the fold as a producer—devoted themselves to being true to Torres and his vision. Even if they had to go around Torres to achieve that. Once the movie was in development, Torres wrote a script, but Bregman rejected it, and brought in screenwriter David Koepp, who'd also scripted a 1993 release titled *Jurassic Park*. "He was a teenager," Torres recalls, which is not quite accurate. The still-youthful-looking Koepp was about thirty. Torres didn't tell me exactly why his script was rejected, but a clue might lie in an exchange he had with Martin Bregman after watching *Carlito's Way* for the first time. Torres picked a lot of nits about it, and Bregman said, "Edwin, if we had made the film exactly as you'd wanted it, it would be twelve hours long."

If the life of Torres's creation had an epic sweep to it, that's because Torres's own life does. "When I relate these narratives to you, sometimes I can't believe it myself," Torres told me about forty minutes into our conversation. "How did I get to the State Supreme Court?"

The L.P. Hartley novel *The Go-Between* opens with a much-quoted observation: "The past is a foreign country. They do things differently there." The latter portion of that statement may hold true from Torres's perspective, but not the first half. His recollections are so vivid as to be palpable.

"Anyway, I was born in 1931, on Lenox Avenue, you can imagine. Then my father got an apartment on 107th Street and Madison Avenue, Spanish Harlem. That's where I was raised. That was the time of the gang wars. This before the heroin arrived. Heroin arrived in the '50s. In the '40s, though, when I was growing up, it was gangs, street gangs. I was with them in a sense, friends of mine and so forth, but I was never like a gangbanger, never.

"I was in three different rumbles, one with the Comanches and one with the Scorpions…these were the two Black gangs… and then with the Italian gang on 111th Street… What the fuck was their name? My brain is completely... What was the name of the Italian gang in Harlem?"

Victoria was stuck too. Eventually Torres would recall they were the Red Wings.

"Anyway, I can give you the three accounts. I had a fight with the Comanches on 104th Street and Park Avenue with one guy. The other guy, his buddy came alongside with an ash can handle. They used to take them off the ash can and use them like a brass knuckle. He busted my jaw with that, knocked me out. I fell on top of a Jewish street vendor's cart. I couldn't eat for a week. That was the Comanches. They were from around 100th Street in the projects and whatnot. They just picked on me, I think because I was a spic there. That was the thing. It was ethnic, I guess, what it was.

"Then subsequently, I was in Central Park on 106th Street and Fifth Avenue. On Fifth Avenue, there's a lake there. I was in my teens, early teens, and I was fishing. That's what I was doing at the lake. Then the Scorpions, they were the worst gang...that was the Black gang from 111th Street...they came on bikes, three of them. They sent this little guy, little punk, over to me. He said, 'Let me hold a quarter, motherfucker.' In those days a quarter was money. I remember the exchange. I said, 'I look like your father, motherfucker?' He punched me in the face. I remember he popped me. I remember I jumped him and I was dragging him into the lake. I was going to put his head in the lake and the other three guys, they came up on the bikes, bicycles.

"I said, 'Any one of you motherfuckers, come on down.' You know what I mean? Because I was so hot, I guess. They said, 'We're going to fuck you up.' At that time they had introduced zip guns, which were these homemade 22s. All the street gangs started using them. That was the first equipment. They pulled out the zip guns and they were going to blow my ass away, and so then they chased me to 110th, the end of the park near the lake, but I was known as Fast Eddie in Harlem, because I was quick, so I got away.

"The next day my buddy, Orlando Cordona, comes and tells me that someone, a guy named Big Stoop, had told the Scorpions where I lived. Anyway, they came up and down the block on bicycles. Orlando said, 'They're going up and down the block on their bikes. They're looking for you.' He warned me.

"I was hiding for a few days. I remember I was trying to get my hands on a real pistol. If I had, I might have killed one of these guys. Then one day I was standing on the corner of 107th Street and Fifth Avenue with three brothers, the Gwyn brothers, Robert, Jimmy, and Johnny. They were like, my God, they were the toughest guys in Harlem, three brothers. Johnny, especially, was the Golden Glove champion later on. They're all dead. Anyway, the Scorpions pulled up on bikes again, and they spotted me. Then I remember they were wearing these stingy brim hats, and they going to kick my ass. Then Johnny took the hat off one of them and threw it out on Fifth Avenue. They started to laugh a bit. But they were buffaloed. They were gorillaed. They were scared. They don't fuck with the Gwyn brothers, so I walked behind that one.

"Later on, I was Johnny's lawyer in two murder cases. He got twenty-five to life for one of the murders. He did fifteen. He thought *Carlito's Way* was based on him. He wrote me a letter from prison telling me that.

"Oh yeah, then the third one, because I remember them vividly. I used to go to Jefferson swimming pool on 112th Street and First Avenue. That was all Mafia, Italians at that time, that area. I used to go by myself. I guess I passed for a wop or whatever. I never had any problem. Then I organized a posse on my block, Puerto Ricans. We were all going to go to the pool, because we didn't have a swimming pool, and it was hot as hell. I put a group together. There must have been about eight or nine of us, or ten Puerto Ricans. We're coming all colors. I remember my friend Felino, I always remember him saying, 'Them wops are going kick our ass today.' I said, 'What? There's ten of us here. What are they going to do?' I took the whole posse up on 112th and First Avenue. We stood outside, because you had to be in line to get into the swimming pool. I think before twelve o'clock you didn't have to pay or something. While we're there, the Red Wings, that was the Italian gang—they all became gangsters and were mobsters later on—that was the street gang around there, really bad Italian gang, the Red Wings, there must have been about twenty of them, they jumped us with stickball bats and bicycle chains. No guns yet at that time. This was all in the '40s. One of them wrapped a bicycle chain around my neck. I had a scar there for a year. They kicked our ass. There must have been a whole mob of them. That was the third of the escapades, the rumbles that I was involved in where I got my ass kicked three times." He insists the incidents didn't leave him with any residual racial animus.

"But I never held any bitterness toward any of them because later in life, people that promoted my career and helped me and my closest buddies were Black guys and Italian guys. And that's New York." He credits his father for keeping him from a life of crime. Self-educated, he was an informal ombudsman for the neighborhood, always seeking to do good and never taking a dime for his troubles. "He was a prime example of what man could be and should be. I'd be going to Raymond's Pool Room on 106th Street and Madison Avenue. Raymond's Pool Room was the focal point for all the drugs, all the rackets going on in Spanish Harlem at that time. That was where it started. I remember one time I was in there, shooting pool. I must have been about sixteen. He came by and he looked in the window. He spotted me and he knocked on the window and said, 'Come on out here.' I come out, and this place was full of gangsters. He knew that. They used to keep pistols under the table. He said, 'Go inside, finish your game and you'll never ever set foot in this fucking pool room again. You understand?' I said, 'Okay.' I left the pool room. I never went back. That's the kind of guy he was."

The stories go on. How he lost his best friend Orlando to combat in the Korean War; Torres dedicated *Carlito's Way* to Orlando years later. How he got placed into New York District Attorney Frank Hogan's office on the recommendation of notorious political kingmaker Carmine De Sapio. How he and a Black assistant DA were sort of "representation" hires in the prosecution of the notorious late 1950s "Capeman" case, in which Salvador Agron, a gang banger from Spanish Harlem, was accused of killing a couple of Irish-American kids he mistook for members of a rival gang. "They brought me into the case as a showpiece, I guess, a show, because they were all Puerto Ricans, Sal Agron, the Capeman, Antonio Hernandez, the Umbrella Man. They were in the headlines. I'm in the trial with Bill Logan, who's a Black guy who was a great lawyer. He was top assistant DA in the homicide bureau, but he'd been there about twenty years. He tried the case. I couldn't try shit. But I'd be sitting next to him. I guess he wanted the ethnic factor that they would see Puerto Ricans or some shit. But I remember vividly Sal Agron, the killer. He's the one that killed, stabbed two kids. He was seventeen, skinny little, a skinny fuck.

"Luigi Longo, that was his name, he was the court interpreter, because some of the defendants claimed they didn't speak English, which was bullshit. They were Puerto Rican, but they were here. Luigi told me that he had said to Sal Agron, 'See that guy over there, that DA? He's a Puerto Rican just like you. They're not all against you. He's a Puerto Rican.' Sal, he didn't take it that way. They marched them past where I was seated with Logan, past the DA's desk. This is in the fucking courtroom. I think he was in cuffs, yeah. As they're going by, he leans over the table and I'm there with Logan, and he says, '*Alca huete.' Alca huete* is a Puerto Rican idiomatic expression, which means like stool pigeon, flunky, low life. It's a real insult. You get the drift?"

I did. Torres even spelled it out for me. "I remember I jumped up… I was still in Harlem, don't forget…and I said something, the equivalent of your mama's an *alca huete*. I remember he went to throw down and I went into my Golden Gloves dance, too, but they kept us apart. I remember Bill Logan telling me, 'Eddie, stay upstairs tomorrow. Don't come.' Later on they wrote books about this fucking trial."

And Paul Simon wrote a musical, which starred singer and actor Ruben Blades, who also contributed music to the film of *Q&A*. "I consulted with Ruben on that. I went to his house and worked on the part." At the time the musical premiered, protestors objected that the show somehow glorified Agron. I asked Torres what he and his wife thought of it. They more or less shrugged. "It was good."

I said to Torres that the gangs he tangled with in his youth fed directly into the stream of adult criminality he portrays in his *Carlito* books. He remembers when dope came to the neighborhood; "All of a sudden guys I grew up with are driving these big cars."

It was still in the neighborhood when the production of the movie was going into gear. "I took David Koepp to Harlem one day on a Saturday afternoon. We had a little entourage. De Palma was with us. He was dazzled by everything going on in the street. I'm walking them up, I think it was Lexington Avenue, around 110th Street, and there were a lot of junk dealers out there. We're walking past them and this dealer, I didn't know him, but I'd seen him around. I'd see everybody sooner or later. Anyway, he saw Koepp was this young white guy, and he looked at him and he said, 'I got your stash right here, babe.' David's walking with me, he's next to me, and the guy goes on, 'I got your shit right here. You can bet.' Koepp got wide-eyed and nervous, and the dealer saw his reaction and he said, 'Well, how about a Valium?' The motherfucker said, 'How about a Valium?' De Palma was behind us. I said, 'No, listen dude, be cool. We're okay.' I'll never forget that. 'How about a Valium?'"

In an email, David Koepp confirmed the story while allowing he remembers it, "of course," differently. "We'd had a number of tours around the old neighborhood, but on this one I thought I was alone with Hizzoner. In any case, the dealer ran through a number of various drug-of-choice options, as I remember, before looking me up and down and suggesting, 'Valium?' I thought it was very sweet of him to prescribe for me."

Torres told me he would close up his courtroom early to go up to Spanish Harlem and visit Pacino's trailer and run lines with him. "Al wanted to do Carlito as me." Pacino is not Puerto Rican, I interjected, and Torres replied, dryly, good point.

"That caused a bit of static. Tony Gorilla, the legendary Tony Gorilla, Tony Roach. One day I'm in the trailer with Al and who should visit but the legendary Tony Gorilla, Tony Roach, one of the biggest guys on the street. He comes knocking on the door with about three or four guys. Al's security tells me, 'This guy wants to see you, Judge. He says he grew up with you.' I go outside and it's Tony Roach surrounded by his crew. He says, '*Carlito's Way*.' I said, 'What?' 'You're making *Carlito's Way*, right?' I said, 'Yeah, we're shooting. We're in the middle of it.' 'Well, you got this fucking wop playing a Puerto Rican. Why couldn't you get a Puerto Rican?' He's giving me that shit in the street, right on Park Avenue. I said, 'Tony, the biggest star in Hollywood wants to play this role. His name is Al Pacino. You want me to tell the producer, "You can't use him. You got to use…"?' Then I came up with some obscure Puerto Rican names, of bit actors or whatever, '"You got to use," so-and-so, so-and-so, "instead of Al Pacino." Is that what you want?' I remember Tony Roach, he looked at those other guys and they like…" Here Torres shrugged. "That's settled then."

Pacino did have his own ideas early on, including tonsorial ones. He was wearing his hair shoulder length as he prepared for the role. "Michael called the trailer one day. Pacino was sitting in there rehearsing, me and him, because he was going over the lines. I picked up the phone. Michael is in a panic. 'Brian says, he's quitting the film.' I said, 'What are you talking about?' 'He can't stand that fucking hairdo that Al was wearing. He can't stand that. He's going to quit unless he cuts that hair. You got to do something about that.' I said to myself, 'What the fuck am I going to do?' But I said to Michael, 'Okay.' Pacino said, 'What does he want? What does he say?' I said, 'No, no, it's okay. It's okay.' I put the phone down."

It was still early days, and Torres had arranged for Pacino, co-star Sean Penn, De Palma, and some other cast and crew members to come up to a pool room and bar on 106th Street to meet some of the actual gangsters who'd inspired Torres's tale. He could not pull in "One Eyed Benny" or "Crazy Willy," but he did indeed draw Tony Gorilla.

"Let me tell you the kind of people these guys were. Tony Roach's brother Nicky, he murdered the wife of Johnny Gwyn, who was one of my closest friends. When Johnny went up for that murder, his wife Norma, she was fooling around. Beautiful girl. I took her around a lot. I remember what happened was, Nicky was stoned, coked up. There was a party going on and he had his gun out and somebody said, 'Oh, you ain't shit.' Nick said, 'Yeah? Well, I'll show you.' Boom, and he shot her, Norma, Johnny Gwyn's wife, and he killed her. He killed her in front of everybody. I knew it, but nobody ratted up. Nobody gave him up. He beat that fucking rap. But Johnny Gwyn was brought down from prison to the funeral and all that shit. It must have been like twenty years after that, and Johnny Gwyn was paroled. He's with me in this club on 125th Street, run by a friend of mine who got shot in the spine not long thereafterwards and was paralyzed. Nicky was there with his brother, Tony, and these other guys at the other side of the bar, and they sent over a drinks.

"Now Johnny Gwyn's wife was murdered by this fucking guy, Nick. Johnny said, 'Take those drinks back.' Now, I was shitting green then. I said, 'No, no sir.' Somebody's going to get killed and I'm going to be in the fucking middle of it. This on 125th in Harlem. They came over. I don't know. Tony Gorilla came over. This was, 'Listen, Johnny, this was a mistake. It was a big—' 'Get away from me,' Johnny said. Johnny always carried a pistol. What am I going to do, dive under the table? I don't know what the fuck I was going to do. I don't know how, but Johnny didn't kill him, and Johnny killed a lot of people.

"And now Tony Roach, brother of Nicky Roach, is having drinks with Al Pacino and other Hollywood luminaries. We're sitting around the table with Sean Penn and Pacino—the bomb! It's hard to believe these people were all with them, but there we were. And I got an idea. I pointed to Al, with his hair down to his shoulders, and I said to Tony, 'What do you think of Al's hairdo? What do you think? Tony, how would that work upstate?' Hah! 'How would it work upstate?' Tony looked Al up and down and said, 'The motherfucker would be wearing ballerina slippers.' That's what he said. 'The motherfucker would be wearing ballerina slippers.' Pacino smelled a rat and he's looking at me. And I'm going like, 'I don't know what the fuck this came from.' The next day the hair was gone. That's a true story."

David Koepp was working under a deal with Universal when he was approached by Martin Bregman to work on *Carlito's Way*. "Marty was an extremely effective producer, and there aren't a lot of those around anymore," he recalls. "He was adept to dealing with the studio. He wasn't afraid to mix it up with the director, but he would always back the director. He was good with material and, in this case, Al Pacino respected him, and that helped move things forward. By the time I worked with him, though, he had a tendency to shut down what could be really constructive conversations. My least favorite go-to phrase of his was, 'You're dead wrong and I'll tell you why,' which he usually offered when you were only about a third of the way through the thought you were trying to convey. But I was young, I was in my late twenties, was probably twenty-nine when I was doing this. He was not. He'd done a million things." At the time *Carlito's Way* was set up at Trans-World, but Koepp had an out of his Universal deal that he could exercise if he wished, and once he read the two books in Torres's *Carlito* saga—*Carlito's Way* and *After Hours*—he did indeed wish. "They were so specific and the voice was so vivid and the characters were vivid. Obviously, whoever wrote it knew these people. I felt unafraid to take on something that was way out of my wheelhouse, because I knew that what I was going to bring was largely structural and cinematic, but the characters were all there and vivid. But I did say there's no way I can do it if the author of the books doesn't want to talk to me, because I need him and I need him to like me, and I need him to take me around and tell me stuff. Fortunately he did. I speak Spanish and was at the time married to an Argentine woman, and Edwin loved that. So we got along very well.

"We did a few drafts, quite a few drafts. It took a while. We got off to a very good start. My first draft went over well, but it needed a lot of work. So Marty had a lot of very specific thoughts about what would make it 'street.' I got tired of hearing about what's 'street' and what isn't, and at one point I was very cheeky and said, 'Marty, your street is Park Avenue.' He said, 'Well, it wasn't always,' which is true. So then we started meeting with directors and Brian was his early and favorite choice, but the feedback he was getting from, I guess it would've been Marty Bauer, his agent at the time, was he's not doing another gangster movie. Finally, Marty got him to read it, and Brian was suitably impressed with the script and said, 'Okay, well, maybe this gang.'"

At the time De Palma was embarking on *Carlito's Way*, he said it was a "very conventional" movie. "Otherwise you find you get reviews like 'it doesn't make sense,' 'it's ridiculous,' or 'it's laughable.'" It's true that the movie plays things straight, but it also has a time structure that's not entirely linear—the narrative of the picture plays via Carlito's dying flashback—and the movie is dynamic in a way that only De Palma could make it. It being made in 1993, it had the weight of ten years' worth of post-*Scarface* gangster movies on top of it. Koepp found himself leaning on certain conventions unconsciously.

"Al, while being very sweet, was concerned about every particular point. His attitude was, 'This is what I do and I can't fuck it up. I've played gangsters before and I got to get this just right.' And he likes to rehearse. Sean Penn had strong opinions and always felt kind of maltreated, maybe that's how he feels in life, I don't know. But I think he always felt like he was being treated as second fiddle. And in a sense he is. I mean, his name's not in the title, the other guy's is. So we rehearsed every weekend through shooting, through a fourteen-week shoot. Every movie has one, but there was a scene that became the bone of contention, which was the scene when Carlito goes to the hospital. And as initially written, it was about six lines.

"He tells Kleinfeld"—the lawyer played by Penn—"'You betrayed me.' And that's really fucked up. And he takes the bullets out of the gun without us knowing and leaves. It's a scene that both the actors really fixated on as the key to everything. I rewrote it dozens of times. It got six pages, it got three pages, and no one could ever be quite satisfied with it."

Pacino became frustrated and farmed the scene out to another writer, a playwright friend. Koepp is slightly embarrassed to relate how poorly he took this attempted revision. "I called the playwright and I had words with the playwright." For the purposes of this anecdote, he is designated "Ira."

"Then ten minutes later, Al called me and said, 'Did you tell Ira you were going to kill him if he ever rewrote one of your scenes again?' And I said, 'I did. But I was very upset, Al, I was...' And he just sort of sighed in a very world-weary way and said, 'David, you can't tell people you're going to kill them.' And I wanted to say, 'You of all people...'"

"You were in your twenties," I said to Koepp, trying to sympathize.

"I know I was. I've settled down a lot since."

The problem was not yet solved, in any event. "So I've now got dozens of versions of this scene. I came to rehearsal and they read one, and I thought it was beautiful. I was like, 'That's the one.' And Al said, 'I don't know.' And I said, 'Why? It's great. What did you not like?' And he said, 'This part here where I tell him he broke my heart.' I said, 'Yeah, that's the best part.' He said, 'I said something very similar to that in another movie.' I was like, 'Oh, shit.'

"I had just written the Fredo scene in *The Godfather Part II* without even realizing it. So that one didn't make it. Then it came to the day to shoot. I was talking to Brian and an AD came out and said, 'Al wants to see you guys in his dressing room.' So he had *not* come out to do the scene. Brian and I went to his dressing room and he said, 'I think I figured out the problem with the hospital scene.' And we said, 'Oh, okay.' And he said, 'Carlito would never go to the hospital.' And. Long pause. Brian finally says, 'Go to hell, you *built* the hospital.' The scene they shot was strikingly similar to the very first version of it."

16

SAY GOOD NIGHT TO THE BAD GUY

"The idea of progress is a secular version of the Christian belief in providence," the commentator and philosopher John Gray writes in the foreword to his 2003 book *Straw Dogs: Thoughts on Humans and Other Animals*. "That is why among the ancient pagans it was unknown. Belief in progress has another source. In science, the growth of knowledge is cumulative. But human life as a whole is not a cumulative activity; what is gained in one generation may be lost in the next." Gray's musings, which bear some similarity to those of Robert Musil in his unfinished novel *The Man Without Qualities*, conclude that the idea of progress is a chimera, and the communally held notion that knowledge liberates us is laughable. Humankind, Gray holds, remains ever "prey to every kind of folly."

Had the overt purpose of *Scarface* been a didactic one, the state of the world forty years after its release would stand as powerful testimony against the idea of human progress. Although persons of a certain age and disposition might, from experience, shudder at the mere thought of a bump of cocaine, the drug is still very much with us. According to the United Nations Office on Drugs and Crime's *Global Report on Cocaine 2023*, "The COVID-19 pandemic had a disruptive effect on drug markets. With international travel severely curtailed, producers struggled to get their product to market. Night clubs and bars were shut as officials ramped up their attempts to control the virus, causing demand to slump for drugs like cocaine that are often associated with those settings. However, the most recent data suggests this slump has had little impact on longer-term trends. The global supply of cocaine is at record levels. Almost 2,000 tons was produced in 2020, continuing a dramatic uptick in manufacture that began in 2014, when the total was less than half of today's levels. The surge is partly a result of an expansion in coca bush cultivation, which doubled between 2013 and 2017, hit a peak in 2018, and rose sharply again in 2021. But it is also due to improvements in the process of conversion from coca bush to cocaine hydrochloride." In June 2023, reporter Mitchell Prothero wrote for *Vice* about the expansion of the cocaine market into heretofore relatively unaffected sectors of Europe: "[T]his business has burst from the underworld to the streets in this wealthy part of northern Europe, where overall crime rates are amongst the lowest in the world." We need not comment on the current prevalence of guns and gun violence in the United States.

Still, *Scarface* was, ultimately, not a didactic film. Its numerous dimensions contain of course a dimension of distance, a deliberate withholding of certain kinds of depth, and an occasionally detectable sardonic tone. But what it aims for is phenomenological intensity—a spectacle!—and it achieves it.

One thing that makes De Palma so confounding for some of his critics is an ostensible ideological inconsistency. De Palma's earliest movies did not overtly espouse but certainly examined a radical politics; *Scarface* and *The Untouchables*, on another hand, could be seen as out-and-out refutations of the liberal humanism that John Gray so disdains. Mamet's script for *The Untouchables*, written well before Mamet announced his shift from political liberalism to some peculiar species of conservatism, is practically an endorsement of fascist authoritarianism. The humanism of *Carlito's Way* derives from Torres and Pacino, abetted by Bregman and Koepp; De Palma allows it to function in the film's atmosphere because he's keeping faithful to the source, and because he knows it moves audiences. Luis Buñuel once stated that while he did a lot of work for hire in the Mexican phase of his filmmaking career, he never once made a film that went against his own moral principles. And despite the contradictions that teem in his work, I think that De Palma could credibly make the same claim. Because De Palma understands the potential for ideological mess that cinema affords its creators. And that whatever a movie may "say," it is saying it as a movie. The form itself contains a lot of escape hatches. As crowd-pleasing as the hooray-for-the-cops bits in *The Untouchables* are, the movie-movieness of the picture allows viewers so inclined to take it as a kind of kidding on the square. Because it's De Palma, *The Untouchables* can feel like an impeccable reproduction of a fascism-endorsing work rather than an actual fascism-endorsing work.

I needn't tell you that such considerations are indeed what you can call rarefied and have little to do with how most of the people who've made *Scarface* an iconic film process the movie. The internet made *Scarface* a meme, because of course it did. Around the time that energy was revving up, the culture critic Ken Tucker published a book called *Scarface Nation*, which set out to examine, as he put it in his introduction, "a series of loops and twists" delineating the "disruptive saga" of the movie itself and its subsequent reputation. The tale "takes off in a number of directions, making its mark in other media (video games, novelizations, TV shows, comic books), in politics, and most pervasively in movies." This was a book I myself avoided while composing most of this look at *Scarface*. Anxiety of influence and all that. But Tucker has ever been a searching and astute critic, and this account packs in a lot of insight.

The sports and pop culture enthusiast Shea Serrano is one of the most prominent social media boosters of the De Palma picture. On Twitter in 2020, he called *Scarface* the most rewatchable Pacino movie. A snarky respondent to a Serrano tweet in 2022 invented this exchange between Serrano and perhaps himself: "My favorite movies are *Scarface* and *The Godfather*."

"Oh yeah? Well my favorite foods are lobster...and Skittles."

Promoting his 2019 book *Movies...and Other Things*, Serrano assembled some pals and made a video called *15 Best Gangster Movie Moments*. (I discussed this feature at some length in my book about *Goodfellas*, and I don't want to belabor my points too much here, but duty demands some attention be paid.) Inspired by his work in sports journalism and bracketing, Serrano has some rules for enumerating such moments, including one eliminating Robert De Niro, because he's just too definitive a gangster portrayer. There is also what he calls "The Kleinfeld Rule." (Which comes from *Carlito's Way*, although to say just how is kind of a spoiler.) "Simply put, this says that we're not allowed to select any moment where a primary guy dies. In it. For example. Scarface at the end of *Scarface* he gets shot in the back, he's dead. You cannot pick that. However, something like *American Gangster*, Denzel Washington, when he shoots Idris Elba in the head, you can pick that one if you want."

This does not rule out *Scarface* altogether. And so, coming in at number six, "the Success Montage" from *Scarface*, as it is deemed. We watch a little of it with the gang. Hey, it's the tiger! "I really like the Success Montage the most out of *Scarface* because of what it seems to represent," Serrano says. "What I mean is the movie itself is about a hundred and seventy minutes long. And the first part of the movie, where he's building himself up into this icon, takes about a hundred and three minutes. And that makes sense because we're going from the sort of immigrant, just getting into America, he's just gotta build himself all the way up until he becomes this drug kingpin. And then we have the montage. And then the third part of the movie. And the third part of the movie takes about sixty minutes. And that's when everything falls apart. That makes sense." Yes it does. "The upward trajectory takes the longest. The downward trajectory is a little bit shorter. About sixty minutes. And the Success Montage, which is the only part of the movie where everything goes exactly right"—and which, Serrano here continues to neglect to mention, features a *tiger*—"is only sixty seconds long. And that seems to imply that when you're a gangster, the best part of this is gonna be for a very small very short period of time. I love that they snuck this sort of moviemaking trick in there"—right, this is what that Russian dude Andrei Tarkovsky called "sculpting in time."

"Also it's just fun to watch Tony Montana just, own a fucking tiger?" FINALLY.

Serrano is Mexican-American, and he has no complaint about Pacino playing a Cuban character. *Carlito's Way* is not mentioned in the video, except in relation to the Kleinfeld Rule. Arguments about representation in the arts, and especially about white American performers taking roles of specific ethnicities not their own, are today so common as to be set-your-watch predictable. And they've grown ever more specific and persnickety. Complaints are not limited to the choices of white Americans. There was widespread criticism of Javier Bardem, an actor from Spain, playing the Cuban bandleader and comic actor Desi Arnaz in a film about Arnaz and Lucille Ball in the 2021 film *Being the Ricardos*. Only two decades before, Bardem was praised for his, you know, "courage" in portraying the gay poet Reinaldo Arenas—you may recall, the guy who was on the Mariel boatlift, evicted from his country on account of his sexual orientation—in Julian Schnabel's 2000 *Before Night Falls*. A gay Cuban poet, that is.

For some Cuban-Americans, *Scarface* remains a thorn in the side. In 2018, Monica Castillo, a writer with whom I am friendly, wrote "How *Scarface* Transformed the Way Cubans Were Perceived in the U.S." for the website *ReMezcla*. After recounting her own experience of the movie—for some time Castillo was enjoined from watching it by her Cuban mother, and once she did see it, it made her "skin crawl," and continues to do so—she quotes several sources. One Cuban drug dealer, speaking on the condition of anonymity, goes the "better to be feared" route of estimation, saying that the image of Cubans had changed from "cleaners or superintendents" to that of "hard-core, badass drug dealers."

Filmmaker LeAnne Russell told Castillo, "Seeing and hearing Al Pacino imitate a Cuban accent, phrases, and mannerisms in such a cartoonish, blatantly culturally insensitive way really made me wonder why so many Miami Cubans find pride in this film." Her disapprobation reaches a level of near-piety as she continues: "For Cuban-born actor Steven Bauer—also in the film—to dismiss what he calls 'old-school Cubans' who took offense to the depiction of Cuban refugees in the film and say that it is 'only a movie' is naive and sad to me." (I thought of dangling this quote before Bauer for my second interview with him, but thought better of it, and in any case I've got a pretty good idea of how he might have responded.) Others in the piece discuss Pacino/Montana's boisterousness, his braggadocio. Castillo concludes, "As with everything else with the Cuban community, it's complicated."

These accounts do raise the question, in my mind at least, as to whether Pacino actually *leads* with ethnicity in his performance. Given his vocalizations, it's difficult to argue that he doesn't. And certainly Muni's immigrant notes in the 1932 *Scarface* are pronounced, and Pacino was deliberately emulating Muni's register. But when I replay Pacino's performance, it's the swagger and the slump, the physicality, that seems the most salient point of the portrayal. Of course, it probably need not be stated, I'm a white male (of Italian and Irish extraction, although quite honestly I've never cared much about the stereotypes associated with either ethnic group; I do remember in my childhood one of my uncles, a Polish-American, getting it with both barrels in the joke department from both the red sauce and corned beef components of the clan), and so I can't claim to feel what Cuban-Americans might. The hardcore Pacino-ites who packed the 92nd Street Y offered no questions on the matter of representation. The fact of his performance, and of his performance as a Puerto Rican in *Carlito's Way*, is what it is. (In 2022, the Colombia-born American actor John Leguizamo allowed that he felt some discomfort during the shooting of *Carlito's Way*, in which he had a supporting role: "I know he's trying and he's a great actor, so brilliant, he was my hero," he said of Pacino. "But it was odd, man. It's an odd experience to be a Latin man in a Latin story written by a Latin man and the lead guy's a white guy pretending to be Puerto Rican.")

Reflecting on his father's relationship with Al Pacino, Michael Bregman said, "It was hot and cold. You know, it was a hot and cold relationship. And it's a shame because if you look at the movies they made together, those were just better pictures. But they had a confrontational relationship at times. I think they would have been both better off working together more often. *Carlito's Way* is the last thing they ever did together." Michael himself gave filmmaking a shot with the 2005 direct-to-video prequel, *Carlito's Way: The Rise to Power*, which starred Jay Hernandez, a Monticello-born actor of Mexican descent, in the role of young Carlito. Bregman, possibly finding filmmaking a less than congenial overall pursuit, now works in real estate.

Brian De Palma's last film as of this writing was 2019's *Domino*, on which he clashed with the European producers. Watching the picture, you can understand why—the ambitions of this paranoid thriller came up short against the means De Palma had at his disposal. Shortly prior to that film's release, my friend Charles Ardai at Hard Case Crime published *Are Snakes Necessary?*, a novel De Palma wrote with his partner Susan Lehman, a former *New York Times* reporter. The title comes from the book that Henry Fonda's character is so absorbed in before he is seduced by Barbara Stanwyck in Preston Sturges's immortal long-con screwball comedy *The Lady Eve.* The plot is typically twisted, the perspective cosmically sardonic. My communications with the director suggest strongly that he's highly frustrated that he's not directing at the moment. One hopes that circumstances improve to the extent that he's able to get in the batter's box again.

Pacino remains Pacino, albeit in an increasingly eccentric way. Karina Longworth's treatment of his career, *Anatomy of an Actor: Al Pacino*, published in 2013, ends with a consideration of his farcical self-portrayal in the 2011 Adam Sandler comedy *Jack and Jill.* "The question of selling out reverberates throughout *Jack and Jill* on both a narrative level and as meta-text. Pacino's very participation in the movie could be (and was, by many journalists) considered a sellout, and an unusually blatant one; the text of the film itself seems to roll its eyes at anyone high and mighty enough to act as though a sellout, in today's corporate culture, is still anathema. Indeed, it was interesting to see third parties suggest that Pacino should feel shame for taking the part, when Pacino himself has historically been incredibly open about the compromises inherent in maintaining his lifestyle—he's always contextualized his initial return to the screen after his mid-1980s hiatus as compelled by the need to pay bills—as well as the fact that even he, one of our greatest living actors, cannot always pay those bills by making quality pictures." (Of course, lifestyle is in many respects a matter of choice, and in 2023, at the age of eighty-three, Pacino made the choice to father a child, his fourth.)

One can lament that "they" no longer make movies like *Scarface* or *Carlito's Way*, but then again, Martin Scorsese's *The Irishman*, in which Pacino, as Jimmy Hoffa, gave a performance as electric as anything he's ever done, was released only a few years ago. (*The Irishman* does have its detractors, but as the saying goes, real heads know.) So there's always hope, or something like it.

For the 1983 *Scarface*, Robert Warshow's words, first published in 1948, hold as true in their odd way as they did for the 1932 *Scarface*: "At bottom, the gangster is doomed because he is under the obligation to succeed, not because the means he employs are unlawful. In the deeper layers of the modern consciousness, all means are unlawful, every attempt to succeed is an act of aggression, leaving one alone and guilty and defenseless among enemies: one is *punished* for success. This is our intolerable dilemma: that failure is a kind of death and success is evil and dangerous, is—ultimately—impossible. The effect of the gangster film is to embody this dilemma in the person of the gangster and resolve it by his death. The dilemma is resolved because it is his death, not ours. We are safe; for the moment, we can acquiesce in our failure, we can choose to fail."

★ ★ ★ ★ ★

NOTES/SOURCES

Prologue

"Five years of Prohibition": H.L Mencken, cited in, among other articles, Weber, Will-Mark, "Raise a Glass to FDR & Repeal Day," *USA TODAY*, December 5, 2014

"When Prohibition was introduced": John D. Rockefeller, letter to *New York Times*, June 12, 1932

"seminal 1948 essay": Warshow, Robert, "The Gangster As Tragic Hero," in *The Immediate Experience: Movies, Comics, the Theatre and Other Aspects of Popular Culture*, 2001, Cambridge: Harvard University Press, p. 97

"Over the years Capone": Okrent, Daniel, *Last Call: The Rise and Fall of Prohibition*, 2010, New York: Scribner, p. 365

"Cocaine: The Champagne of Drugs": Crittenden, Amy and Ruby, Michael, *New York Times Magazine*, September 1, 1974

Chapter One

"I never once had one of those successful hits and thought I was God": Thompson, Anne, "The Filmmaker Series: Brian De Palma," *Premiere*, reprinted in *Brian De Palma: Interviews*, Knapp, Lawrence F., editor, 2003, Mississippi: University of Mississippi Press, p. 157

"He was a bit surprised": *De Palma*, feature documentary directed by Noah Baumbach and Jake Paltrow, 2015, distributor A24

"more important than anything else in 'Blow Out'": Canby, Vincent, "Travolta Stars in 'Blow Out'," *New York Times*, July 24, 1981

"De Palma had seen directors come and go": Tarantino, Quentin, *Cinema Speculation*, 2022, New York: HarperCollins, p. 185

"The death-dealing, all-voyeurism-all-the-time world": Kenny, Glenn, "'Domino' review: All Voyeurism, All the Time," *New York Times*, May 30, 2019

"a disappointed revolutionary's professional interest in power": Christgau, Robert, Consumer Guide, at http://www.robertchristgau.com/cg.php

"I found myself on talk shows": Vallely, Jean, "Brian De Palma: The New Hitchcock or Just Another Rip-Off?" *Rolling Stone*, October 1980; reprinted in Knapp, p. 69

"As soon as I get this dignity from *Scarface*": Hirschberg, Lynn, "Brian De Palma's Death Wish," *Esquire*, January 1984; reprinted in Knapp, p. 82

Chapter Two

"who the hell is Howard Hawks": Wollen, Peter, "Who the Hell Is Howard Hawks," in *Paris Hollywood: Writings on Film*, 2002, London: Verso, p. 55

"a boy of privilege": McCarthy, Todd, *Howard Hawks: The Silver Fox of Hollywood*, 1997, New York: Grove Press, p. 35

"It may be perverse": Wood, Robin, *Howard Hawks*, new edition, 2006, Michigan: Wayne State University Press, p. 52

"Well, Ben, I've got an idea": McBride, Joseph, *Hawks on Hawks*, 1982, California: University of California Press, p. 45

"As reworked by Hecht": McCarthy, p. 137

"It was after midnight": Trail, Armitage, *Scarface*, 2019 reprint, New York: Dean Street Press, pp. 41–42

"The original story": McBride, pp. 45-46

"The movies are one of the bad habits that corrupted our country": Hecht, Ben, *A Child of the Century*, 1982 edition, New York: Primus, p. 458

"a thousand dollars a day": Hecht, p. 486

"The work I did for Hughes": Hecht, pp. 486-487

"my favorite picture": McBride, p. 43

"height of the gangster craze": McCarthy, p. 153

"He remembered the film vividly all his life": Wollen, p. 57

"*Scarface* is a passionate, strong, archaic photographic miracle": Farber, Manny, "Howard Hawks," in *Negative Space*, 1998, New York: De Capo, p. 25. The cover of this particular edition is a very attractive still from Hawks's film, showing Karen Morley's Poppy looking confused and slightly bereft after being abandoned mid-dance by Tony, who has become enraged at seeing his sister in the nightclub dancing with another man. The image from the still, however, does not occur in the film proper.

"the frightening discrepancy": Wood, p. 54

Chapter Three

"I love what Wallenda said": Grobel, Lawrence, *Al Pacino: In Conversation with Lawrence Grobel*, 2006, New York: Simon Spotlight Entertainment, p. 50

"We were a public company": Hawley, Tom, "Martin Bregman," in *Making Films in New York*, December 1975

"you got your midget": Evans, Robert, *The Kid Stays in the Picture*, 1994, New York: Hachette

"the Italian biographers": Kezich, Tullio, and Levantesi, Alessandra, *Dino: The Life and Films of Dino De Laurentiis*, 2004, New York: Miramax

"long-discounted": Yule, Andrew, *Life on the Wire: The Life and Art of Al Pacino*, 1991, New York: Donald I. Fine, Inc., p. 75

"I was impressed with his busy secretaries": Stone, Oliver, *Chasing the Light*, 2020, New York: First Mariner Books, p. 106

"Bugsy Siegel": Stone, p. 111

"Stories had it": Stone, p. 119

"It was a series of events": Yule, p. 147

"I've had screaming fights with Marty": Farber, Stephen, "Martin Bregman Juggles Projects to Make a Movie," *New York Times*, July 19, 1987

"He was going to make Cornelia Sharpe a star": Author conversation with Barbara De Fina, November 18, 2022

"It was a difficult film to write": Guarino, Ann, "Riding a Hot Streak," *New York Daily News*, November 8, 1976

"Driving down Sunset Boulevard": Yule, p. 207

"Most people don't know what a producer does": Kissel, Howard, "Producer Bregman Knows His Role," *New York Newsday*, September 14, 1982

Chapter Four

"when Grobel asked him something similar": Grobel, p. 45. The exchange with Grobel went thusly: "Before *Serpico* you were up for Best Supporting Actor for *The Godfather.* Do you feel you were in the wrong category?" "Oh sure. Definitely. That was outrageous. It's things like that that gets you a little sour. I decided to pass the ceremonies by. There were certain people around me who wanted to write a letter, who wanted me to announce that I would not accept the nomination. I would always say, 'Let it go. Let it go. Don't make waves.' But then, even though I didn't go, I watched it on TV. I felt bad. I didn't care for that kind of contradiction."

"Are you kidding me?" Al Pacino at the 92nd Street Y, April 21, 2023, Author's notes

"I think Al would like to take *Scarface* off his filmography": Author interview, Michael Bregman, July 15, 2022 "the whole role dwells in his eyes": Butler, Isaac, *The Method*, 2022, New York: Bloomsbury, pp. 324-325

"When Pacino was finally offered the part": Lahr, John, "Al Pacino's Driving Force," *The New Yorker*, September 8, 2014

"Al responded to the idea…": Winkler, Irwin, *A Life in Movies*, 2019, New York: Abrams, pp. 113-114

"Sometimes people who are not really meant to be together…": Grobel, p. 91

"did very well on cable": Grobel, p. 93

Chapter Five

"Well, Brian had been a very successful horror director…" and so on: Author interview, Oliver Stone, October 13, 2022

"the film is more important than any single one of us": Zoller Seitz, Matt, *The Oliver Stone Experience*, 2018, New York: Abrams, p. 116

Chapter Six

"Spiegel states": Spiegel, Maura, *Sidney Lumet: A Life*, 2018, New York: St. Martin's Press, p. 286

"Photographically, this is one of the most interesting pictures I've done": Lumet, Sidney, *Making Movies*, 1995, New York: Alfred A. Knopf, p. 87

"Apart from the corny elements": Yule, pp. 210-211

"I walked away from Sidney": Yule, p. 211

"When Brian and I first started talking about it": Author interview, David Rabe, January 18, 2023

Chapter Seven

"I did not have a lot of work under my belt for sure," and so on: Author interview, Michelle Pfeiffer, April 24, 2023

"I remember Al and I had dinner one night": Weinraub, Bernard, "Michelle Pfeiffer's Blue-Plate Special," *New York Times*, October 6, 1991

Chapter Eight

"I sat almost in the second row," and so on: Author interviews, Steven Bauer, January 18, 2023, and July 6, 2023

"When the movie came out": Kenny, Glenn, "'America the Beautiful': Treat Williams and William Forsythe Remember Sergio Leone and 'Once Upon a Time in America'," RogerEbert.com, October 7, 2014

Chapter Nine

"I've never talked about this before," Persall, Steve, "Scarface Scabs Remain," *Tampa Bay Times*, April 4, 2008

Perez letter: "Miami Official Objects to Cuban Refugee Film," Jaynes, Gregory, *New York Times*, August 24, 1982

"a very stupid man": Houston, Frank, "Scarface in Miami," *Miami New Times*, April 3, 2008

"definitive quote from Ned Tanen,""Getting Tough with Scarface," Beck, Marilyn, *New York Daily News*, August 30, 1982

"they chased me out of the state": Trachtenberg, J.A., "De Palma: Paying the Price for 'Scarface'," *Women's Wear Daily*, September 15, 1983

Alonzo quotes on *Scarface*: Cleaver, Thomas McKelvey, *American Cinematographer*, December 1983

"All right! He's hired. OK?": Ziesmer, Jerry, *Ready When You Are, Mr. Coppola, Mr. Spielberg, Mr. Crowe*, Maryland: Scarecrow Press, 2003, pp. 390–400

"Brian was a cold man": Stone, pp. 176–181

"De Palma's naps were legendary": Salamon, Julie, *The Devil's Candy*, New York: Houghton Mifflin, 1991, p. 162

"It was a funny thing," and so on: Author interview, Lou Stroller, August 2, 2022

Chapter Ten

"the live adult entertainment emporium called the Pussycat": If you are interested in the author's own experience of the Pussycat, a piece called "Going Through the Motions" in the literary magazine *Black Clock*, issue number 19, will fill you in a bit.

"There were peepshows all over the place": Author interview, Bill Pankow, November 1, 2022

"split screen can be interesting": Hirsch, Paul, *A Long Time Ago in a Cutting Room Far, Far Away*, Chicago: University of Chicago Press, 2020, p. 6

"A director deserves": Hirsch, p. 166

"I'd worked for Jerry as apprentice and assistant": Author interview, David Ray, September 12, 2022

"a 2022 article in *Mixdown*": Macniece, Sam, "Gear Rundown: Scarface Soundtrack by Giorgio Moroder," *Mixdown*, December 5, 2022

"And now we've moved": Commentary by Paul Schrader, *Hardcore* Blu Ray, Twilight Time

"They had an IB Technicolor print": Author interview, Jay Cocks, April 13, 2023

"I started very early to play piano": Author interview, Sylvester Levay, June 1, 2023

Chapter Eleven

"the whole thing was kind of exhausting": Author interview, Bill Pankow, November 1, 2022

"Malibu": Author interview, Jay Cocks, April 13, 2023

"The hardest thing": Author interview, Lou Stroller, August 2, 2022

"The X ruling": Harmetz, Aljean, "Movie 'Scarface' Receives X Rating," *New York Times*, October 30, 1983

"'I'm ecstatic'": Harmetz, "'Scarface' Gets an R Rating on Appeal," *New York Times*, November 9, 1983

Chapter Twelve

"Before we boarded": Arenas, Reinaldo, *Before Night Falls*, New York: Viking, 1993, p. 283

"*Scarface* was so ubiquitous": Servin, Jim, "Harris Yulin: The Outlaw," *The Purist*, Fall 2014

"All right, you say you believe in indiscriminate violence": Jones, Kent, "Hail the Conquering Hero: Andrew Sarris," *Film Comment*, May-June 2005

"article on the *Forbes* website": St. John, Allen, "The Guns of Breaking Bad," *Forbes*, August 23, 2013

"Patricia Norris recalls": Tucker, Ken, *Scarface Nation: The Ultimate Gangster Movie and How It Changed America*, New York: St. Martin's Griffin, 2008, p. 60

Chapter Thirteen

"I hung out in Central Park": Author interview, Michael Bregman, July 15, 2022

"the most stylish and provocative": Canby, Vincent, "Al Pacino Stars in 'Scarface,'" *New York Times*, December 9, 1983

"grandiose modern morality play,": review, *Variety*, November 3, 1983, taglined "Cart," presumably Todd McCarthy

"Kurt Vonnegut walked out after 30 minutes": McMurran, Kristen, Hutchings, David, and Lansden, Pamela, "The Famous Turn Out (and Some Are Turned Off By) the Bicoastal Previews of Al Pacino's Bloody 'Scarface,'" *People Magazine*, December 19, 1983

"So much more and event than a movie": Sarris, Andrew, *Scarface* review, *Village Voice*, December 20, 1983

"And Frank's henchman": Kael, Pauline, "A De Palma Movie for People Who Don't Like De Palma Movies," *The New Yorker*, December 18, 1983 (the online version changes the title of the piece to "The Fake Force of Tony Montana")

"The entire emphasis is on Tony": Denby, David, *New York Magazine*, December 9, 1983

"It is boring": Gelmis, Joseph, *Scarface* review, *Newsday*, December 9, 1983

"Explosive": Corliss, Richard, "Say Good Night to the Bad Guy," *Time*, December 9, 1983

"The violence is endless": Reed, Rex, "Pacino Leads Pointless Bloodbath in *Scarface*": *New York Post*, December 9, 1983

"facile, flashy cynicism": Kaufmann, Stanley, *Scarface* review, *The New Republic*, December 1983

"How Should We React to Violence," Canby, Vincent, *New York Times*, December 11, 1983

"shot out of his seat": Fagen, Cynthia R., "Three Knifed at Flick as *Scarface* Bleeds," *New York Post*, December 13, 1983

"Scarface Died for My Sins": Fernandez, Enrique, *Village Voice*, December 13, 1983

"There are many Cuban-Americans": Perez, Miguel, "*Scarface* Murders a Reputation," *New York Daily News*, January 15, 1984

Chapter Fourteen

"They said it would help promotion": Dutka, Elaine, "The Healing of 'Scarface,'" *Los Angeles Times*, September 17, 2003

"I'm aware of *Scarface*": Author interview, Harry Allen, June 29, 2023

Chapter Fifteen

"working a lot": *De Palma*, Baumbach and Paltrow

"I was never a big fan of the television series": Art Linson, *A Pound of Flesh*, New York: Avon Books, 1993, p. 65

"Dave, don't you think?": Linson, p. 67

"tell that greasy bastard": Linson, p. 75

"Because if I kill off Sean Connery": Linson, p. 127

"I wanted to use Don Johnson…it's going to be expensive": Baumbach and Paltrow

"I was born in 1931": Author interview, Edwin Torres, July 3, 2023

"Marty was an extremely effective producer": Author interview, David Koepp, April 19, 2023

Chapter Sixteen

"The idea of progress": John Gray, *Straw Dogs*, New York: Farrar, Straus, and Groux, 2003, pp. xiii-xiv

"The COVID 19 pandemic" *Global Report on Cocaine 2023: Local Dynamics, Global Challenges*, United Nations Office on Drugs and Crime. https://www.unodc.org/documents/data-and-analysis/cocaine/Global_cocaine_report_2023.pdf

ACKNOWLEDGMENTS

Joseph Veltre and Peter Joseph, agent and editor, the starters on this book and on my prior book, excellent men who provide superb support and who are also great company. I'm very lucky to have them as collaborators. I also owe a lot of gratitude to Joseph's and Peter's respective staffs. Eden Railsback in Peter's office has been, almost literally, a life saver. A very long time ago I worked on a possible book about this film with Jud Laghi, and while we didn't get it off the ground, I'm grateful for his belief and encouragement at that time.

Brian De Palma gave his support and time and insight, without which I could never have started, let alone finished, this project. Jay Cocks, a mutual friend, was sometimes my bridge to Brian, as well as a remarkable interview subject. My monthly lunches with Jay and my great friend Farran Smith Nehme are always fun, enlightening, and sustaining. Farran has been a stalwart supporter of all my enterprises.

My wife, Claire, is my great love and is so close to the work she deserves a co-byline.

My friend Davitt Sigerson is a tireless and inventive consigliere in all matters, including writing. Our friends B. and D., who for certain reasons might prefer not to be named in this text, have also provided wise counsel. Ethan Iverson, crime fiction aficionado (among other things), helped me flesh a few things out.

Steven Bauer became a friend during the long months we were negotiating interview times. Michelle Pfeiffer and her publicists Annett Wolf and Jessica Mallari were extremely helpful. There is nobody in the world like Oliver Stone. Thanks to him, and thanks to Matt Zoller Seitz for getting us together. (And much else.) Sylvester Levay was kind and helpful. I owe Tim Greiving, whose liner notes on the two-CD *Scarface* score (on La-La Land Records) are incredibly astute and informative. Gary Gersh and Stan Rosenfield: Thank you for trying. Thanks also to Lou Stroller, David Ray, William Pankow. David Koepp was a great help from the moment I reached out to him and well after we concluded the formal interview. Michael Bregman is a great guy and I forgive him for dispensing with his father's archives. Justice Edwin Torres is one of the most amazing men living on this earth.

There was a lot of loss in my life while I was writing this book. My father, my oldest friend, and my mother-in-law are commemorated in the book's dedication. I also mourn Nicole Busch, who compelled me to sit through *The Rocky Horror Picture Show* at midnight on dozens of occasions in 1978—she was working the concession stand at the Oritani Theater in Hackensack—and Debra Buhay, who said "It reminded me I need to do my laundry" after we saw a midnight show of *Eraserhead* at the Waverly Theater (now the IFC Center) in late 1979.

Ron Goldberg and Joe Mulligan, Stewart Wolpin, Colin Ungaro, John Fahey, and Kenny Altman are old friends who serve in good stead to this day. Ron in particular. He and the late Joseph

Failla is/was the biggest De Palma head[s] in my life. I think we all saw *Scarface* together and one of us—it wasn't me—actually did guffaw at the Hawks/Hecht dedication at the movie's end. It was really the timing of the dedication, I think, but what are you going to do. I thank my brother and sister, and all the Kenny and Petrosino families, who've lived with my preoccupations for years and have been pretty supportive for the most part, I must say.

I owe Neil Burger a thank you for something that he did for me for my prior book, and I forgot to include him in the acknowledgments there. Thank you, Neil. Thanks to Steven S. for lending his ear when I needed to vent about a particular issue that had been consuming me as I neared the end of composing this text. And thanks to Ed Solomon, who knows all and also knows everybody, for a last-minute connection that helped preserve my legal fundament.

Thanks to Brian Tallerico, Chaz Ebert, Stephanie Goodman, Mekado Murphy, Ben Mercer, Liz Helfgott, Mark Graham, Tim Apello, and the Tisch School of the Arts at New York University, who each in their way helped me keep body and soul together.

During the writing of this book, I was visited by an eye affliction—something that a person who leans unusually heavily on his sight does not welcome. Dr. Gonzalo Ortiz at East Jefferson Hospital in Metairie, Louisiana, was the first physician to help me with this problem; back at home, Dr. Yasha Modi and Dr. Peter Weseley at NYU Langone, and the entire staffs at the ophthalmology and ambulatory care departments, helped me get back to full vision and made me feel secure and comfortable during the process. I thank them deeply. And thanks, Larry Blake and Eva Contis, for driving Claire and me to the emergency room and sitting with us when all should have been having dinner. It's on me next time.

INDEX